DOWNTOWN USA
Urban Design in Nine American Cities

DOWNTOWN USA
Urban Design in Nine American Cities

By Kenneth Halpern

WHITNEY LIBRARY OF DESIGN
an imprint of Watson-Guptill Publications/New York

The Architectural Press Ltd/London

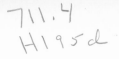

This book was made possible through grants from:

The Graham Foundation for Advanced Studies in the Fine Arts
The Kaplan Fund
The National Endowment for the Arts

First published 1978 in New York by Whitney Library of Design,
an imprint of Watson-Guptill Publications,
a division of Billboard Publications, Inc.,
1515 Broadway, New York, N.Y. 10036

Library of Congress Cataloging in Publication Data
Halpern, Kenneth S., 1944
  Downtown USA.
  Bibliography: pp. 239–244
  Includes index.
1. Cities and towns—United States—Case studies.
2. City planning—United States—Case studies. I. Title.
HT123.H33   1978   309.2'62'0973   78-18339
ISBN 0-8230-7154-5

First published 1978 in Great Britain by The Architectural Press Ltd.,
9 Queen Anne's Gate, London SW1H 9BY
ISBN 85139-173-7

Manufactured in U.S.A.

First Printing, 1978

Edited by Sarah Bodine and Susan Davis
Consultant editor: Jeanne M. Davern
Designed by James Craig, Bob Fillie, and Peter Musgrave-Newton
Composed in 9 point Vega Regular

To my mother and father
and New York City

Acknowledgments

This book has been an immense undertaking, and would have been impossible without the early support, guidance, and encouragement of several people. In particular, I would like to thank Jonathan Barnett, Sarah Bodine, Roberto Brambilla, Susan Braybrooke, Susan Davis, John Golden, Fernando Jimenez, Gianni Longo, Wilhelm von Moltke, Jacquelin Robertson, Richard Weinstein, and the late Duccio Turin.

Special thanks must also be offered to Carter H. Manny, Jr., of the Graham Foundation, Joan Davidson of the Kaplan Fund, and Robert McNulty of the National Endowment for the Arts for their personal support and financial commitment that helped make this expensive project a reality; to Jeanne M. Daverne for her invaluable editorial work on the final manuscript; to William West for editorial direction on the early manuscript; to Adolph Plachek for the generous permission to use Columbia's Avery Library; to Peter Musgrave-Newton for graphic design work; to John P. West III for his patient reading and comment on the manuscript's content; and to Michael Sheckman and John Tagler for typing and proofing the final manuscript.

Furthermore, I would like to acknowledge the generous cooperation of numerous public officials, architects, planners, urban designers, and friends in the cities surveyed. They primed me with information, fed me, and, on occasion, housed me. I am especially indebted to:

New York
Michael Bailkin, Richard Baiter, William Bardel, Richard Basini, Ross Burckhardt, Robert Flahive, Fred Kent, Michael Kirkland, H.T. Kuo, Edgar Lampert, Norman Marcus, Don Miles, Bill November, Lauren Otis, Michael Parley, John Philips, Stephen Quick, Alfi Radzicki, Raquel Ramati, Alfred Schimmel, Peter Seidel, Colin Stewart, David Vander, William H. Whyte, Arthur Zabarkas.

Chicago
John Costonis, Jim Curry, Robert DeVoy, Pam Dunlop, Michael Gelick, Charles Halpern, Dennis Harder, Meg Kershaw, Elayne Kilgore, Maurine McAvey, Harry Manley, Abbott Nelson, David Norris, Stephen Roman, Jared Shlaes, Eric Yondorf.

Philadelphia
Edmund Bacon, Zui Barzilay, John Bower, Alan Levy, Patty and Jay Piersol, Jeff and Pat Ryan.

Houston
Joseph Chow, Tony and Adele de Santos, D. Glasser, Lorraine Jeter, Richard Somerville, Carolyn Thompson.

Washington, D.C.
Frank Ditter, Ron Eichner, Robert Harris, Ron Margolis, Anne Meglis, Joanne Neuhaus, Joe Passoneau, Jim Sandell, Steve Sher, Nancy Taylor, Jeff Wolf.

San Francisco
Bernard Averbuch, Don Carter, Larry Doane, Bill Duchek, Kris Eggen, Audrey Emmons, Don Emmons, Bob Feldman, Ralph Gigliello, Charles Gill, Sylvia Gill, Ed Green, Peter Groat, Don Haagstad, Dick Hedman, Frank Hendricks, Roger Hooper, Allan B. Jacobs, Susan King, John Kriken, Gunilla Lerup, Lars Lerup, Ed Michael, Dick Olmsted, Derek Parker, Robert Passmore, Dave Sablin, Paul Schwartz, Peter Svirsky, Bill Weber.

Boston
William Fain, Deborah Gottland, Charles Hilgenhurst, Richard S. Joslin, Vicki Kaiser, Garhard Kallmann, John Sloan, Mase Weiniger, Kyn Sung Woo.

Atlanta
George Blevins, Roy and Tappy Frangiamore, Eric Harkness, Sharron Humble, Manual Padron, Raunda Pitney, Tom Shuttleworth, Ron Sineway.

Minneapolis
Gail Bronner, Ken Brunsvald, Dan Gill, Max Goldberg, Joel Goodman, Lawrence M. Irvin, Tim McCoy, Richard Morrill, Dale and Jan Mulfinger, Stephen Murray, Leonard Parker, Ralph Rapson, James Stageberg, Perry Torvec, John and Gracy Waugh.

Contents

Foreword

We are a nation of cities, in a world that grows increasingly urban. Nearly three-quarters of the people in the United States now live in metropolitan areas, and for 50 years these regions have absorbed virtually all the nation's population growth. But within these areas there has been a shift of both population and employment from the urban centers to the suburban fringe, which has had a devastating effect on many of the nation's older cities.

This dispersion of activity has weakened the concentration of opportunities in the downtown, and has thus drained the economic strength and individual commitment needed for the downtown's continued renewal. The reasons for the shift away from the center city are many, but they include national policies that have favored the automobile, single-family detached homes, and new construction and subsidies that concentrate the poor and dependent in central cities. At the same time, for these and other factors, an enormous number of jobs have relocated to the suburbs.

Fortunately, many of these national policies are now being reconsidered in the light of their unintended effects. Furthermore, a growing concern for the environment, for the conservation of energy, and for the proper use of resources is leading to a better understanding of the advantages and efficiencies of cities. We are also beginning to appreciate the practicality of maintaining and reusing our urban investments in downtown areas, rather than abandoning them and starting anew elsewhere.

As Mayor of The City of New York, I am concerned with how well this city continues to play its role as a national and international center of commerce and with the steps that can be taken to maintain or enhance its suitability as a forum for socially constructive activity. An essential aspect of this concern is the built environment and the organizational, legal, and design tools that are used to achieve its betterment.

Kenneth Halpern's review of urban design as it has been practiced in the downtowns of nine of this country's larger cities is both complimentary to New York—in that it shows the city to have been a leader in its innovative concern for the built environment—and instructive in its descriptions of the achievements and failures elsewhere and its suggestions of what remains to be done in all these cities.

As has been carefully illustrated in *Downtown USA,* planning and development in an established urban center is a complex and difficult art that requires sensitivity to physical and social constraints and a particular kind of continuity and dedication over long periods of time. It requires realistic plans that build gradually towards a few simple and widely shared goals. It requires a mutually constructive partnership of government with business and community interests, and it requires the participation of people who understand the evolving purposes of cities and how to encourage and guide necessary physical change in an increasingly complex society.

The success with which cities continue to serve our needs depends in large part on decisions that are beyond local control. However, to the extent that local efforts can be responsible, the accomplishments of some of the cities described in this book bode well for the future, while developments in other cities pose serious questions about where we are going as an urban society. In New York, we will continue to build on a firm foundation of creative urban design, broad community participation, and the services of committed professionals who realize that, for better or for worse, government is ultimately responsible for the quality of our urban environment.

Edward I. Koch
Mayor of The City of New York

Preface

Thirty-five American cities have a population of 400,000 people or more. Including their respective regions—often defined as Standard Metropolitan Statistical Areas (SMSAs)—40 percent of the U.S. population live either in or around these 35 cities. This book is a comparative analysis of urban design policies over the last 20 years in the downtown areas of nine of these cities. Alone, the nine urban centers presented here are the nucleus of regions equal to about 20 percent of the total American population. Employment in these nine urban centers ranges between 80,000 and 1 million people.

The cities selected for analysis were chosen because they are both old and new; they are located in a variety of climate zones that range from frigid (Minneapolis) to torrid (Houston); and for people to get to work downtown, they vary from an almost total dependence on the automobile (Houston—86 percent) to an almost total dependence on public transportation (New York—96 percent). The impact of these conditions on the built form are illustrated in part through the various urban design solutions the cities have adopted to deal with these phenomena.

Each chapter of the book is devoted to one city. The chapters begin with a brief discussion of that city's population characteristics and its historical development as it relates to its plan and are followed by an analysis of its zoning and urban design policies for new construction, landmark preservation, transportation, and open space.

Most important, the cities surveyed present a spectrum of urban design policies along with their implications. In New York and San Francisco comprehensive urban design requirements are incorporated into the zoning ordinance. In Boston, most urban design controls are a result of the leverage of urban renewal, tax incentives, and planned unit development. Houston has no zoning, and (although arguments to the contrary are presented) may, as a result, be denying its citizenry the quality of urban life that transcends the mere collection of disparate developments along a highway, no matter how well designed any individual piece may be. Chicago and Atlanta have zoning so lenient that there is no control at all over new development; in the case of Chicago, this policy is at the direct expense of saving that city's important landmarks. In Washington, D.C., the zoning's height and bulk restrictions have forced the downtown to spread over a vast amount of urban land. In Minneapolis some of the most successful examples of urban design in the country are the result of private initiative. And finally, in Philadelphia, guidelines of a usually nonbinding comprehensive plan have been followed for 30 years.

Few cities anywhere, whether in the United States or abroad, have exercised urban design control equal to the magnitude of the problems they are facing. But those cities that have established at least some urban design policies for their centers have created more pleasant urban areas; automobile traffic has been restricted on certain streets allowing linear parks to be created in their stead; in San Francisco and Munich, major urban spaces have been created in conjunction with new rapid transit systems; and in Rome, important existing urban spaces such as Piazza Navona and Piazza Farnese have been recaptured for pedestrians. In all these cases, air and noise pollution have been drastically cut. Furthermore, retail business has improved in virtually all American, Canadian, and European cities where such policies are in effect. This is because more people are coming downtown as new transportation systems and regulations for the improvement of existing systems make it easier to do so and as the renewed urban streets make it a more pleasant experience once there.

In the time available to research this book it was literally impossible to cover all the American cities that may have made a significant contribution to the evolution of urban design theory and its practical implementation. But the nine cities surveyed here offer at least a good cross section of the state of urban design thinking and show some of the problems of those cities that have failed to utilize urban design as a tool to guide development.

Prologue

Those who work in downtown America spend at least half of their day there, five days a week. Yet, today the central areas of most large American cities lack the viable integration of housing, offices, convenient shops, and restaurants that is still common in Europe; and few American downtowns possess the sense of order, beauty, interest, and vitality of European centers. This is true, in part, because of the way most American cities developed.

Territorial expansion and population growth in the United States coincided with the industrial revolution. Industry staked out the best locations in terms of transportation—getting raw materials in and shipping finished goods out. Around these industries grew cities. Usually the best location for these industrial centers was next to the great lakes and rivers. The cities located quickly across the country wherever there was something to "harvest," be it trees, ore, coal, or corn and where there were the means to get these "crops" to a centralized location, from which boats and trains could get them to the rest of the nation and abroad.

Inevitably, the nature of many of these early industrialized cities changed. When the pillaging was done, when the trees were all cut down, or when the ore was all mined, many cities died. Still other cities were able to adjust, finding new industries upon which life could be sustained.

The chaos of early American cities was often overwhelming. If a city had no plan of its own, it often adopted the U.S. government's organizing framework—the rectangular survey—a grid. The rest was up to individuals, and although in small parts of some cities there were restrictive covenants tied to land ownership, it was not until 1916 that the first zoning resolution sought to place minimal restraints upon just what an individual could build between that gridiron network of streets.

So, quite obviously, American cities bear little resemblance to older more ordered European cities—although it was not always for want of trying. The French planner, L'Enfant, was hired to design Washington, D.C., and his classical plan for the city endures in spite of compromises in its structure to accommodate the automobile.

Other American cities too, once they were secure in their wealth, turned to Europe as a model for plans that could tie all the disparate architecture into a unified, grand city. Daniel Burnham, an American version of L'Enfant, was a man who could produce such plans. Chicago, Minneapolis, and San Francisco all hired him—or his long-time associate, Edward Bennett—to rearrange their abused landscapes. Only Chicago seriously adopted his plan, but one of the plan's recommendations—a fixed cornice line—soon succumbed to the emerging possibilities of steel cage construction and elevators, as well as (not least of all) real estate speculation.

By the time the industrial revolution began in Europe, the great capital cities of that continent were mostly built; and many had even been remodeled several times according to the latest planning fad. Because cities like London, Paris, and Rome were the seats of government for their entire countries, this gave them the power to prevent

1

2

3

5

6

7

4

noxious industries from encroaching too far upon their regal splendor. Yet they could still benefit from the wealth produced by their industrializing countrysides. Similarly, part of America's wealth is Washington's wealth. And like London and Paris, Washington can afford to be regal with disregard for what it spends to build new government buildings—although maintenance of its inherent beauty leaves much to be desired.

Out of respect for their cultural heritage, Europeans maintained their cities intact during the 19th and 20th centuries. Even following wars, important historic sections were often rebuilt precisely as before. For this reason it is helpful to look to Europe for examples of urban design elements that have survived the centuries and have produced distinctive, humane cities: the canals of Amsterdam and Venice (1); the boulevards of Paris and Vienna; the octagonal intersection grid of Barcelona; the arcades of Berne and Bologna (2); the gallerias of London (3) and Milan (4); and the piazzas of Rome (5), to name only a few examples.

It is important to remember that all these urban design structuring elements were practical, pragmatic solutions to basic functional requirements—mostly transportation, shopping, and the need for large numbers of people to congregate at one time. But these "structuring elements" were also much more than merely "functional," and today are viewed as amenities: a point often missed when similar utilitarian structures are created in American cities.

For example, in many of the towns in central Europe built by the Dukes of Zähringer, the major street served as a market. Arcades were a part of the flanking buildings, offering weather protection then, as they still do today, 700 years later. The provision of the arcade did not produce a dull uniformity, for each building interpreted the arcade in its own subtly different way (6, 7).

In Rome, in the late 16th century, it was religious concerns that prompted Pope Sixtus V to connect the significant churches by thoroughfares that plowed a path across the maze of old Rome so the pilgriming flock would not lose their way as they paraded to the resting places of their favorite saints. In front of each of the churches,

many of which were actually built by Sixtus V, was a huge gathering place, a *piazza*, upon which Sixtus saw fit to place an obelisk—borrowed centuries earlier by roaming Romans who had made their way to Egypt (8). The obelisk served as a focal point, a marker for the church that lay at the end of the thoroughfare. And the system of thoroughfares became the structure upon which Baroque Rome was built. Recently in Rome, the effects of policies carried out by anonymous civil servants to close much of the center of old Rome to the automobile rivals any of the great building periods of that city's long history (9).

In Barcelona, with its rigid grid plan and octagonally shaped intersections, Antonio Gaudi has shown in his Casa Milá, built in 1905, that architects can be architecturally creative and yet still build within urban design constraints deemed in the interest of the larger community (10, 11).

There is, of course, a danger of being overly romantic when viewing some European cities. The boulevards of Paris, for instance, were designed to give the French generals strategic points from which to control the unruly Parisians—who became even more unruly after countless housing quarters were condemned to make way for the boulevards. As grand as the Paris boulevards appear today, they worked havoc on those who had to sacrifice the sound housing in their route. Much of the new housing that was built, now in an architecture subservient to the streets, became quickly overcrowded. There were tiny, oddly shaped rooms that deferred more to the shape of intersecting streets than to the shape of a dining room table or a bed (12). The saying "when a good American dies he goes to Paris" will be of little comfort to the one who gets buried in the back of one of Haussmann's town houses!

Regardless of the motivation behind the urban design structuring elements of European cities, modern America, with few exceptions, has generally turned its back on these examples. In the last 20 years alone, massive urban highways and the ubiquitous "cobra head" street lights have been allowed to brutally scar the landscape of the most American cities, creating irreparable damage (13). Few highways—if indeed any

1   Venice was settled in the midst of a lagoon primarily for defense and a livelihood based on fishing. But the canal system, although developed from prevailing water routes within the lagoon, was formalized over the centuries as an internal servicing network for the city.

2-3-4   Shopping in Bologna, where by law every building in the old center has an arcaded front (2); London, the Burlington Arcade (3); and Milan, the Galleria (4).

5   Urban spaces such as Piazza Navona—historically created as gathering places for civic and religious functions—have in recent years been declared off limits to automobiles.

6-7   The arcades in Berne and other Zähringer towns, whose economies were based on marketing, were added to the fronts of existing and once uniform buildings so that vendors and shoppers alike would have weather protection, a consideration no less important today.

8

9

10

12

13

14

New York City

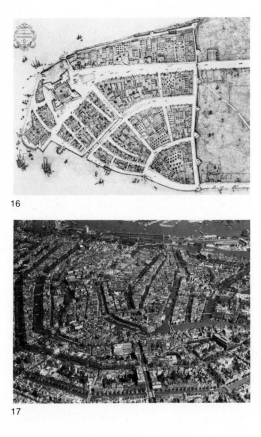

16

17

New York is the largest U.S. city. With San Francisco, it has been the most effective city in utilizing principles and techniques of urban design to guide its development over the last 10 years. New York City has put forth urban design proposals for many aspects of urban problems, including the reorganization of transportation and the transfer of air rights to protect landmarks; but its main contribution to the theory and practice of urban design comes from its innovative use of incentive zoning to encourage or require developers to build according to prescribed urban design guidelines.

Population and geography

Spread unevenly among its five boroughs—a land area of 333 sq miles (850 sq km)—New York City has a census population of about 8 million people. In addition, it is estimated that there are as many as 1 million illegal residents in the city. Although the population of the surrounding 26-county region, at 10.4 million people, is only slightly more than that of the city, the region—divided among over 550 municipal governments and at least 900 special districts—is spread across 12,500 sq miles (30,000 sq km), an area almost 40 times the size of New York City. New York has two primary business centers, Midtown and Lower Manhattan (15).

Historical development

Lower Manhattan grew from the original plan of the early 17th-century Dutch settlement, New Amsterdam, patterned closely after Amsterdam (16). The density of old Amsterdam has remained more or less constant over the past several centuries and by European standards is considered high even now (17). New Amsterdam (renamed

New York in honor of the Duke of York, when the Dutch, under threat of attack from the English, peacefully surrendered the colony in 1664) has grown up as well as out (18, 19). Today, approximately 500,000 people work within the confines of the original Dutch settlement in Lower Manhattan, a ½-sq-mile (1.3-sq-km) area. With few changes, the same network of narrow streets remains to serve this incredibly dense area. It is able to function because 96 percent of those working in Lower Manhattan commute by some form of public transit.

North of Lower Manhattan, the streets are laid out on a grid that was adopted in 1811 (20). It was thought at the time that the major movements would be east-west, between the two rivers, and so 155 streets running river to river were laid out at 200-ft (60-m) intervals (21). The 12 north-south avenues were each 100 (30 m) wide, and they were laid out at intervals ranging from 650 to 920 ft (200 to 280 m). According to Sibyl Moholy-Nagy, ". . . nothing had ever been attempted that equalled in brutality the grid stencil to be clamped over the cliff and ravine studded granite shelf."[1] Later when the shipping trade failed to move much beyond its well-entrenched location in Lower Manhattan and when it became apparent that the major movements were north-south, two more avenues, Madison and Lexington, only 80 ft (24 m) in width, were spliced into the original grid.

The Midtown business district, which runs roughly from 30th to 60th Streets, developed because of its convenience to the two major rail terminals in Manhattan, Pennsylvania Station and Grand Central Station. One million people work in 1 sq mile (2.6 sq

15   Within the ½ mile (.8 km) square core area of Lower Manhattan, 500,000 people work, and over 1 million work in the 1 sq mile (2.6 sq km) center of Midtown. Ninety-six percent of those in Lower Manhattan and 92 percent of those in Midtown arrive at work by public transportation.

16   The 1660 Castello Plan shows how closely New Amsterdam was patterned—at least for a while—after its mother city, Amsterdam.

17   Amsterdam's density has remained constant for centuries, but is still considered high by European standards.

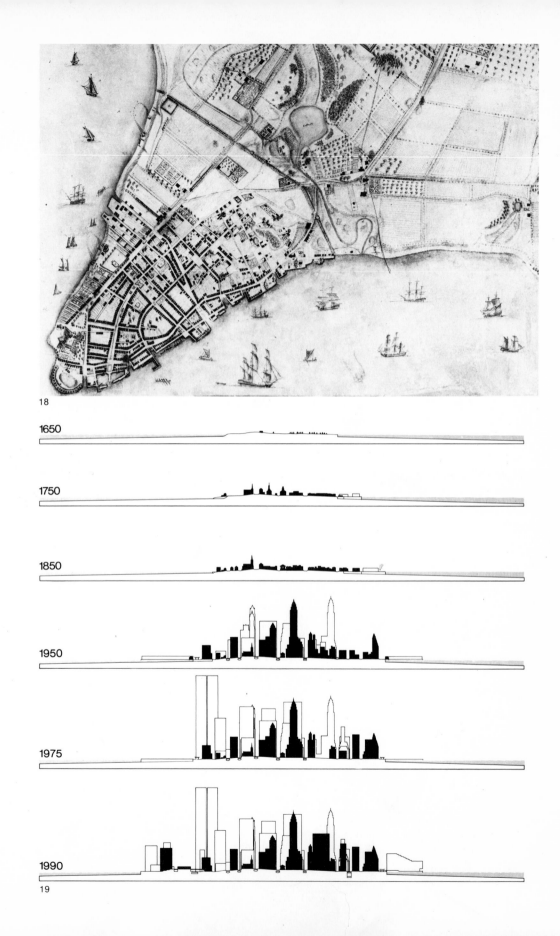

18

1650

1750

1850

1950

1975

1990

19

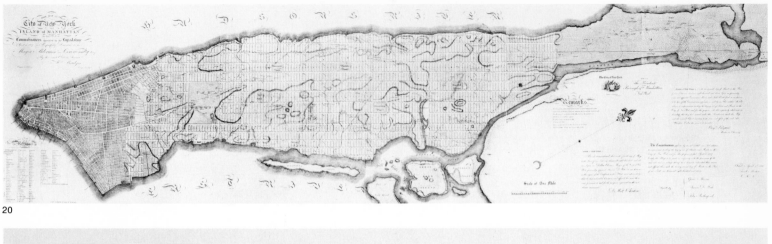

20

21

18   By 1743, New York was rapidly acceding to its changing role from a colonial settlement to an international port city.

19   Historic elevations of Lower Manhattan show that New York was allowed to grow with little control. It is only since the late 1960s that urban design policies have been established to ensure that with future construction historic features are preserved and past mistakes avoided.

20   The 1811 commissioner's grid plan for New York, brutally imposed over Manhattan's rocky terrain, provided a structure for unparalleled growth. However, the provision for primarily east-west movement was based on the mistaken assumption of continued shipping activity along the length of the two rivers flanking the island.

21   Composite elevation of Midtown in 1970 by Jerry Spearman is from the Hudson River looking east.

22

23

24

22-23-24 The results of the 1916 zoning ordinance: the Empire State Building (1931) is the epitome of what can be built under its regulations (22), while the McGraw-Hill Building (1930) by Raymond Hood is considered one of the most elegant solutions built within the zoning law (23). In general, the "Ziggurat Revival" style is the architectural by-product of the 1916 zoning ordinance's height and setback requirement and has had a profound effect upon New York's landscape (24).

km) of Midtown. Like Lower Manhattan, Midtown continues to function because 92 percent of the commuters arrive by public transit.

New York has been a pioneer in zoning legislation since it passed the nation's first zoning ordinance in 1916.

In 1915, the Equitable Building opened in Lower Manhattan. The massive 42-story tower cast a 7-acre (2.8-ha) shadow, cutting off sunlight from neighboring 21-story buildings. The negative impact of the building was so great—tenants started moving out of adjacent buildings because of the lack of sunlight and view—that realtors joined reformers to support what became the first zoning ordinance in the United States. Although the city proposed the ordinance under pressure to limit the ill effects of urban congestion, it continued to encourage intensive development of tax-generating properties.

The 1916 zoning ordinance attempted to resolve the long-standing conflict of two principles of English common law. The first was the position put forward by Coke in the early 17th century of the right to build upwards unencumbered by legal restriction: *Cujus est solum, ejus est usque ad coelum* (whoever has the land possesses all the space upward to an indefinite extent). The second principle was the Law of Ancient Lights, which dates back to the time of Richard the Lion Hearted in the late 12th century and is thought to be the earliest attempt to protect a landowner's right to sunlight by giving him the right to file suit against an adjacent landowner who erected a building that cut off his sunlight. However, in a 1596 case, *Bury vs. Pope*, the plaintiff lost his suit as the court held it was the complaining landowner's "folly to build his house so near to the other's land."[2] In American law, the Right to Light fared equally badly. New York's highest court ruled in 1838 that the right to sunlight ". . . cannot be applied in the growing cities and villages of this country, without working the most mischievous consequences."[3]

The 1916 zoning ordinance invented the setback. It sought to strike a balance between the rights of a landlord and the rights of his neighbors that would reflect both the

weight of prior law and the realities of modern building technology. Under the ordinance, a developer could build upon 100 percent of his land, but only up to a certain height, whereupon the building had to set back. Then up again and another setback. This " "height and setback" requirement was to conform to an established angle, measured from the center of the street, that was calculated to let more air and light onto the streets and surrounding properties. When the building set back to a point where the tower portion covered no more than 25 percent of the site area, the tower could go up forever. From whence cometh the Empire State Building (22), the McGraw Hill Building by Raymond Hood (23)—perhaps one of the most elegant solutions to the zoning ordinance—and a landscape of buildings around New York that constitutes one of America's unique contributions to the history of architecture: "Ziggurat Revival" (24).

Despite its supposedly social concerns, the 1916 ordinance was so generous that if New York were built to its zoning limitations, it would house a residential population of 77 million people and the commercial districts could accommodate 344 million people. As this was almost twice the population of the United States at that time, planners used these statistics to push for a limit on a building's allowable floor area and hence its density.

A new zoning resolution in 1961 encouraged open space in commercial areas with mixed results.

In 1961, New York City adopted a new zoning resolution designed to correct some of the perceived inadequacies of the 1916 law. The permitted densities of residential districts were revised downward to the point where the city now has a theoretical capacity for 11 million people. The resolution's effect on density in the business districts was less substantial. To win the support of the real estate community for the overall legislation, the planners proposed a basic floor area ratio (FAR) of 15 in the densest commercial zone.

FAR is a ratio between the site and the amount of building that can be put on it. For example, at an FAR of 15, if a developer has

25

26

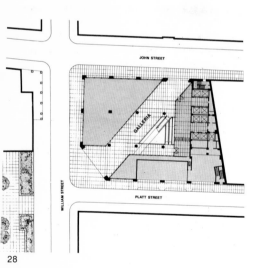

28

29

27

a site of 10,000 sq ft (950 sq m), he may build a building 15 times that area, or 150,000 sq ft (14,200 sq m). This floor area may be distributed in a variety of ways. For instance, assuming other regulations did not prevent him, the developer could build a 15-floor tower covering the full 10,000-sq-ft (950-sq-m) lot, a 30-floor tower covering half the lot, a 60-floor tower covering one quarter of the lot, and so on.

Real estate developers had been building profitable commercial structures around the size of FAR 15 since the end of the Second World War, so the new zoning resolution worked no hardship on them. What really got the real estate community behind this new law, however, was a bonus which allowed the developer up to a 20 percent increase in the size of his building if he provided a plaza. A developer might therefore increase his FAR from 15 to 18 simply by covering less of his lot and building a taller building.

Although the equivalent of three full-lot floors may seem an overly generous bonus, it is not without its rationale. The bonus is necessary in part to offset the additional costs of a taller building, which is more expensive because of the significant increases in costs of mechanical equipment, especially elevators. Furthermore, the city genuinely wanted more open space in its densely populated commercial areas. With land in the central business district ranging from $300 to $1,000 per sq ft, the city did not feel it could afford to buy up land for park space, nor could it afford to have that land off the tax rolls. In exchange for a significant amenity, the city had to provide a significant bonus.

The plaza bonus also pleased the architectural community. Two buildings of the 1950s had a profound effect upon the architects' push for the new zoning resolution: Mies van der Rohe's Seagram building (25) and the Le Courbusier-influenced United Nations building (26). The United Nations was a tower sitting in a park. No setbacks, just a pure tower. The Seagram building, with lower buildings tucked behind it, is not quite so pure a solution; but it does present itself as a tower sitting on a plaza. Architects did not accept "economic realities" as an excuse for imposing a predetermined

form; and they thought any zoning rule which imposed setbacks upon buildings was a form of aesthetic rape. They were also strongly convinced of the need for more open space in Midtown.

But under the 1916 ordinance, a tower is a very expensive solution in terms of land costs. The Seagram tower occupies exactly 25 percent of its site, and thus under the old zoning it could have been built to the stars, except that the building would have been all elevator shafts and no floor space. The 1961 resolution took away the unlimited height provision and substituted a 40 percent allowable tower coverage for the old 25 percent, which made for more workable towers in terms of the mechanical system and the land costs.

The plaza bonus has been a success in the sense that many developers have elected to build plazas in order to pick up the bonus. Indeed, since 1961, the city has added a number of other bonus provisions to the zoning resolution. Among these are through-block connections, both covered and open to the sky (27), arcades, and gallerias. The galleria in the 100 William Street building in Lower Manhattan, by Davis, Brody and Associates and Emery Roth and Sons, is an outstanding example of what good architects can do with these bonus elements (28, 29).

Unfortunately, much of the building in the 1960s was not so sensitive as 100 William Street. Many of the new plazas seemed designed to discourage people from using them. Important opportunities to provide arcades, shopping areas, and subway connections were missed. Often, new structures failed to achieve simple harmony with neighboring buildings.

Mayor John V. Lindsay was troubled by this problem, and early in his administration he established the Paley Commission to study the problem of urban design in New York City. Among the recommendations of that commission was the establishment of urban design as a discipline within the City Planning Department. It was recommended that staff members be primarily architects who either had graduate training in urban design or through the practice of architecture had worked on large-scale urban projects.

25-26   Two examples of the push for a new zoning ordinance without height and setback requirements are Mies van der Rohe's Seagram Building (1958), a tower sitting on a plaza without apparent setbacks (25), and the United Nations Building (1952), a tower without setbacks (26) sitting in a park, both of which influenced the direction in which New York architects sought to build.

27   Amendments to the 1961 zoning ordinance were intended to encourage the construction not only of plazas and arcades but of other urban design amenities, including open and enclosed through-block connections. These were a way of breaking up the long Midtown streets and reflected recommendations of urban critic Jane Jacobs.

28-29   The galleria space in 100 William Street is one of the better examples of an urban design amenity built under New York's zoning incentive program.

30

32

26

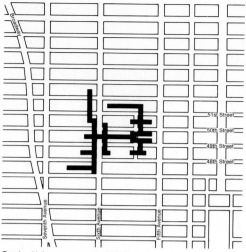

Scale: ⅛ in. represents 200 ft

 Underground concourse
31

30-31-32 Rockefeller Center (started in 1931), one of the finest examples of urban design in the United States, occupies a 24-acre (9.6-ha) site. Its 21 buildings are all interconnected by an underground shopping concourse and connect with the subway. The original buildings in the grouping also maintain street-level shopping and are juxtaposed to provide for a variety of major urban spaces.

Under the guidance of the chairman of the Department of City Planning, Donald Elliot, and with the counsel of Norman Marcus, the Urban Design Group in City Planning was started in 1967 by Jonathan Barnett, Jaquelin Robertson, Richard Weinstein, and Myles Weintraub. In subsequent years, six other urban design offices for special areas of the city were created.

Zoning in its broadest terms only regulates the use and bulk of a building, but the urban design offices have found imaginative ways to make zoning a more responsive tool to improve the quality of building in the city. Aside from zoning issues, these urban design offices have also familiarized themselves with transportation and open space issues and have effectively challenged conventional approaches by other city agencies, significantly altering many city projects.

More importantly, as Jonathan Barnett explains in his book *Urban Design as Public Policy*, the Urban Design Group established methods for making urban design part of the process of public policy planning and implementation, institutionalized it through the civil service, and initiated a graduate program of professional education in urban design at City College of New York with internship in New York City urban design offices.

A new kind of incentive zoning—the "special zoning district"—was invented by the Urban Design Group to establish public policy for large-scale development in specified areas.

Through its special zoning districts, New York is attempting to provide the unifying hand to large-scale development that was provided by the developer in Rockefeller Center. In this way the city hopes to benefit from the amenities that only become possible when development is conceived on a large scale.

In many ways, Rockefeller Center is the finest urban complex ever built in the United States. It is carefully designed to fit within the predetermined street grid (30). It has an underground shopping concourse that connects to all buildings within Rockefeller Center and to the subway (31). The center

also maintains the nature of Fifth Avenue and all the side streets as shopping streets. It does this by tying lower buildings in with towers—something Eero Saarinen opposed doing in his solution for the CBS Building on Sixth Avenue. The massing of the buildings also creates Rockefeller Center Plaza, one of the most significant urban spaces in New York (32). Finally, the streets are lined with trees, and there is a continuity of style, material, and detail.

Few areas of New York, or any city for that matter, have been conceived on such a grand scale. And few areas are as well organized or as exciting.

Rockefeller Center has served as a benchmark for the special zoning districts in New York, illustrating both the opportunities and the obligations of new development—opportunities in the sense of improving environmental quality through the creation of usable and exciting urban spaces; obligations in the sense of making subway connections or allowing for future connections, continuing shopping streets, and, where humility is called for, ensuring that buildings modestly yield to existing urban qualities rather than compete with them.

Within the urban framework there can be distinctive architecture. But with few exceptions—like public monuments, churches, and museums—judgment of a building must take into consideration how well the building relates to the context in which it is built.

Lincoln Center Special District became a prototype.

Although it was the second special zoning district in New York following the Theater District, the Lincoln Center District was the first to impose urban design controls, and it became the forerunner of the many special zoning districts throughout the city.

The need for zoning controls in this area of the city arose when the developer of a building exactly opposite the plaza of the Lincoln Center for the Performing Arts proposed to set his building back and mirror the Lincoln Center plaza, the easiest, most obvious way to take advantage of the plaza bonus (33). The Urban Design Group felt that a second plaza would deny the first its sense of enclo-

33

34

33-34 The development directly opposite Lincoln Center was originally designed to be set back, creating a plaza similar to the one in Lincoln Center (33). In 1968 the building became the focus of the first major fight to impose urban design controls to regulate new buildings in significant urban locations. A detail of the first project in New York built under urban design controls (34) shows that it was constructed along the Broadway diagonal with a continuous shopping arcade. The tower is set back from the lower portion of the building to maintain the scale of the neighborhood.

sure and that a building which continued the street wall on the east side of Broadway would be a more appropriate backdrop for the existing plaza (34). The treatment of Broadway was an issue because Broadway is the only diagonal street within the Manhattan grid and this element of irregularity has helped to create some of the more distinctive architecture in the city. Because of the obvious problems that would arise if the proposed building was built in a way that did not respect these existing conditions, a special zoning district was quickly drafted to ensure against such a possibility.

The special district requires:

–Buildings along the easterly frontage of Broadway and certain buildings along Columbus Avenue build to the street line up to a height of 85 ft (26 m). This would be about 6 stories, which is within the human scale of perception, and is consistent with the residential buildings in the neighborhood, the buildings in Lincoln Center, and many older buildings along Broadway which set back at the 85-ft height as was required under the first zoning resolution.

–At the 85-ft height, the tower portion of the building must set back from the street wall.

–An arcade 17 ft (5.2 m) wide with an average height of 20 ft (6 m) must be provided along the front of each building built on these streets. Although the arcade is mandatory, it is also bonused.

–To protect neighborhood shopping, the ground floor must be devoted primarily to active retail frontage. Uses like banks are prohibited from occupying more than 40 ft (12 m) of a building's ground floor frontage.

Normally, with all the bonuses, a building in this neighborhood could reach a maximum FAR of 12. The building could be all apartments, all offices, or a combination of both. In response to pressure from developers to build even larger buildings in this area than was allowed, the Lincoln Center Special District grants up to a 20 percent increase in floor area above the FAR of 12. Furthermore, the 20 percent increase is tied directly to the provision of public amenities such as plazas and galleries at specified locations on a developer's site. Developers

who seek this extra bonus must first obtain a special permit from the City Planning Commission. This provision is an administrative headache for both the city and the developer, but it was thought necessary for the Lincoln Center District in order to closely monitor the generous bonus provisions and to ensure responsible interpretations of the district's objectives.

Fifth Avenue Special District preserves the walls of a great shopping street and encourages mixed use for a 24-hour community.

Fifth Avenue is another place that needs a street wall more than it needs plazas. This internationally significant shopping street is also the most important ceremonial street in New York and the location of many of the city's finest landmarks—the Plaza Hotel, St. Patrick's Cathedral, Rockefeller Center (35).

When Best & Company and the DePinna Company, two prominent department stores located within one block of each other on Fifth Avenue, sold their respective buildings to real estate interests that were surely planning to construct office buildings, a tremendous concern about the future of Fifth Avenue grew among the avenue's merchants. Department stores are quite naturally the anchor points of shopping centers, which rely on them as magnets to draw people to an area of comparison shopping. Many observers felt, therefore, that the loss of these two department stores could have a substantial impact on the future of the avenue as a shopping center. And aside from the impact of new construction, there was the problem of changing ground-floor uses in existing buildings, where shops were gradually being replaced by banks, corporate showrooms, airline ticket offices, and lobbies, to the point where these uses accounted for almost 22 percent of the avenue frontage (36). Today, three of the top five categories of use on Fifth Avenue are nonretail. Although department stores remain first in total frontage, banks are a close second, followed by office entrances and airline ticket offices. Many of the travel agencies and corporate showrooms are able to outbid the traditional shops for what they consider to be the prestige of a Fifth Avenue address

36

35 Fifth Avenue, aside from its role as a major shopping street, is New York's main ceremonial street and the location of many of the city's finest landmarks and urban spaces.

36 Two major threats to the urban design structure of Fifth Avenue are the changes in ground-floor uses in older buildings and newer buildings which destroy the urban wall. Over 20 percent of the Fifth Avenue frontage has changed to banks, corporate showrooms, airline ticket offices, and building lobbies—uses antithetical to the pursuit of comparison shopping.

and hence the advertising value of this location. Although they often do not make sufficient sales to justify the rents, the difference can be written off as a public relations expense.

New buildings that do not provide retail frontage have a doubly negative effect on a shopping street. First, they displace numerous smaller shops. Second, the redeveloped site with its substantially higher density increases the market for standard lunchtime service shops even while it reduces the available retail frontage. A specialty shop cannot normally afford the rent that a chain hot dog stand will gladly spring for in a good location. With the market thus manipulated, the result is inevitable: some people make money, but everybody else loses.

The dangers presented to Fifth Avenue by redevelopment and changing uses were exacerbated by the relatively small size of the existing buildings along the avenue when compared with the densities that the zoning allows there. The possibility of rebuilding at a substantially increased density on a prime site is a possibility dear to the heart of the New York real estate developer, and it was widely expected that the Best and DePinna sites would be only the first in a long line of sites on Fifth Avenue that would rapidly undergo redevelopment. This expectation was based on, among other things, the rate at which land was changing hands. Land transactions are a matter of public record; and despite the standard practice of developers of using different dummy purchasing organizations when assembling sites, it was clear that a great deal of assemblage by major developers was going on. There was a very real possibility that the nature of Fifth Avenue would be irreversibly altered in only a few years.

In urban design terms, Fifth Avenue has a fabulous urban wall that frames Central Park and continues down through Midtown to Washington Square (37). At 59th Street, a critical point on the wall, sits the General Motors Building, which sets back to create a sunken plaza and which has an automobile showroom at the ground level resembling a marble garage (38). The GM Building is kitty-corner to Central Park, one of the largest central-city parks in the world, and it

is directly across the street from the elegant Grand Army Plaza in front of the Plaza Hotel. It is the last place in New York where another plaza was needed; and unfortunately, it is suggestive of a development trend in New York (39, 40).

The GM plaza raises a fundamental issue about zoning. One of the basic precepts of zoning law is the right of expectation. In other words, a person has a right to build a building precisely the size and type of his neighbors' buildings, if he so desires. The right of expectation is a reasonable principle when viewed in its natural context, which is a zoning ordinance that treats the lots in any given zone as if they were interchangeable and allows no deviation from its blanket, zone-wide prescriptions. The plaza bonus, however, introduces a new element. The developer is permitted to build a bigger building and thereby place a greater burden on the public infrastructure in exchange for the provision of a public amenity, the plaza. In other words, the developer gets something of value—more floors on his building. Shouldn't the public therefore have the right to ensure that *it* receives something of value? If the public receives a plaza where it is worse than useless, as it did in the GM plaza, the public is clearly getting gypped.

The successive special zoning districts in New York City may be seen as increasingly sophisticated tools designed to ensure that the public receives *meaningful* amenity in exchange for the developer's bonus, without infringing on the developer's legitimate rights and expectations. One of the basic ways the special districts protect the developer is by laying out the terms of the district in advance, so the developer knows what to expect, even though he may have to expect different things—in exchange for a bonus—from lot to lot.

The basic urban design goals for Fifth Avenue were clear: maintenance of the urban wall and the attendant shopping at its base. As the Office of Midtown Planning and Development (OMPD) proceeded with its urban design analysis of the Fifth Avenue area, another design opportunity presented itself. It was noted by OMPD's director, at that time Jaquelin Robertson, and the Fifth Avenue study's project director, Steve Quick, that the major urban spaces associ-

37

38

39

40

37-38 Buildings along Fifth Avenue form an urban wall that frames Central Park and provides the necessary frontage for continuous shopping as it passes through Midtown. However, the General Motors Building at 59th and Fifth Avenue (38) is set back, thus weakening the shopping street while using a public bonus to provide an open space directly across the street from Central Park and Grand Army Plaza in front of the Plaza Hotel. It was the last place New York needed another open space.

39-40 Saarinen, discussing the CBS tower (39) on Sixth Avenue, has said: ''A plaza allows a building to be seen. Our buildings should be seen because they are monuments of our time.''[4] This is the kind of thinking that destroys the urban street and that has been detrimental to Fifth Avenue. The Grace Building on 42nd Street (40) breaks the delicate urban continuity established by the four older buildings on that block. It changes the scale, color, and material as it also destroys the urban wall that frames Bryant Park. Its lobby and ground-floor banks interrupt the shopping character of 42nd Street.

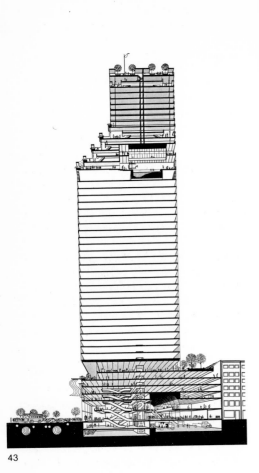

43

41

41　Paley Park, one of the few truly usable open spaces in Midtown, is located on a side street just off Fifth Avenue.

42　The urban design framework for Fifth Avenue was based on an analysis of existing urban conditions.

43　Prototypical Fifth Avenue mixed-use building.

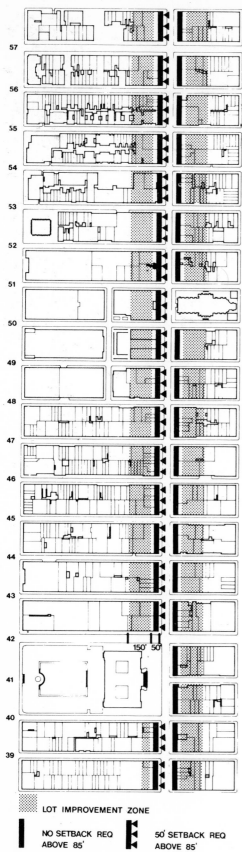

LOT IMPROVEMENT ZONE

NO SETBACK REQ ABOVE 85'

50' SETBACK REQ ABOVE 85'

ated with Fifth Avenue were actually on side streets: Paley Park is on 53rd Street between Fifth and Madison Avenues (41); Bryant Park sits behind the Public Library, which fronts on Fifth Avenue between 41st and 42nd Streets; and Rockefeller Center Plaza is tucked behind the buildings that front on the avenue. Continuation of this method of providing open space near the avenue seemed appropriate, and the open space provisions of the special district were written accordingly.

The main provisions of the Fifth Avenue Special District (42) are as follows:

—All buildings in the district, which extends from 38th Street to 57th Street, have to build up to the lot line on the avenue.

—Buildings on the east side of Fifth may build straight up in the plane of the street wall if it is so desired; but if a setback is preferred, that cannot occur before the 3 story height. Buildings on the west side of the avenue must be built to the lot line to the height of 85 ft (26 m); at that point they must set back a minimum of 50 ft (15 m). This last requirement will provide tower separation between the east and west walls, letting more light onto the street in the afternoon, the time of peak usage. It also picks up the height of the existing setbacks on the Rockefeller Center buildings. A modest bonus is available if these setbacks are landscaped—as are those in Rockefeller Center—and also accessible to the public.

—One point of the allowable floor area bulk, roughly equivalent to two floors of a new building, must be devoted to retail uses selected from a special use group written around the most characteristic types of shopping on a shopping street. The list excludes corporate showrooms, and it limits banks and airline ticket offices to occupancy of not more than 15 percent of ground-floor space.

—Building lobbies cannot be located on Fifth Avenue; rather they must be located on the side streets at least 50 ft (15 m) behind the avenue.

—The plaza bonus can be used, but any plaza has to be located at least 50 ft behind the avenue. An extra incentive is offered if

the urban space developed is a galleria—a through-block connection between two side streets which is covered, has natural light, and is flanked by retail shops. The entry to the building can also front on this space.

—A special incentive is given to a development that provides retail space in addition to the minimum requirement. The incentive provides an increase in bulk of up to 20 percent, and the tower portion of the building can be up to 15 percent "fatter" than the zoning normally permits (this would ultimately allow the building to have fewer floors and therefore be less expensive). However, the bulk so gained can only be devoted to residential or hotel use (43).

Fifty years ago, Fifth Avenue was primarily a residential area, with several luxury hotels. Office buildings replaced most of the residential buildings in the core, attracting even more hotels in the process. Construction of new residential space in the core will help give the area more vitality after 5 P.M.

The concept of the 24-hour community, to which the mixed-use building is tied, is more than a cute idea. It is a practical and energy-efficient way to take advantage of an extensive infrastructure of subways, bus lines, and gas, water, sewer, steam, electric, and telephone systems that now sit virtually idle after 5 P.M. New dwellings along Fifth Avenue will make use of this excess capacity and produce needed tax revenues. Consider the cost—often as much as 50 percent of the total development—of providing a new public infrastructure in an outlying area to serve a similar residential density.

Olympic Tower, designed by Skidmore, Owings and Merrill (SOM) and developed by Aristotle Onassis, is the first building to be built under the district guidelines. Located at 51st and Fifth Avenue, Olympic Tower has 3 floors of retail space, 19 floors of office space, and 27 floors of cooperative apartments (44). In exchange for the public amenity bonus, the building includes a galleria with a fountain, small shops which normally would not be able to afford the price of Fifth Avenue frontage, and a cafe.

The building also does something else special. Its galleria is sited to line up as closely

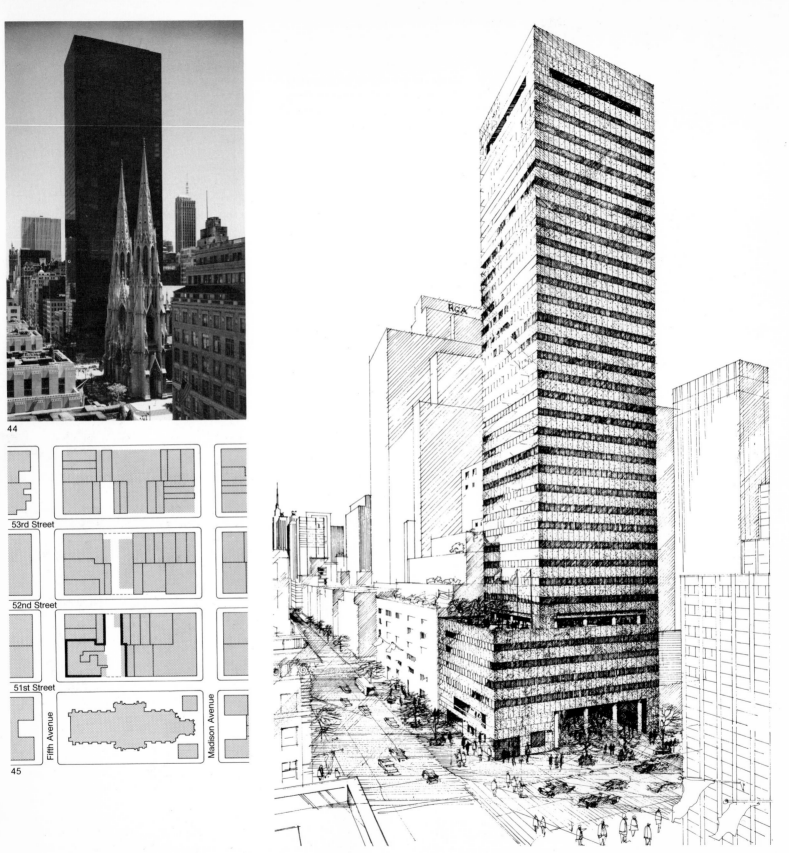

44

53rd Street

52nd Street

51st Street

Fifth Avenue

Madison Avenue

47

48-49   The 57-story Galleria is the first mixed-use building to be constructed in a transitional zone between
areas which are either all housing or all office. The building provides a through-block shopping way (49) as its
major public space.

50   Times Square is a neon zoo which is symbolic of the
tourist industry, the second most important aspect of
the city's economy.

be argued that the mixed-use legislation
does not constitute an entirely new depar-
ture.

The main provisions of the new mixed-use
zoning are as follows:

–To be eligible for a mixed-use building, a
zoning lot must be at least 20,000 sq ft
(1,800 sq m) in size. This provision seeks to
ensure that there will be enough space at
the ground level for two lobbies—one residential, the other commercial—as well as
retail activity.

–Each building must provide—without
bonus—5,000 sq ft (465 sq m) of recreational space for the exclusive use of residential tenants and their guests without admission or membership fee. The area
required is approximately the size of Paley
Park, but it may be developed as one or
many spaces, with portions covered or enclosed. Areas open to the sky must be landscaped, with the remainder of the space devoted to sitting or recreational facilities.
Design and locational flexibility were deliberately allowed to provide the possibility of
indoor spaces for winter and outdoor
spaces for summer.

–Each mixed-use building is required to
provide a covered pedestrian space, a galleria, a through-block arcade, a plaza-con-
nected open area, or any additional amenity
or combination of amenities that generates
a bonus equivalent to 2.5 FAR. The building
is required to do this whether or not it actually uses the bonus. Fulfillment of this requirement along with the requirement for
tenant recreational space will produce
more open space than is provided either by
an all-residential structure or by an all-of-
fice structure. However, the architect will
have considerably more flexibility in designing the space than was provided under the
1961 zoning.

–All setback areas occurring in the commercial portion of the building, including its
roof, must be landscaped if they are more
than 20 ft (6 m) deep.

–Because automobile ownership in the
central city is extremely low, the residential-
zone requirement that there be parking
spaces for 40 percent of the apartments has

been waived. (More recently a moratorium
was declared on construction of new parking spaces in Midtown, except under special circumstances.)

The Galleria, designed by David Kenneth
Spector, is the first building in New York
built under these new mixed-use provisions
(48). Located on 57th Street, an important
crosstown shopping street and thoroughfare, the 57-story building has 9 floors of office space below 36 floors of residential
space that contains 250 apartments. The
5,400-sq-ft (500-sq-m) tenant recreation
space is on the roof of the building, half of
which is enclosed. At the base of the building is a through-block skylighted galleria
that is 100 ft (30 m) high in places (49). The
galleria is flanked by shops, and in addition
there is a multilevel cafe bordering the central atrium.

**Times Square–Theater District, first of New
York's special zoning districts, offers a
space bonus for incorporating theaters in
new office buildings, but still lacks urban
design controls for developers who do not
elect the bonus option—and most do not.**

Times Square is difficult to define precisely.
Named after *The New York Times,* which
still has its main office in the area, the
"square" is certainly not square. In shape,
it may be likened to a somewhat bedraggled
bow tie. The largest space in the area, a
triangular traffic island, is called Duffy
Square. As for atmosphere, only seeing
could be believing (50).

Physically, Times Square may be defined
roughly as the large open space created by
the intersection of Broadway and Seventh
Avenue. Conceptually, Times Square is the
entertainment district that stretches along
42nd Street from Sixth to Eighth Avenues,
runs up Broadway and Seventh Avenue
from 42nd to about 53rd Street, and bleeds
out along all the in-between side streets.

Symbolically the center of the tourist industry, Times Square ranks second in economic importance in New York City only to
the neighboring garment industry.
(Psychoanalysis is a close third.) Times
Square is the home of the Broadway theater—it is also the entertainment center for
the low- and moderate-income groups of

51

52

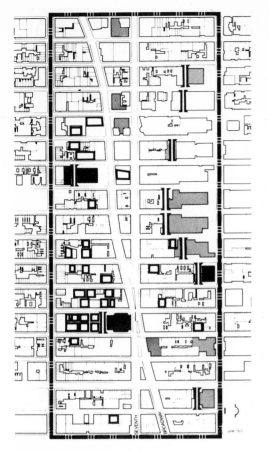

Existing theaters
New development
New development with theaters
Midblock pedestrian passages

53

51-52 The W. T. Grant Building, which houses the Minskoff Theater, was the first building to include a new theater in exchange for a bonus of additional office space. The lower floors of the W. T. Grant Building, with active retail on the ground level, banks and office lobby at the second level, and a Broadway theater above (52), have proved to be an excellent prototype for a new zoning proposal that would regulate all new buildings in Times Square and would also insist on large signs for each building.

53 Since the inception of the Theater District in 1967, four theaters valued at over $12 million have been built and others are planned.

the city. For example, on 42nd Street between Sixth and Eighth Avenues there are approximately 20 movie theaters, most of which show first-run films at one-third the price of the more fashionable East Side theaters only a mile away. Open seven days a week and almost 24 hours a day, the movie theaters are critical to the economic vitality of the area. In contrast, a Broadway theater only puts on about 10 shows a week.

By the mid-1960s several large sites in the theater area had been assembled; and as the boom of speculative office development continued, it seemed that Times Square was to be the next major concentration of new office buildings. The new buildings were being planned for sites that occasionally exceeded 2 acres (.8 ha) in size, which meant that one building had the potential of demolishing many of the small theaters in the area, which tend to cluster and are typically 2-story structures on 10,000-sq-ft (950-sq-m) lots. In fact, the assemblage pattern showed that many of these older theaters were part of larger development sites. The fear was that the city would lose its Broadway theaters, which are a central part of New York's economic and cultural life. Without the theater, actor Joe Silver warns, New York would be just two huge Toledos.

Before it was built, the W. T. Grant Building became the center of an attempt by the Urban Design Group to try to work an incentive around the provision of a new theater in a major office building. The developers, in this case the Minskoff Brothers, were reluctant to try what they felt was a high-risk experiment. Their architects had assured them that a theater would increase the time and expense of development by virtue of the theater's complex construction and the need to hire special consultants. However, Mayor Lindsay was excited by this first attempt to demonstrate what urban design could do and by the possibility that the demonstration could be realized in a short period of time, on a grand scale, and without costing the city any of its precious tax dollars. The developers remained adamant, and finally, after several unproductive meetings between the developers and the urban designers, the Mayor was asked to intervene. According to Richard Weinstein, who at that time was a member of the Urban Design Group, Mayor Lindsay convinced the

developers that any delays caused by building a theater would be nothing compared with the delays they would experience if they attempted to get a building permit from the Department of Buildings for a building without a theater. Whereupon the developers saw the wisdom of the Mayor's position and, in a dramatic turnabout, became great patrons of the arts, to the extent that they saw fit to name the theater after themselves.

The Minskoffs also agreed to follow a number of urban design guidelines established by Richard Weinstein and Jaquelin Robertson. In exchange for providing the theater and for adhering to the design standards, the Minskoffs received a special permit under the spanking new Special Theater District, the first of the city's special zoning districts. The permit allowed them to increase the bulk of their building by 20 percent, above and beyond the existing bonus for provision of public amenities.

The result of all these alarums and excursions has been a very satisfactory building, from an urban design point of view. The ground-floor Broadway frontage has retail shops that all remain open until very late in the evening. The rear of the building contains a restaurant that fronts on Shubert Alley, which the building, by setting in, has widened by 20 ft (6 m). A bank was placed on the second level with a better-than-average chance of success because the lobby for the 50-story tower was also placed on the second level, accessible from the ground level by escalators located at either end of the Broadway frontage (51, 52).

Since the time the Theater District legislation was passed in 1967, three buildings have incorporated a total of four theaters: The Minskoff Theater with 1,650 seats, the Uris Theater (another developer-patron) with 1,850 seats, the Circle in the Square Theater with 600 seats, and the American Place Theater with 299 seats (53). Several other developers have expressed their intention to build new theaters if there is a pick-up in the building market. All this represents a very pleasant turnaround. The four theaters are the first theaters to be built in the area in over 40 years. Between the 1920s and the mid-1960s, the number of theaters in the Times Square area actually decreased from about 80 to 33, with many

55

54

54 New zoning proposals would encourage the location of taller buildings along the avenues to preserve midblock theaters on the side streets. Zoning has been used this way before in New York to save midblock townhouses.

55 Although it provides two theaters and went through a design review process by the City Planning Commission, the Uris Building illustrates what can happen in the absence of specific urban design controls in an area like Times Square.

of those left for sale, and only about half open with Broadway productions. The new theaters represent not only confidence in the future of the theater, but also an indirect subsidy to the arts estimated at from $12 to $15 million.

Under the circumstances, the substantial bonus provided to the developer seems reasonable. With its excellent network of subways, Times Square can accommodate the increased number of commuters. Aesthetically, the added floors are a bearable burden. And in terms of fairness, it is necessary to offer a developer a substantial bonus in exchange for a theater. The additional construction costs are high because of the long spans and transfer beams that are required, not to mention the many consultants who must be brought in. Then again, a theater is definitely a dicey business proposition. A show can open on Friday, get slaughtered in the morning *Times,* and not live to the Saturday matinee. That may leave a theater empty for the rest of the year.

A review of the nine-year history of the theater district reveals three main problems.

First, there are still no provisions in the special zoning to save existing theaters, many of which are fine old buildings. Although not of historic architectural significance per se, these theaters are an integral part of New York's cultural life and certainly an attempt should be made to preserve them. To resolve this problem, an extremely simple zoning amendment has been proposed that would encourage a developer to build around an existing theater (54). The amendment would offer the developer the same bonus he would get if he were building a new theater, in exchange for renovation and preservation in theater use of the existing theater as long as it is a contiguous part of the zoning lot being developed. It was calculated that 30 percent of the existing theaters were adjacent to development parcels large enough to utilize this amendment. It has been estimated that successful employment of this measure, coupled with the recent construction of new theaters and the continued existence of theaters which do not appear to be threatened by new construction, could ensure that a minimum of 25 Broadway theaters would remain in use for the forseeable future.

The second problem is that the theater district is the only special zoning district without specific urban design controls. Out of 13 buildings erected in the special district, only 3 elected the option to build a theater and were thereby subjected to design review by the City Planning Commission. Even this design review is not completely satisfactory because the seven-person commission usually has only one architect and one professional planner as members. Nor do the commissioners have the leisure to analyze in depth the designs that are presented for their approval. So although the Uris Building at 50th and Broadway does have two theaters and a pedestrian through-block connection, it also has two useless sunken plazas fronting on Broadway, and its Broadway frontage is devoted to banks and lobbies (55). The ten new buildings that were not subject to design review were built under the existing provisions of the zoning resolution, which, in Times Square, offered many of the same problems that cropped up on Fifth Avenue (56, 57, 58).

The third problem with the theater district has to do, again, with the deleterious effects of the 1961 plaza bonus. For example, even though one of the two sunken plazas in front of the Uris Building does connect to the subway (while being very careful not to admit any light to the station), these are essentially useless spaces that detract from Times Square.

Furthermore, the city plans to implement a modified version of a plan by Van Ginkel Associates to close a section of Broadway and create a series of plazas (59). The street right-of-way for almost all north-south avenues, including Broadway, is approximately 60 ft (18.5 m). When Broadway and Seventh Avenue—120 ft (37 m) of roadway divided into 12 lanes of traffic—merge to six lanes at 45th Street, a bottleneck is created. No more than six lanes of cars can pass through this bottleneck, so there is no point in feeding any more than six lanes into the bottleneck (60). OMPD proposed to close Broadway to traffic between 45th and 48th Streets, diverting traffic on upper Broadway over to Seventh Avenue. Removal of a traffic island that forces Seventh Avenue to neck down to 30 ft (9 m) would restore Seventh Avenue to its original width of 60 ft

56

57

58

59

57   As most new buildings in Times Square do not elect to include a Broadway theater, they are free from all urban design controls. The results, like this building at 43rd and Broadway, are buildings which are anathema to the ambiance of Times Square.

58   John Portman's design proposal for a hotel in Times Square contains two huge interior spaces and a legitimate theater, but fails outwardly to acknowledge the existing qualities of the area. In exchange for the bonus to build the theater, the Planning Commission insisted that the hotel have small shops at its base and large signs covering part of the lower levels of the building.

59   Under the supervision of OMPD, the city built a discount ticket booth to aid the ailing Broadway theaters. The highly successful project shows the need for increased public space in Times Square.

60-61   The combined 12 lanes of traffic of Broadway and Seventh Avenue narrow down to six lanes at 45th Street. No more vehicles can pass through Times Square than can pass through comparable points of adjacent avenues. By diverting traffic on upper Broadway to Seventh Avenue and removing one traffic island, the same number of vehicles can pass through Times Square as do presently, but a huge urban space is created in the process (61).

60

61

62

63

65

66

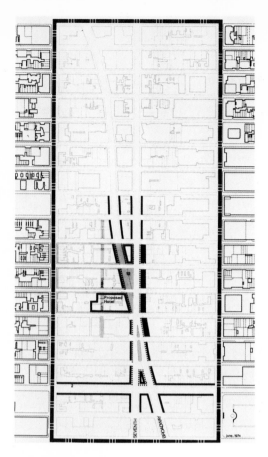

— Frontage controls
...... Major signage
▓ Through block connections and Broadway Plazas
■ Second-level shopping loggia

64

62   Part of what makes Times Square so exciting is the contradiction between public gestures toward civic art and an exploitative backdrop of lively and adventurous commercial signage. It is that positive inherent quality of this unique urban space which the zoning regulations seek to protect.

63   Richard Anuszkiewicz's painting in the Times Square area, part of Doris Freedman's City Wall's program, has a profound impact on the streetscape.

64   A new plan for Times Square would require all buildings to have large signs and active ground-floor retail space. Construction of new theaters would still be encouraged, as would the retention of older theaters.

65-66   OLMD was established by executive order to implement the Lower Manhattan plan. The plan provided an image of what that part of the island could become and, among other things, recommended housing on landfill areas (66), which would have a continuous pedestrian promenade at the river's edge. There would also be unobstructed views from the depths of the core area out to the river. OLMD has codified many of the plan's original objectives.

(18.5 m); and six lanes of traffic would be able to pass through Times Square, the same amount that can go through now. This simple rerouting of traffic creates a nearly 2-acre (.8-ha) area of pedestrian space, a hidden city-owned land bank valued at close to $10 million (61).

It makes no sense to give a bonus for a plaza that fronts on another plaza, a lesson that should have been learned from the GM Building, with its sunken plaza that faces Grand Army Plaza and Central Park. So it would therefore seem reasonable to enact urban design controls specially adapted to the unique situation in Times Square, as was done for Fifth Avenue.

Times Square is unique. It is a neon zoo, and as such it is a valid expression of one side of the character of one of the world's great cities. This is not a stately avenue, like Fifth Avenue, where mink-swathed matrons may browse for baubles before tea at the Plaza. It is the original from which Las Vegas was copied. As Picasso is reported to have said about his imitators, "You do something new, and then somebody else comes along and does it pretty." Architects who design for Times Square should be encouraged to respect this environment, rather than be allowed to attempt a replication of Fifth Avenue (62, 63).

Accordingly, a series of urban design controls has been written for Times Square. The controls would apply to any building along Broadway or Seventh Avenue from 41st Street to 53rd Street and along 42nd Street from Sixth Avenue to Eighth Avenue. They are written as amendments to the existing Theater District, although they have not yet been approved (64). The major provisions are as follows:

—All buildings along Broadway, Seventh Avenue, and 42nd Street must build to their respective building lot lines. This provision takes away the developer's option to use the plaza bonus in front of his building.

—In lieu of a plaza, new developments on the west side of Broadway may elect to continue Shubert Alley, as a new hotel by John Portman proposes to do.

—There must be at least one level of retail use integrated into the pedestrian circula-

tion system. The uses must be part of a special use group that excludes banks, loan offices, and corporate showrooms. Without this provision, the large plazas the city plans to build might quickly be surrounded by banks that close at 3:00 P.M. Travel agencies, excluded from the Fifth Avenue Special District, were felt to be appropriate to Times Square and are therefore among the permitted uses.

—Any development fronting on a subway must make an appropriate and visible connection within its property and remove the entrance on the sidewalk.

—All new developments fronting on Times Square must certify to the planning commission that signs characteristic of Times Square will be an integral part of the building's facade. There is no bonus for providing the sign, but there is an incentive: rental incomes, which in some cases are as much as $150,000 per year.

While there is much that can be done to improve Times Square without new construction, the goal of the zoning is merely to ensure that if there is to be new construction, buildings recognize, at their lower floors, the essential and unique qualities of Times Square and add to the signs, shops, restaurants, and theaters. This simple principle of adding or reinforcing long established and obvious qualities of unique areas in the city is the reason for all special zoning districts in New York.

A new phase of New York's pioneering effort to make urban design an instrument of public policy began with the establishment in 1967 of the Office of Lower Manhattan Development (OLMD), the first of several offices which were to be created by Mayor Lindsay to guide and monitor development in all five boroughs for the Office of the Mayor.

In a 1965 interim report to the City Planning Commission, consultants recommended that landfill be added to the U.S. Pierhead line clear around Lower Manhattan and that housing and office buildings be built (65, 66). The housing for 60,000 residents would at least offer some of the 500,000 downtown workers a chance to live within walking distance of their offices. And it would add life

1650
1776
1850
1973
1980
67

68

67 For more than three centuries, the growth of Lower Manhattan has occurred with taller buildings and landfill. (See also 19.)

68 Most buildings in the core area of Lower Manhattan are built on 100 percent of their sites and, accordingly, align themselves to fit along the subtle curves and angles of the historic street plan.

to and take advantage of an area of the city that has incredible resources but virtually shuts down at 6 o'clock in the evening.

For the past 300 years, landfill has been used to reinforce this tightly organized area of the city that needed to grow circumferentially to take advantage continuously of the waterfront rather than expand only towards the available land masses to the north (67).

The consultant's final report to the City Planning Commission in 1966 contained a graphically illustrated master plan for Lower Manhattan, with a series of recommended policies the city should adopt before leasing any of its land. After the Lower Manhattan Plan was presented, New York State announced interest in developing a landfill area at the western edge of Lower Manhattan. The project was to be called Battery Park City, but the plan produced for the 91-acre (36.8-ha) site had little resemblance to the city's new master plan. And worse, the project had ignored many of the major recommendations of the plan, which included a continuous pedestrian esplanade at the water's edge, with direct and visible connections from the center of the core to those walkways.

When Mayor Lindsay established the Office of Lower Manhattan Development (OLMD), it was charged with the implementation of the Lower Manhattan Plan. OLMD's director, Richard Buford, a lawyer cognizant of the city's leverage in the debate by virtue of its ownership status, simply wrote into the lease with the Battery Park City Authority that the original Master Site Plan must be followed precisely. Some of the city's consultants for the Lower Manhattan Plan were then hired to augment the state's design team; and a new site plan was created that certainly lacked the visual interest of the Lower Manhattan Plan, but did adhere to its basic requirements.

The original goal of Battery Park City was to provide a racially and economically mixed community with the 15,000 housing units split evenly between upper-, middle-, and lower-income families. For a variety of reasons—including the difficulty of raising sufficient subsidies and also the fear that the upper- and middle-income units might be

unmarketable because of the mix of so many lower-income units—the city allowed the economic composition to be altered to allow for maximums of 30 percent in luxury units, 56 percent in middle-income units, and a minimum of 14 percent for low-income units.

The Buford lease provisions cleverly left the door open for his successor, architect Richard Weinstein, to provide a more precise set of guidelines based on the need to interpret the aims of the Master Plan into legal language that the developers could understand and that architects could easily design within.

At the same time, Richard Weinstein's staff began to make detailed urban design recommendations for the easterly side of Lower Manhattan, which was to be called Manhattan Landing. The Manhattan Landing development was administered quite differently from Battery Park City. Several clearly identifiable development parcels were to be leased to different developers who agreed to work within the city's urban design framework. Because the city owned both waterfront sites, maximum residential densities and office bulk were established from the beginning. There was to be no additional bonused space for the provision of public amenities as is *pro forma* with zoning in New York. Instead, the developer had to follow a detailed set of requirements that allowed some flexibility in how they could be met. For example, both Battery Park City and Manhattan Landing required an internal north-south pedestrian easement through their respective centers. But this might be accomplished by stringing together a variety of established urban design elements such as arcades, loggias, galleries, parks, and so on. Because of their similarity, Battery Park City and Manhattan Landing basically have the same set of requirements, although they have been modified somewhat to reflect design considerations that vary on the two edges of Lower Manhattan.

Many of the urban design controls for the proposed developments along the river find their genesis in a carefully constructed analysis of the core, where many buildings have traditionally aligned themselves with the delicate curves of many of the original

69

70

71

69   The view corridors that have been established throughout Lower Manhattan must be respected by all new construction. Coupled with view corridors, the requirement that buildings are constructed up to prescribed lines will ensure that several existing urban spaces remain well defined.

70-71   Wall Street (so named because it was the northern wall of the old fortified town of New Amsterdam) is one of several of Lower Manhattan's canyonlike streets that will greatly benefit from a perpetual view of the East River and access to the morning sun.

72-73   This detail of a proposed development for the northern site in Manhattan Landing has been designed within the established urban design requirements of that particular parcel (72), taking into special consideration its proximity to the South Street Seaport.

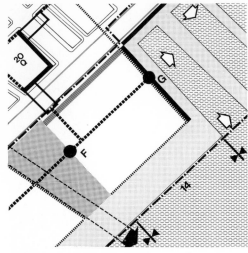

--- District boundary
▶◀ Parcel line
▬▬ Build-to line
▭▭▶ Visual corridor
▭▭◇ Window
•▬●▬ Pedestrian corridor
▭▭ Pedestrian bridge
▓▓▓▓ People-mover corridor
░░░░ Esplanade, pedestrian way
▒▒▒▒ Pedestrian space
▪▪▪▪ Pedestrian circulation improvement

72

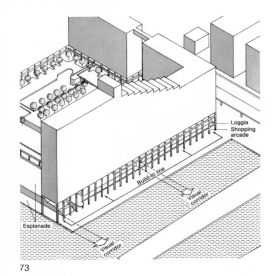

73

streets of Lower Manhattan, especially Broadway and Broad Street (68).

To maintain a respect for the historic development of Lower Manhattan, which many buildings of the past two decades have denied, and to take advantage of the new opportunities presented for the active use of the river front, the following urban design controls have been established:

–View corridors (69). The view corridor is a defined "volume" or "envelope of space" that reflects the existing street pattern and is extended as a visual easement through the perimeter development sites. There can be no development within a view corridor. This urban design technique will ensure that a visual continuity is maintained between the existing core and new development; it will keep the views of the river from the depths of the core open to a future when these edges will actually be accessible (70, 71)—in fact, it is a mandatory requirement that there be a pedestrian connection to the river's edge through that part of a view corridor that passes through the development sites; it will enable the corridor in the east-west direction access to morning and evening sun; and, finally, it establishes an armature for new development.

–Build-to lines. To ensure that view corridors do not "bleed out" as they cross into the proposed developments and to define better the major public open spaces that the overall plan creates, certain key corridors have been identified, requiring that building walls of new developments be built parallel to and along these established lines. This also applies to areas within the core, specifically to protect existing spaces—City Hall Park and Battery Park.

–Pedestrian circulation system. A pedestrian circulation system has been established for each of the major development districts setting forth a network of pedestrian paths which is linked to the downtown core at specific locations. This will permit direct pedestrian access and circulation between the waterfront and the center of the island. Pedestrian bridges are generally specified at established elevated pedestrian levels, like the World Trade Center and the Greenwich Street Special District. The bridges are invariably along the visual corri-

dors or connect open spaces and park areas. In either case, they are meant to move the pedestrian safely across the heavily traveled vehicular arteries that flank both major waterfront projects.

–Esplanade. All waterfront projects will provide an easement at the river's edge for an esplanade. This continuous pedestrian walkway will extend from the base of the Brooklyn Bridge, which marks the northern end of the Seaport Historic District, southward along the edge of Manhattan Landing, around and through the existing Battery Park and then northward along the river's edge of Battery Park City. The esplanade along Manhattan Landing must have a minimum width of 150 ft (45 m), although limited sections of it can be spanned by buildings.

In addition to these urban design considerations, specifications have also been established for a variety of other elements including arcades, loggias, galleries, open and enclosed pedestrian bridges, and enclosed pedestrian shopping bridges. Within the overall urban design framework, a particular element may be specified at certain locations (72, 73).

To encourage both preservation and renovation of one historic district, OLMD devised zoning amendments which freed development rights from the parcels of which they were a part and even permitted them to be "banked" for future sale and used as credit against present indebtedness.

The South Street Seaport sits at the northeastern edge of the financial center (74). Once the center of 19th-century New York's thriving shipping industry, today it is a historic district under renovation, with its slips offering berths for classic ships of the past and its 18th- and 19th-century buildings reserved for museums, restaurants, small offices, craft shops, artists' studios, and apartments. The preservation of the Seaport is a unique undertaking, combining several legislative elements from special zoning districts and historic districts coupled with a few innovations of its own, cleverly sewn together by Richard Weinstein and Edgar Lampert, chief council for OLMD.

In the Seaport transactions, the zoning resolution was amended in 1972 to provide, for

74

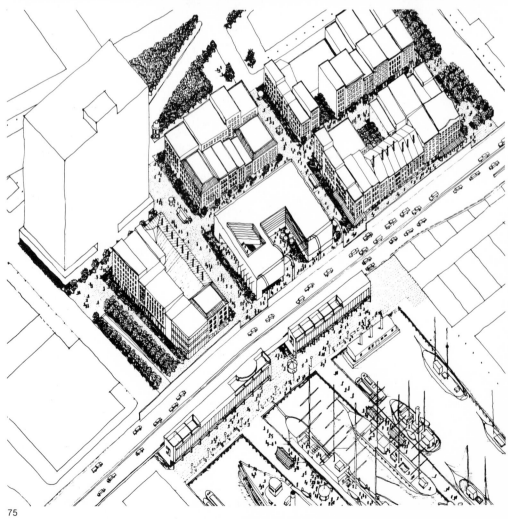

75

74-75 The South Street Seaport, now a historic district, was threatened by the growth of office buildings in Lower Manhattan. Urban design techniques were instituted to remove speculative pressures from the Seaport area, protect the uses within, and ensure that surrounding new development would be sympathetic to the scale of the Seaport's lower buildings.

the first time in the city and perhaps for the first time anywhere, for development rights to be freed from the parcels of which they were a part. The development rights could be transferred not only to an adjacent parcel but to any individual or corporate entity to ''hold,'' as long as that individual or corporation would ultimately transfer the development rights to what were designated as ''receiving lots'' within the special zoning district (75).

Within the Seaport, the average blocks contained 5-story buildings covering 100 percent of the site. These blocks, called ''granting lots,'' had unused development rights. A receiving lot could purchase enough development rights to increase its maximum allowable bulk by 20 percent. Through a conversion technique it would be possible to buy even more development rights, thereby increasing the buildings' tower coverage.

Originally, in 1968, a corporation on behalf of the Seaport acquired four blocks of the Seaport area to create a historic district. To do so, the corporation borrowed $10 million to finance the acquisition of the property. As a business venture—even though non-profit—the Seaport could not get off the ground. The corporation was not even able to pay interest on the loan, which had accrued almost $2 million. Apart from these properties, one of the most prized blocks in the area, the Schermerhorn Row, was still in private ownership along with a few other significant parcels.

The city, through the urging of Richard Weinstein, actively tried to save the Seaport. Using its urban renewal powers, the city agreed to purchase all outstanding parcels, including the Schermerhorn Row and the original 4 blocks the Seaport Corporation held, for a total of $8 million. Of that sum, about $3 million went for the original Seaport blocks. In turn the Seaport Corporation handed these funds over to the banks to reduce the $12 million mortgage to $9 million. Additionally, all development rights from what were now city holdings, including the development rights from several streets in the district that were to be closed to create a pedestrian precinct, were transferred to a consortium of banks. In return, the banks agreed to release the mortgage

lien from the Seaport properties so that the city could purchase them free and clear.

An important feature of the South Street Seaport, one which might serve as a useful precedent for other historic districts, was that air rights were not required to be directly transferred from a granting lot to a receiving lot because there was no market for development rights at the time of the Seaport transactions. Therefore, the banks served as an intermediary to hold or ''bank'' these development rights. As though by magic, all these events occurred simultaneously. The city then leased all its newly acquired holdings back to the Seaport Corporation under a 99-year lease. Besides the $3 million the banks received from the Seaport Corporation, they now possessed 1,200,000 sq ft (114,000 sq m) of development rights that they could sell to any designated development parcel within the Seaport Special District. In this way, they may eventually recoup the remaining $9 million they had invested in the area, provided the office market picks up.

To match the city's vested interest in the Seaport, a series of urban design controls were established in an attempt not only to clearly define the Seaport area, but also to ensure that new construction at its periphery creates a transitional scale relationship. The main urban design definition of the Seaport will come from a mandated build-to-line required of the proposed building at the northern edge of Manhattan Landing. The building must also respond to a cornice articulation at its + 45-ft (13.5-m) elevation, the cornice height of the Schermerhorn Row. To retain unimpeded views from the esplanade of the splendid Brooklyn Bridge, nothing may be built in the Seaport district within 150 ft (45 m) of the pier head line.

For the Greenwich Street Special Development District, OLMD developed an overall urban design plan and a comprehensive system of incentives and controls for blanket approval by the City Planning Commission and the Board of Estimate, eliminating the special permit a developer was required to obtain under the earlier special district zoning legislation.

The Greenwich Street District is the most complicated of the special zoning districts.

This is so because Greenwich Street is also the most comprehensive urban design district in New York, according to John West, who, under the direction of Richard Weinstein, was one of the chief designers of the district and helped draft its legislation.

Besides mandating primary pedestrian connections, bonusing a series of optional subway improvements, reinforcing an important shopping street, and maintaining the overall character of Lower Manhattan—the Greenwich Street District also establishes for the first time where major open space should be located (76). This is a condition related both to the opportunity to create it and to the need for it.

From the developer's point of view, the district is important because it is self-administering. In the past, developers may have wanted to build certain urban design elements, such as covered pedestrian space, not only for altruistic reasons, but also for the higher bonus rate. But they often did not because it required a special permit from the Planning Commission, a lengthy process that presented the same problems of delay and uncertainty as the previous special zoning districts that also required a special permit.

The Greenwich Street District was the first special district that did not require the developer to obtain a special permit first. This was because the Greenwich Street District was presented *in toto* to the Planning Commission and the Board of Estimate. They were aware of the inclusion of items that normally require special permits and approved the district because these items were carefully detailed and, more important, were part of the overall urban design plan. It only remained for the Department of Buildings to make sure the building, with its attendant urban design elements, conformed to the letter of the zoning law before a building permit would be issued.

In the late 1960s, Lower Manhattan experienced the same development pressures as Midtown. The 110-story twin towers of the World Trade Center were well under construction, shifting new development to the west of the established center (77). South of the World Trade Center it was possible to build a building 10 times the area of the zon-

ing lot, which was 50 percent less than that allowed in the commercial center. But developers recognized that this area, also flanked by the proposed Battery Park City, was to be the next area of redevelopment—therefore, they were busy assembling land with the expectation that the city would upzone this area to be consistent with the density of the World Trade Center. In fact, the Fisher Brothers had assembled a rather large tract of land divided by a small public street, and asked the city to close the street and sell it to them. In this case the developer needed the support of the Office of Lower Manhattan Development for an upzoning. But Richard Weinstein was concerned that too much of an upzoning on this one favored site could constitute spot zoning. The developers would have a better chance for an upzoning if it were part of an areawide plan. The urban design controls established for the Fisher Brothers' building would have the double responsibility of responding to present conditions, such as the World Trade Center's elevated pedestrian deck, and of serving as a prototype for future buildings in the district.

The first objective of the Greenwich Street Special District plan was to improve circulation for pedestrians, emergency and service vehicles, and subway accessibility. Also the Lower Manhattan Plan recommended the location of three main east-west pedestrian bridge connections over the highway from Battery Park City to the Greenwich Street area), he could build a 500,000-sq-ft corporate. Greenwich Street itself is an important local shopping street, but in need of reinforcement.

An analysis by Al Shimmel, the city's real estate economist, on the impact of a 50 percent upzoning showed that the residual value to the developers would reach millions of dollars. For example, if a developer has a site of 50,000 sq ft (4,700 sq m) and the present zoning allows the developer to build at an FAR of 10 (10 times the site area), he could build a 500-600-sq-ft (47,500-sq-m) building, excluding bonuses. But if the developer knows he can market an even larger building of 750,000 sq ft (71,200 sq m) and therefore had to purchase more land surrounding his existing site to build the additional 250,000 sq ft (23,700 sq m), he would need to buy another 25,000 sq ft (2,000 sq m) of land. If it were $200 per sq ft, the additional land alone would cost $5 million. Therefore, granting an upzoning on this original site would save the developer $5 million initially and would also bring a return on the extra square footage. It is impossible, however, to determine precise figures, since the developer buys the land at an inflated price because the seller believes there is sufficient market pressure for the city to upzone. At issue here is what benefit the city should derive from an upzoning that has a clear, if not a precisely calculable, value for a developer.

It was decided that significant public improvements to the transportation system should be the *quid pro quo*. Therefore, for a developer to receive an upzoning from an FAR of 10 to an FAR of 15, he must refer to his specific site in the zoning text and build all mandatory pedestrian circulation improvements that are listed. For the most part, these improvements are pedestrian bridges that connect his site to others. The developer is often, but not always, free to choose from a variety of bridge types—the more elaborate the bridge, such as a glass-enclosed, heated, and air-conditioned shopping bridge, the greater the bonus. The costs of the different types of bridges and other improvements have been converted into the amount of additional square feet the developer may add to his building by constructing such an improvement.

If the provision of all the mandatory pedestrian improvements does not equate to sufficient floor area to construct a building at an FAR of 15, the developer then refers to an appendix in the zoning resolution that lists nine major subway improvements within the Greenwich Street Special District. The improvements range from construction of tunnels (under various streets that connect subway platforms) to entrance modernizations. If a developer builds the required pedestrian improvements and the highest-ranking elected subway improvement as required and is still shy of reaching a floor area ratio of 15, he may make up the difference by contributing a sum of money based on the difference, although he is not obliged to do so. If the developer works his way to a floor area ratio of 15, he is eligible to take advantage of the zoning's standard 20 percent bonus provisions, which would

allow a maximum floor area ratio of 18. However, nothing in life is easy. There are strings to this second set of bonuses.

At an FAR of 15, the developer, referring again to a description of urban design requirements for his particular zoning lot, must construct the listed mandatory improvements. Each block is part of the overall district plan, and on the west side of Greenwich Street, for example, each of the northern 4 blocks in the district must, among other things, construct a shopping way. This urban design feature is also germane to Manhattan Landing. It consists of a shopping arcade at the ground level, a glass-enclosed climate-controlled shopping way at the second level, and clearly marked escalators connecting the two levels every 150 ft (46 m) (78). Other sites in the district may select from among arcades, loggias, and elevated plazas, but must always provide certain prescribed urban design elements.

In Greenwich Street, the provisions of all the amenities and circulation improvements that would be in the public interest and justify the upzoning would be too numerous for the standard 20 percent bonus. Therefore, another bonusing technique was created that would increase public amenities and was clearly advantageous to the developer, but without ill-effects to the public. This bonus increased tower coverage that the zoning presently limits to 40 percent of the site. A conversion was worked out between the value of percentage increases of tower coverage from 40 percent to a maximum tower coverage of 55 percent to the provision of public amenities. Buildings of high coverage are characteristic of Lower Manhattan and are less expensive to build.

Because of the significance of "the Greenwich Street approach" in planning for rapidly expanding areas of central cities, it is useful to illustrate how the district works.

The Bankers Trust Building was the first building constructed within the guidelines of the Greenwich Street District. As mentioned earlier, the site consists of 2 complete blocks—54N and 54S—that could now be developed as one contiguous parcel, as the city had agreed to sell to the developer the street that divided the two sites (79).

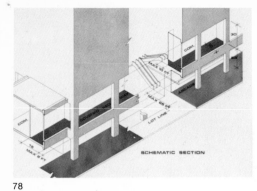

SCHEMATIC SECTION

78

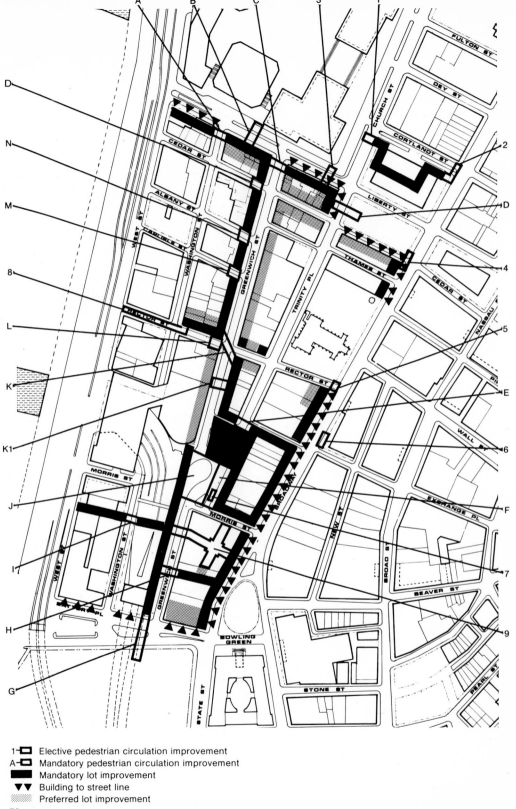

1 ▭ Elective pedestrian circulation improvement
A ▭ Mandatory pedestrian circulation improvement
■ Mandatory lot improvement
▼▼ Building to street line
░ Preferred lot improvement

76

76   The Greenwich Street Special Development District provides a comprehensive urban design framework that maintains the overall character of Lower Manhattan. The district legislation mandates primary pedestrian connections, bonuses subway improvements, reinforces shopping streets, and determines where open space should be located.

77   The World Trade Center lost out to the Sears Building in Chicago (117) in the tallest-building olympics, but sparked new development in this section of Lower Manhattan, which led to the Greenwich Street District.

78   A "shopping way" is an urban design element required of all new buildings locating on Greenwich Street.

77

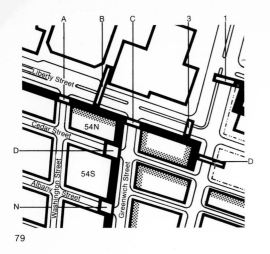

79

In order not to disrupt the normal east-west pedestrian movement through the site, a condition was that the developer provide a through-block arcade approximately along the alignment of the closed street.

The site is approximately 66,000 sq ft (6,200 sq m). The FAR permitted a building 10 times that area, or 660,000 sq ft (62,500 sq m). However, by providing all bonus features available, the developer could achieve an upzoning and ultimately construct a building 18 times the lot size, or 1,188,000 sq ft (118,700 sq m). The developer in this case knew he could successfully market a building with an FAR of 18 and also he could take advantage of increased tower coverage because the major tenant required substantial back-office space for computers.

Therefore, the developer had to first provide specified public improvements or amenities equivalent to the difference between FAR 10 and FAR 15, or 330,000 sq ft (31,300 sq m) of bonus space. The first requirement was to construct all pedestrian circulation improvements shown on the zoning map. There were five mandatory pedestrian bridge connections between the 2 blocks. However, because the sites are now combined, the pedestrian bridge over Cedar Street was unnecessary. Also because the sites to which bridges A, C, and N were to connect have not as yet been redeveloped, those bridges automatically become the responsibility of the adjacent sites as redeveloped. This leaves only connection B to the World Trade Center to be constructed. The zoning resolution describes this connection as a 165-ft (50-m) open pedestrian bridge. The bonus for this type of bridge is 100 sq ft (9.5 sq m) of additional floor area per linear foot of bridge. This produces 16,500 sq ft (1,550 sq m) of bonus floor area. (Eventually, it will be possible to walk at the same level from Broadway, which is at an elevation of +30, through the Greenwich Street area while the ground falls away as you approach the Hudson River. Finally, there will be the bridge connections over the highway to Battery Park City, from which point the pedestrian will be brought back down to the river.)

Next, the developer selected the first item from a ranked list of elective or optional

subway improvements, a pedestrian tunnel under Church Street, connecting the World Trade Center with the new U.S. Steel Building (number 1 in figure 79). The tunnel cost approximately $2 million. It is not directly connected to the developer's site, but represents a basic precept of the district: an improved transit system benefits everyone.

The tunnel produced a floor area allowance of 303,500 sq ft (28,828 sq m). At this point, the developer was within 10,000 sq ft (950 sq m) of an adjusted floor area of 15. As no elective pedestrian circulation improvement was that small, the developer chose to contribute to the Greenwich Street Development District Fund, which was established for this purpose. At $6.75 per sq ft (this figure is based on the assessed value of 60 office buildings and is revised annually according to a formula in the zoning resolution), the remaining 10,000 sq ft required a contribution of $67,500. These funds are being used to make modest subway improvements within the special district.

Once the developer has worked his way to an FAR of 15, he is eligible for the standard 20 percent bonus, the equivalent of three additional points of FAR, for the provision of public amenities. The developer is obliged to build certain urban design features whether or not he wants the additional square feet of building their provision would allow him to build. The mandatory lot improvements in this case are a shopping arcade approximately 100 ft (30 m) long to compensate for the closing of Cedar Street, a shopping way approximately 185 ft (56 m) long, and a pedestrian connection at the elevated level to connect the bridge from the World Trade Center with the shopping way and the bridges to be built in the future. Although the zoning permits the pedestrian connection to be a minimum of 15 ft (4.6 m) wide, the developer decided to take advantage of building an elevated plaza which offered a larger bonus and was coupled with a bonus for a required number of trees on the plaza. Among the shopping arcade, the shopping way, the elevated plaza, and the trees, the developer earned approximately 318,000 sq ft (30,150 sq m) of bonus floor space—space that could be used to increase either the floor area or tower coverage of the building.

80

The developer converted 171,293 sq ft (16,123 sq m) of this allowable floor area to increase the tower coverage from 40 to 53 percent. The remaining floor area increased the FAR from 15 to 17.4. To build to the maximum FAR of 18, the developer chose to provide two discretionary lot improvements—an arcade along Liberty Street and a plaza on Washington Street.

Other, more fundamental requirements are not bonused but are of considerable benefit to the public and of relatively little cost or inconvenience for the developer to provide. These include reserving 2.5 percent of the total building floor area exclusively for certain shopping uses at the lower levels; restriction of access to parking and loading facilities from specified streets; and the positioning of some buildings on their sites so as to reinforce both the shopping street and the edge of a defined urban space.

In sum, the completed building (80) contains urban design features the average developer would neither have contemplated providing in this project himself, nor, in all likelihood, permitted his architect to include in his design, even assuming that the architect had the knowledge and foresight to understand the need for such urban design elements and would elect to do them if he were not so mandated.

An air rights transfer provision enacted into law in the continuing struggle to save Grand Central Station is an important new tool for New York landmarks preservation, though it was not enough to prevent protracted litigation in the Grand Central case which puts New York's 1962 landmarks preservation law itself in jeopardy.

In support of the efforts of the Landmarks Preservation Commission, the Planning Commission in New York has passed a variety of zoning laws designed to facilitate achievement of the objective of the landmarks law—the preservation of landmark buildings. Perhaps the most important of these amendments to the zoning resolution has been the air rights transfer provision that has figured so prominently in the Grand Central preservation battle.

With several hundred designated landmarks, New York's record of preservation

seems impressive, but closer examination reveals its weakness. Of the approximately 300 landmarks designated by 1970, 80 were churches, 69 were public buildings, and 45 were residences. The Landmarks Preservation Commission even designated seven cemeteries, a bridge, and one lonely tree. What it did not designate in great numbers were truly endangered buildings—in particular, privately held structures on prime sites, where the zoning would allow redevelopment at significantly higher densities.

The aim in the early years was to build up a large inventory of designated landmarks with little controversy. It has been a general policy of the commission to get the owner to agree to designation before it acts. Because of its policy of cooperation and because it had avoided designating buildings located on prime Manhattan sites, where the tax abatement provision in the Landmarks Preservation Act is an insufficient incentive to reduce development pressure, the Landmarks Commission has avoided court tests of the basic legal issue presented by the landmarks law—whether a landmark designation, by infringing on the landowner's right to redevelop his parcel to its maximum potential, constitutes an illegal taking without compensation of the landowner's property. In those cases where the issue has come up, the courts have been hard-pressed to say it was other than a taking without compensation. Judicial opinions have generally held that either the city should let the owner build on his land to the zoning limits, or it should compensate him for not allowing him to build. Compensation, of course, is something the city wants to avoid. If the city has to pay cash for its landmarks, rather than provide some other carrot such as tax abatement, there aren't going to be very many landmarks.

With Penn Station lost to the wrecker's ball in 1962, landmark designation of the city's other great railroad terminal was timely, for it came only one month prior to the announcement of plans to construct a 55-story office building over Grand Central Station. Under the existing zoning, a truly enormous building is possible on the Grand Central site because the terminal building is built at an FAR of only 1.5, whereas the zoning allows the site to be developed to an FAR of 18.

79   The developer who owned this 2-block site successfully petitioned the city to sell the development rights from the intervening street. The site—like all sites in the Greenwich Street District—is tied to a series of urban design requirements carefully described on a block-by-block basis in a special section of the zoning ordinance.

80   As part of the urban design requirements, the Bankers Trust Building had to include in its construction a continuous shopping way (a ground-level shopping arcade connected by escalators and stairs to an elevated and enclosed shopping way) and a plaza that has a bridge connection to the World Trade Center.

81

82

83

In 1968, the Penn Central Railroad entered into a contractual arrangement with a developer in which it transferred to him the right to build a tower on top of the Grand Central Station terminal. There was also a provision in the lease with the developer which would have imposed a penalty of $1 million if he failed to either construct the building within a certain time period or litigate the question of its construction to its ultimate conclusion—one of the factors that put a lot of pressure on the developer to continue to try to resolve that question, even at a time when the economy was perhaps not strong enough to warrant going ahead with the building.

Marcel Breuer was the architect, and his first proposal would have cut right through the main space of the terminal (81). According to the developer, the solution adhered to the landmarks law, which at that time only protected facades. But when people yelled and screamed that a 700-ft (215-m) high modern facade placed atop Grand Central was certainly an alteration of that landmark's classic facade (82) and destroyed the interior space as well, Breuer tried to make peace with his public by presenting an alternate design, still perched over, but now straddling, the station (83). To some, no doubt, this second scheme was an ingenious solution designed to preserve a substantial part of the interior concourse. But both designs were found to be unacceptable to everyone on the Planning Commission as well as the Landmarks Commission.

In 1968 the Planning Commission passed an amendment to the zoning resolution to permit the distribution of air rights to lots which were in the same ownership but separated by public roadways. The previous legislation would have permitted the transfer of Grand Central's 2 million sq ft (190,000 sq m) of air rights only to immediately adjacent sites in common ownership. It was thought that the Penn Central would be satisfied once it was permited to transfer air rights off the site to adjacent sites in the same ownership, even though across streets. Because the Penn Central owned virtually all the buildings within several blocks of the station, it would be able to use its air rights to build a number of very large new buildings.

The air rights transfer also made sense from a planning standpoint. The literally thousands and thousands of people who would work in a building located directly above Grand Central would all arrive at, and depart from, the already very crowded terminal at the same time. If the 2 million-sq-ft mass was built away from the terminal at varying distances, people would arrive in a staggered sequence, alleviating the pressure on the terminal. Also the distributed bulk would allow Grand Central to remain a light well, a sort of air park, for the surrounding tall buildings.

There were several problems with this approach. First, the neighboring sites were for the most part already intensely developed; and second, the air rights transfer legislation prevented such a transfer from increasing the bulk of a "receiving" structure by more than 20 percent. The amount of development rights available from Grand Central was so great that, with this restriction, it would have taken many new buildings and long years before the owner of Grand Central would have realized the economic value of the Grand Central air rights.

Once it became clear that this amendment would not satisfy the developer or probably the courts, another amendment was introduced before the Planning Commission, but failed to pass. This amendment would have given the commission discretionary power to restrict the bulk of any new building within the city's three transportation centers, one of which conveniently was Grand Central, to 80 percent of that allowed in the zoning ordinance. This limitation would have made the office tower economically unfeasible.

In late 1969, the developer, his lawyer, and a representative of the railroad held discussions with Jaquelin Robertson, Bill Bardel (then counsel to OMPD), Don Elliott (chairman of the City Planning Commission), and Norman Marcus (chief counsel to the City Planning Department) about still another amendment to the zoning resolution, which was subsequently passed. In a reversal from its previous attempt essentially to rezone to lower densities the overly dense areas of the city, the new amendment waived the limit on the maximum amount of development rights that could be transferred to any

81-82   Grand Central Station is one of the few great enclosed public urban spaces left in New York. Several alternate design solutions for nearby sites proposed by the city's urban design staff made it unnecessary to alter the interior space or exterior facade. The city's urban designers argued that as a low building, Grand Central Station (82) served the taller surrounding buildings with an "air park" that provided sun and view for thousands of office workers.

83   Marcel Breuer's proposal for a building above Grand Central Station sought to preserve most of the interior space but was unacceptable both to the Planning and Landmark Commissions and to common sensibilities.

84

85

| NEW YORK | WASHINGTON, D.C. |
| CHICAGO | LOS ANGELES |

86

one site and permitted the full allowable bulk from Grand Central to be built on one site in addition to that site's allowable bulk.

Although this solution appeared to be spot zoning, it was not contested. So once again, Breuer produced design schematics, this time for a site other than Grand Central, which utilized this new amendment. Apparently the developer was interested in pursuing this alternative to Grand Central, and the law suit which the developer had brought against the city suing for damages and for the right to go forward with the construction of the building was adjourned at the developer's request while meaningful discussions took place with the city on these alternatives.

However, serious complications began with the combination of a poor office market and the Penn Central's bankruptcy, which made unclear just what the railroad was permitted to do with its properties. As a result there was no attempt by the developer to get the city formally to approve his most recent proposal; and the lawsuit was once again actively litigated because the developer was concerned about the penalty provision in his lease with Penn Central and feared Penn Central would be less able to tolerate his delays now that it was in bankruptcy. Also there was a federal judge seeing to it that the railroad collected every possible cent that it was owed.

The developer argued in court that the Landmarks Commission's designation of his site was unconstitutional in that it took away value from his property because he was prohibited from developing it fully. It was therefore, according to the developer, a taking without compensation. The city, in turn, argued that it wasn't *taking* anything, but was providing the developer with viable alternatives for the transfer of air rights which would have preserved an established landmark and protected the developer's economic interests. The developer's response was that the alternatives weren't close to being the same value as the right to build over the terminal. The alternative site, he said, was so small as to necessitate a building over 60 stories tall, which was prohibitively expensive; and the market value of the site wasn't nearly so high as that of the Grand Central site. Essentially, he ar-

gued that the city never really offered anything as valuable as what he was asked to give up. The city in conclusion argued that the developer had been given reasonable alternatives and that the real reason he didn't pursue them was not because they weren't valuable, but because the office market had turned down so much that he realized he could not go ahead under any circumstances on any site.

The judge didn't announce his decision for about two years. The city assumed it took so long because of the importance of the decision and thought the judge was trying to give the two parties a chance to work out their differences because he didn't want to rule against the landmarks law. But no accommodations were reached during this interim period, and the ruling, when announced, was against the city. The city appealed this decision with the support of citizens' groups and in December 1975, New York's Appellate Division of the State Supreme Court overturned the lower court. In his decision, the judge called Grand Central "a major part of the cultural and architectural heritage of New York City," which, "stripped of its remaining historically unique structures . . . would be indistinguishable from any other large metropolis."[5] In June 1977 the Court of Appeals, the State's highest court, upheld this decision, but the developers have decided to take the case to the U.S. Supreme Court.

A proposal to reorganize midtown Manhattan transportation systems in favor of the pedestrian became a major environmental battle lost to the merchants of Madison and Fifth Avenues; but the story of the "Van Ginkle Plan" and the furor created by the effort to begin with a particular element of it, the Madison Mall, are an essential piece of New York's recent urban design history.

The purpose of the attempt to close Madison Avenue to automobiles was to increase vitally needed walking space; create a major linear park; improve the economic vitality of this important shopping street; reduce noise and air pollution in order to establish a more humane environment; and reorganize surface public transportation.

A typical morning rush hour in New York creates the impression that virtually every-

87

84 The appearance of New York's highways notwithstanding, only about 4 percent of incoming commuters drive to work.

85 The effect of automobile pollution on the environment is devastating.

86 "How to spot some major American cities from the air."

87 What seems to be missing from Midtown is a pleasant place to sit and relax, though a simple administrative action by Mayor Lindsay enabled hundreds of restaurants to open outdoor cafes, creating new street life in New York. Still, cafes are not permitted on the densest streets of Midtown and Lower Manhattan, simply because the sidewalks are too narrow and overcrowded.

body is trying to get to work by automobile (84). The effect of all those automobiles on the environment is nothing short of devastating (85, 86). To make Midtown's air fit for human consumption once again, the federal government has instructed the city that there must be a 72 percent reduction in the airborne concentration of carbon monoxide and an 81 percent reduction in hydrocarbons. As an example of what it would mean to make such reductions, private automobiles would have to be reduced by 80 percent, taxis by 70 percent, trucks by 60 percent, and buses increased threefold to accommodate the passenger-carrying capacity of the removed automobiles and taxis. Even then, the federal standards would only be met if a new, less-polluting bus engine were introduced.

Ironically, over 90 percent of the people who arrive at work in the central business districts below 60th Street already do so by some form of public transportation. Fully 72 percent come by the subway system; slightly over 10 percent come by commuter rail; close to 7 percent by bus; 2 percent by ferry and walking; and only about 8 percent come by automobile. Eight percent of 1 million people generates, nonetheless, a lot of cars, and surveys have shown that no matter how good the public transportation situation, even if it were free, there will remain a hard core of drivers who will continue to drive, if permitted, no matter how expensive it becomes. The simple question put forth by the Madison Mall proposal was: should this 8 percent of incoming commuters continue to control the 40 percent of Midtown's land that is currently used for vehicular movement? And perhaps more important: should they be allowed to continue poisoning the air that everybody in Midtown has to breathe, while actually endangering the entire Midtown community by making adequate emergency services impossible during rush hours? (Compare, for example, *one* subway track which can carry 60,000 passengers an hour with one traffic lane which can carry only 1,500 cars per hour, or about 1,750 people at average occupancy.)

One other problem with the automobile is the conflict with pedestrians; in fact, the density of pedestrian traffic on certain streets in Midtown is so great that it is dangerous because pedestrians often step into

the street, cutting between taxis and buses, just to maintain a normal walking pace. The Regional Plan Association has shown, in studies based upon aerial photography, that Madison Avenue is among several streets considered deficient in this manner. And yet of all surface transit modes, including taxis, private automobiles, and buses, it is the pedestrian who accounts for over 70 percent of the person-miles traveled at midday in Midtown. Despite this fact, of all the land in the public domain, primarily that area between buildings, over 65 percent is given over to people in moving vehicles.

Of the total vehicular movement, taxis typically account for 60 percent of the surface vehicles at midday in Midtown streets. Almost half of these taxis are cruising empty, getting about 6 miles per gallon, while looking for someone to take somewhere. Taxis alone account for 46 percent of the vehicle-emitted carbon monoxide in the air.

While the omnipresent General Motors buses seem to be designed by a midget living in a distant suburb of Detroit, who hates people over 5 ft (1.5 m) tall (the windows are so low, those who stand can never see out to know where they are) and has never been on a bus, let alone in a city, the bus itself is extremely efficient, accounting for less than 3 percent of surface passenger-carrying vehicles in Midtown, but carrying 40 percent of surface passengers. Furthermore, a modern diesel bus carrying 25 passengers (an average midday load) generates 1/100 the carbon monoxide per passenger of a private automobile or taxi.

Finally, what seemed to be lacking most of all from Midtown was a nice place to sit and perhaps have a drink (87). It is true that Mayor Lindsay signed an executive order permitting sidewalk cafes, and in fact, since 1969 over 500 licenses for cafes have been issued. But in the dense areas of Midtown and Lower Manhattan the sidewalks are too narrow and therefore cafes are not allowed. It was obvious that until there was a reorganization of transportation priorities, sidewalk amenities like cafes would not be possible in areas where they would be especially pleasant.

The idea to close Madison Avenue was part of a comprehensive study by Van Ginkel As-

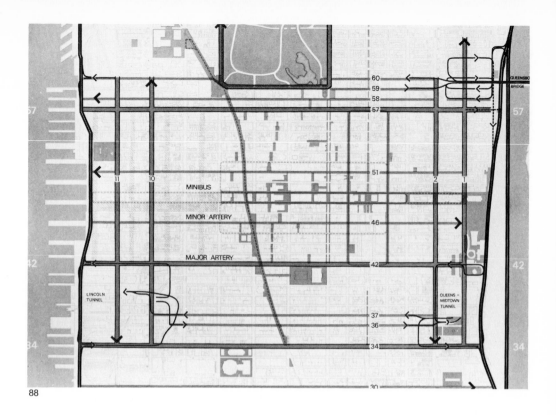

88

89

90

sociates of Montreal, who were commissioned by the Office of Midtown Planning and Development to come up with a proposal to reorganize street priorities and make recommendations that could reasonably be implemented in a short period of time. The Van Ginkels, in studying Manhattan, pointed out that in the business district of central London, with 5 times less density, one was never more than a few minutes' walk from a major open space, whereas in Midtown, besides Central Park which is too far away to be useful to most people working in Midtown, there was only Bryant Park and the beautiful but tiny Paley Park. Despite the proliferation of plazas in recent years, most were less than useless.

The Van Ginkel proposal created a hierarchy of streets, restricting movement along major north-south avenues that pass through the business core and redirecting this traffic to the periphery of the island (88). At the present time, automobiles have equal access along all 12 north-south avenues, even though some of these avenues pass through one of the densest urban cores in the world.

Once traffic was discouraged from entering the core or shifted to its edge, certain streets were freed for use by pedestrians, service vehicles during certain hours, buses, and emergency vehicles. The selected streets were Madison Avenue, Lexington Avenue, and Broadway from 44th to 57th Street, and 48th and 49th Streets from First Avenue to Eighth Avenue. When this network of pedestrian streets was combined with the network of midblock arcades that OMPD was encouraging developers to build, it was found that people living and working in East Midtown would be no more than a 4-minute walk from either a park or a pedestrian street.

It was thought that Madison and Lexington Avenues, with their relatively narrow widths, were of a scale particularly appropriate for pedestrian shopping malls. However, it is also true that the sidewalks along Fifth Avenue are relatively generous at 22-ft (6.5-m) widths compared to the 13-ft (4-m) widths of Madison and Lexington. It was therefore felt that the pedestrians on Madison and Lexington were in the most immediate need of relief.

In earlier times, when Madison Avenue was a series of 4-story row houses, its sidewalks were 19 ft (5.7 m) wide. But by 1921, the department in charge of wrong decisions decided to narrow these vital sidewalks to 13 ft, which they have remained to the present day, despite the growth on the avenue of soaring 50-story buildings with all the accompanying pedestrian traffic.

As an Earth Week experiment in 1971, Madison Avenue was closed to all but pedestrians and buses for 3 hours at noontime. The closure seemed to be an almost total success (89). Noise and air pollution were, for the first time since horse and buggy days, below what were then the 1975 Federal Pollution Standards, with no appreciable increase in pollution levels on the two adjacent avenues. The typical noonday pedestrian count, on the average about 4,500 people passing a point per hour on each sidewalk, remained almost constant, with an additional 11,000 people on the street during Earth Week and no decline in pedestrian traffic on adjacent avenues. It was obvious that thousands of office workers flocked to take advantage of this new space, and a good time seemed to be had by all, except for some merchants who were disturbed by the picnicking in the streets and the so-called hippies playing with frisbees.

Van Ginkel Associates were asked to design a minibus or jitney-type vehicle that would replace the taxis that were to be banned from the mall. It was to be easy for shoppers to step into, no longer than a limousine—which seem efficient only during funerals—and able to seat 14 people. The Van Ginkels designed a handsome pollution-free vehicle, irresistibly named the GinkelVan, that operated on a diesel engine but could convert to electrical power when that became a feasible source of energy (90).

The mall itself was designed by Jaquelin Robertson and his OMPD staff, with construction drawings produced by the Department of Highways. There were many reasons for this decision. Mayor Lindsay was anxious to see the mall built as quickly as possible, and there was some doubt as to whether the Board of Estimate would approve a consultant contract for design. And

91

92

93

91-92 Madison Avenue before surface transportation priorities were to be reorganized—65 percent of the public right-of-way is devoted to moving vehicles (91). The proposed transitway recognizes that 70 percent of the miles logged in Midtown are on foot (92).

93 Conceptually, the design of the Madison Avenue Mall was similar to the *Bahnhofstrasse* in Zurich, with attractive paving on the sidewalk and street (which is reserved for public transit and service vehicles), large trees, benches, new lighting, and graphics.

even if the board did approve, it was a time-consuming process that might have delayed construction toward the later part of the administration, perhaps forcing construction during the Christmas shopping season, something the merchants were very concerned about.

The design for the mall was straightforward (91, 92, 93). Sidewalks were widened from 13 to 29 ft (4 to 9 m), 8 ft (2.4 m) of which, on one side only, could be used by service vehicles during restricted hours. Two lanes of moving traffic were provided, primarily for buses and emergency vehicles. The paving material, hexagonal blocks, had been used successfully in many parks throughout the city for years. Outdoor cafes could now be permitted on the avenue. There were to be many benches and large caliper London Plane trees planted in line wherever possible. The trees were a problem because many of the buildings fronting the proposed mall had vaults under the sidewalk, and it seemed that time and money made it impossible to alter these vault conditions to plant trees in these locations.

There is no question that trees alone can make a substantial difference to a street. But the point of Madison Avenue was not so much the design, because the mall could certainly change over time. (For example, it was thought that a committee could be set up by the many museums in New York for the purpose of lending sculpture to the mall. The problem of trees could also be resolved at a later date.) In the end the Madison Mall boiled down to a major political confrontation between the pedestrian and the automobile.

Planners by this time had numerous examples of successful malls. In Europe there were literally hundreds. Even Rome and Milan were beginning to implement plans that closed virtually their entire respective centers. And London, the European city most comparable with New York, was in the midst of a successful experimental closing of Oxford Street. The plan was conceptually similar to the Madison Mall proposal, with the exception that Oxford Street, as the only major east-west thoroughfare through the entire Byzantine street network of central London, was a far more difficult street to close than Madison Avenue, with its multitude of parallel avenues.

Unfortunately, many merchants along Madison Avenue would have none of these arguments. Europe was foreign and therefore different. Nor were they impressed with documented statistics that the malls in Europe as well as those in the United States had all done remarkably well, increasing retail sales by an average of 15 to 40 percent. Perhaps they had all the money they could use, although this initial reluctance among shop owners seemed to be a general characteristic of many of the malls studied. What many of the more prestigious and vocal merchants feared was a loss of their so-called carriage trade—the well-dressed matron, dripping in minks, who arrives in a very long black car and spends a small fortune. Nonetheless, no shop in the Madison Mall scheme was ever more than 100 ft (30 m) from a crosstown street, about as close as you could get to any shop even with the avenue open.

The Fifth Avenue Association sued the City of New York, and Mayor Lindsay and OMPD in particular, to enjoin them from pursuing the mall. The suit charged that it was not within the Mayor's executive powers to close a street, but rather was a matter to be decided by the Board of Estimate, where the merchants hoped to get a more sympathetic hearing. Mayor Lindsay characteristically argued that he wasn't closing the street, but merely widening the sidewalks. Unfortunately, the Mayor lost this subtle argument; and the Board of Estimate, of which the Mayor is but one of eight members, ruled against the Mayor. The decisive vote was cast by comptroller Abraham Beame, who at that time was under heavy pressure from the taxi industry, which was supporting his candidacy for mayor. Mayor Beame claimed to support the idea of malls, but he couldn't seem to find enough money even to pay Mayor Lindsay's old bills. And so the problem of making use of the city's right-of-ways in Midtown more equitable remains. Though sufficient funds may indeed not be available to make the necessary physical improvements, it would not cost much to make the necessary bus lanes and post restrictions on the use of the automobile.

A critical function of urban design in a city's planning process is illustrated by the OMPD proposal for Manhattan's Queensborough Bridge area which inte-

94

95

96

94 The Queensborough Bridge creates a series of problems. As a major traffic artery, it spews thousands of cars hourly onto the smaller street network of a residential neighborhood.

95 The original public plaza at the base of the bridge became a flourishing neighborhood market in the 1920s and 1930s.

96 The Queensborough Bridge, through coordination of several projects in the area, could once again become an exciting and usable part of the community in which it stands.

grated the separate projects of five separate city departments into a unified design scheme which would not only accomplish those separate objectives but upgrade the whole neighborhood; reorganize traffic to improve both vehicular and pedestrian circulation (and reduce air and noise pollution); and create new amenities for pedestrian and resident alike.

The Queensborough Bridge is the focus of a major urban design project by OMPD and once again illustrates the need for this discipline to be integrated into city government with executive support. In this particular case, the Department of Highways was about to "rearrange" the ramps to and from the bridge; the Metropolitan Transit Authority had let out a contract for the design of a new station for the Second Avenue subway just 2 short blocks south of the bridge; the Department of Cultural Affairs was arranging with other city agencies to grant use of the underside of the bridge and the areas immediately adjacent to the bridge for the City Center Cinematheque; the Urban Development Corporation was constructing a tramway leading from a city-owned parcel just west of Second Avenue to the vast housing project under construction on Roosevelt Island; and the MTSOA (Metropolitan Transit Suburban Operating Authority) was renovating an old trolley car barn under the bridge to be used as a new bus terminal.

Peter Seidel, the project urban designer, and Ross Burkhardt, the project planner, were able to organize these disparate elements into a unified urban design scheme that satisfied the requirements of each agency and also provided a solution to the bridge traffic problem. Bridge traffic is a problem because the bridge is one of the few direct connections between Manhattan and Long Island, and the traffic generated swamps the street network at the Manhattan end (94). If carried out separately, none of the individual projects would lessen the traffic problem, despite the investment of millions of dollars. It is more likely that they would actually exacerbate conditions by attracting more automobiles and pedestrians to an already overcrowded area. The implementation of the urban design plan would not significantly alter the budgets previously approved, but it would require inter-

agency coordination and cooperation, something new for city agencies.

When the bridge opened in 1909, 84 percent of its available capacity was used by mass transit facilities and pedestrian walkways. It was an exceptional piece of bridge architecture, finely detailed, with vaulted "cathedral" spaces beneath the structure, spaces that opened onto a plaza. These qualities made the bridge a popular feature of the neighborhood, and with its open-air markets it was firmly integrated into the everyday business life of the city (95). In recent times, mounting problems of traffic congestion have obscured this civic aspect of the bridge, and it has correspondingly declined as a public gathering place, becoming instead an intrusion and a separate element in its surrounding community. The once-dignified plazas have been given over to parking lots; the vaulted spaces are now closed in and used for storage; and the second-rate uses around the bridge are in sharp contrast to the very high-quality housing, shopping, and entertainment that generally characterizes the area.

The urban design plan calls for bridge traffic to be completely reorganized (96). Construction of a new ramp on the bridge's northern side would free the ground level along the bridge's southern edge, liberating the plaza for pedestrian use once again. The Cinematheque had planned to restore only the plaza immediately fronting its location under the bridge; this new plan calls for renovation of the entire plaza area and installation of complementary uses in the space under the bridge that the Cinematheque does not need. East of Second Avenue, 59th Street would be redesigned and narrowed to serve only local traffic.

The complex traffic movements at the intersection of the bridge and Second Avenue create a snarl of pedestrian-vehicular conflicts that can only be resolved by means of a grade separation of pedestrian and automobile traffic. It is evident that the standard type of "pedestrian bridge" or "pedestrian underpass" does not effectively provide the desired pedestrian continuity, not only in terms of an unobstructed route, but also in terms of the ancillary activities that help create an attractive pedestrian environment. The proposed pedestrian level is

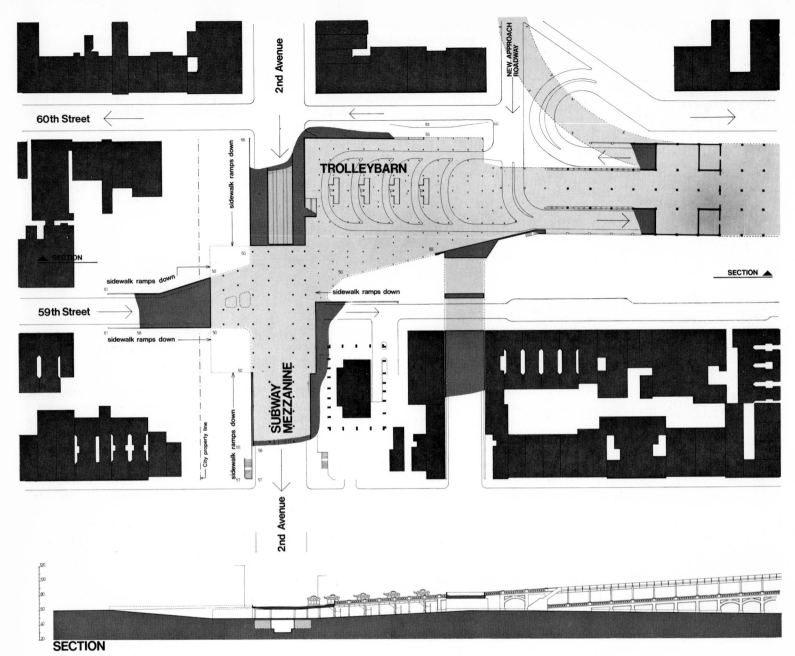

2nd Avenue

60th Street ←

← 2nd Avenue

NEW APPROACH ROADWAY

TROLLEYBARN

sidewalk ramps down

sidewalk ramps down →

SECTION ▲

59th Street →

sidewalk ramps down ←

sidewalk ramps down

City property line

SUBWAY MEZZANINE

sidewalk ramps down

2nd Avenue

SECTION

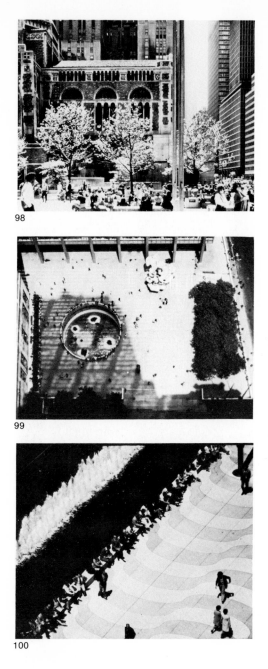

98

99

100

97 By taking advantage of the existing grade changes, a pedestrian level can be created that connects the east and west sides of Second Avenue—including the plaza—via the future Second Avenue mezzanine.

98-99-100 The goal of the new plaza legislation is to provide criteria for future plazas based on a careful analysis of New York's finest existing urban spaces—including the 345 Park Avenue Plaza (98); the Chase Manhattan Plaza (99); and the Time-Life Plaza (100).

designed as a natural extension of the ground level from the plaza at the base of the bridge under the critical 59th Street–Second Avenue intersection (97). At the western edge of this pedestrian level, generous ramps and stairs would guide the pedestrian up to the higher grade. The existing road level would then appear as bridging over a continuous pedestrian area, which would have the essential qualities of ground level and thus encourage development of ancillary activities. Finally, extension of the mezzanine of the Second Avenue subway northward to 59th Street and provision of shops on the mezzanine frontage would be all that is needed to make this new pattern a part of everyday pedestrian and vehicular movement through the area.

The new pedestrian level would provide an important link among the Roosevelt Island tramway terminal, the 57th Street subway station, the Third Avenue shopping-entertainment core, the new bus terminal, and the revitalized bridge plaza area with its Cinematheque and related activities. It is estimated that at least 25,000 people would benefit daily from the improved pedestrian connection.

People-oriented open spaces in Midtown Manhattan were the goal of 1975 zoning legislation revising the plaza provisions of the 1961 zoning ordinance and drawing on studies of use (and nonuse) of existing Manhattan plazas by William Whyte, whose observations—documented with time-lapse photography—indicated that intensity of plaza use can be related to very specific characteristics of seating, planting, accessibility, and retail facilities.

The success, in terms of pedestrian use, of the Earth Week closing of Fifth and Madison Avenues over several years, whereby all vehicular traffic was eliminated except for buses, helped to focus attention on the acute need for more open space in Midtown. Although there are numerous plazas in Midtown, the fact that most of them are unusable is readily apparent to anyone who tries to use them.

The research of William H. Whyte, the author of *The Last Landscape* and *The Organization Man*, provided the basis for a careful analysis of the problem. Whyte, fascinated

with the use of urban spaces in New York, studied major plazas for 2 years, utilizing time-lapse photography. From this work, it was seen that successful plazas measured in terms of the numbers of people using them adhered to some basic, quantifiable principles of seating, orientation, planting, accessibility, and retail facilities.

Working with these findings and other urban design criteria, the Urban Design Group (headed now by Raquel Ramati with Michael Parley as co-director), in conjunction with the Office of Midtown Planning and Development and the Office of Lower Manhattan Development, rewrote the 1961 plaza legislation. The 1975 change in the plaza zoning is significant. For 14 years, as a bonus for providing a plaza, a developer was allowed to build 10 sq ft (.95 sq m) of office space for every 1 sq ft (.09 sq m) of plaza space provided, without many design controls. The result was often an unpleasant strip plaza or a plaza that was poorly oriented or positioned, without even a place to sit. The new legislation seeks to produce a more useful series of urban open spaces. The ideal plaza is now seen as an "outdoor room"—a space very clearly defined by the surrounding buildings—with proper orientation to the sun, ample seating and attractive paving, fountains, trees, small shops, kiosks, and outdoor cafes (98, 99).

The legislation provides for three kinds of urban open space: the urban plaza, the sidewalk widening, and the open-air concourse.

Urban plaza
An urban plaza is defined as "a continuous open area fronting upon a street or sidewalk widening which is accessible to the public at all times for the use and enjoyment of large numbers of people."

To prevent strip plazas, the law requires that an urban plaza have proportions not greater than 3 to 1. In addition, at least 70 percent of the urban plaza's total area must be in one primary space, which cannot be less than 750 sq ft (70 sq m). This provision seeks to avoid the chopped-up nature of some previous plazas where every nook and cranny, no matter how useless, counted toward the bonus. At least 75 percent of the total urban plaza area on a nar-

101

102

103

101   Sunken plazas would be allowed only adjacent to subway stops.

102-103   Nassau Street remains open for service vehicles during the morning and late afternoon but is closed each weekday from 11:30 A.M. to 2:00 P.M. for a pedestrian shopping mall.

row street is to have a southern exposure—that is, in any direction between west-southwest and east-southeast. A through-block plaza must be at least 40 ft (12 m) wide to allow for sunlight to penetrate to the street level and for people to walk in comfort.

Plazas can be successfully located on avenue frontages, but when they come one after another, as has happened along Third and Sixth Avenues, the street fritters away, and so does the plaza. The new law seeks to preserve the street wall and with it the strong linear sense of a street. On shopping streets a sustained frontage of commercial uses is desired to encourage the shopper to perceive the street as a continuous line of attractions rather than a discontinuous series of nodes. The plaza is viewed as an adjunct to the street wall, an outdoor room that punctuates the linear flow of the street.

To preserve the street wall and to ensure that plazas have a sense of enclosure, the law provides that a plaza may be built along the entire avenue frontage of a development only if adjacent plazas within 175 ft (53 m) of any part of the proposed development do not occupy more than 33 percent of that avenue frontage. When adjacent plazas are larger than this size, the proposed plaza is limited to occupying not more than 33 percent of its avenue frontage.

–Obstructions. Depending upon the size of the plaza, there may be a series of permitted obstructions ranging from 33 to 50 percent of the plaza area. Some of these are fountains and reflecting pools, waterfalls, sculptures and other works of art, arbors, trellises, benches, seats, trees, planting beds, bicycle racks, open air cafes, kiosks, temporary exhibits, canopies, and subway station entrances.

–Seating. It was obvious from William Whyte's research that use of a plaza increases in proportion to the amount of seating provided (100). It is, therefore, doubly sad to witness the harsh attempts made to keep people from viewing the great spectacle of the human parade. One fabulous grandstand denied to the public is the ledge in front of the General Motors Plaza which has deliberately been designed so that people may not sit there.

The new requirement of 1 linear ft (.3 m) of seating for each 30 sq ft (2.8 sq m) of plaza is based on Whyte's photographic observations. Long, wide benches are encouraged, and up to 50 percent of the seating can be in movable chairs. Tops of retaining walls and ledges around landscaping also count towards the seating requirement, provided they conform to the established minimum seating dimensions. Steps, although fun to sit on and often a necessary part of plazas with grade changes, cannot be counted toward the total number of required seats.

–Planting and trees. When a development takes advantage of the plaza bonus, it is obliged to plant and maintain trees at least 3½ in. (9 cm) in caliper flush to grade at a maximum spacing of 25 ft (7.5 m) for the entire street frontage of the zoning lot. Potted trees are not permitted.

–Paving. The paving material selected for the plaza must be continued on all public sidewalks adjacent to the development. Although there can be subtle changes in pattern or color to differentiate the two areas if that is felt desirable, this provision may help end the ludicrous distinction between the public/concrete sector and the private/marble sector.

–Retail uses. At least 50 percent of the building walls fronting on a plaza must be devoted to retail uses permitted by the underlying zoning, with the exception that banks, loan offices, travel agencies, and airline offices are excluded. Kiosks for food, magazines, and books are encouraged. It is expected that these retail uses will help make the plaza a lively place to be.

Sidewalk widening
A sidewalk widening must be 10 ft (3 m) wide along an avenue, and not greater than 10 ft nor less than 5 ft (1.5 m) along a side street. These dimensions enable the development to maintain the continuity of the street wall while effectively doubling the capacity of the sidewalk, thereby offsetting the increased density the development creates. The requirements for retail frontage and paving are the same as those outlined for plazas. However, no obstructions are permitted in this area. When an adjacent development already has a sidewalk widening, the new development must continue it.

104

105

106

104-105-106   When architects are free of urban design controls, severe problems and missed opportunities can occur. Kevin Roche argues that this solution (104), which fronts on Nassau Street and raises the building 14 stories off the ground, creates a significant urban space (105) and relates to the old Federal Reserve Building across the street as well as other rectangular towers. In fact what actually happens is that one precious block of retail frontage is lost to be replaced by a building that would pay a premium of an estimated $30 million to create the dubious plaza. The building at 100 Williams Street (106) built along its lot lines with retail facilities at its base would be a better model for the Federal Reserve Building to emulate (see also 28, 29). With only $1 million of the enormous savings gained by such a solution, the entire 4-block shopping area could have been refurbished as a pedestrian mall as the city has wanted to do for years.

Although a sidewalk widening can be an important amenity, it will not allow the development to receive the entire bonus available, and therefore the developer will probably also build either a plaza or an open-air concourse.

Open-air concourse
The open-air concourse was developed as a way of improving pedestrian flow in and out of subway stations in Midtown and Lower Manhattan (101). The concourse will also allow light and air to filter down to the mezzanine, or subway level, integrating the subway station with the street and perhaps making the dashing subway rider feel a bit less like the White Rabbit as he hops down the stairs to the train.

In an open-air concourse, the space at the mezzanine, or subway, level must not be less than 4,000 sq ft (380 sq m) nor more than 8,000 sq ft (750 sq m), with a minimum horizontal dimension of 40 ft (12 m) or 3 times the depth, whichever is the greater. There must be a direct connection up to the street level as well as a direct connection from the mezzanine into the building that receives the bonus. At least 50 percent of a common boundary with a subway station must be open in such a way as to allow light to enter. Permitted obstructions as described in the plaza section may not occupy more than 20 percent of the mezzanine portion. Existing sidewalk subway entrances bordering the new development would have to be removed.

Existing plazas
The new legislation was written primarily for new buildings. At a time when 25 million to 30 million sq ft (2,400,000 to 2,800,000 sq m) of office space sits empty, the most immediate problem seems to be how to make the literally dozens of existing plazas usable. In this connection, an experiment was carried out in Exxon Plaza with Whyte, camera in hand, filming the process. As benches and kiosks offering food and flowers were progressively installed, usage went up—way up. Benches and kiosks are very simple elements that are often inexpensive. In addition, kiosk commerce usually winds up substantially in the black. The new legislation allows existing plazas to have kiosks; under the old legislation they were prohibited. It is hoped that plaza own-

ers will also remove barriers from walls and ledges. Plazas are for sitting.

A four-block segment of Nassau Street becomes a pedestrian way for 3 hours every noonday.

In 1966, the Lower Manhattan Plan recommended that a system of pedestrian ways be developed to accommodate the phenomenal volume of people on the streets walking to and from work in the morning and evening and for shopping and eating at noontime. Some streets were to be closed, eventually, to all vehicles—except minibuses and emergency vehicles—and others were to be remodeled, providing wider sidewalks and eliminating parking and loading.

Of this rather modest, but clearly essential proposal, a mere four blocks of Nassau Street and one block in the Civic Center have been devoted to pedestrians so far, and the Nassau Street closing is only for 3 hours at noontime (102, 103). Nonetheless, Nassau Street has been extraordinarily popular, in part because it is one of the few shopping streets in Lower Manhattan. Although the city would like to remove all physical obstacles in the street, including the curb, and provide a continuous paved surface, new lighting, and graphics, it just hasn't had the money to do so. And in the meantime, proposed new construction which would undermine this important shopping street actually contradicts many of the principles established in New York's special zoning districts (104, 105, 106).

Chicago

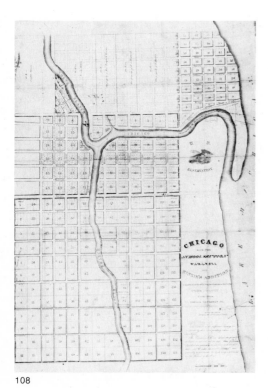

108

107   Chicago's Loop is the second largest employment center in the U.S. Of the estimated 550,000 people who work there, 80 percent come by public transportation.

108   After the fire of 1871, Chicago readopted a grid plan.

Chicago is America's second city and the first home of both modern architecture and the City Beautiful movement. Its downtown remains among the most viable urban centers in the country. But the city has *no* urban design controls; and its zoning—for developers, the most lucrative zoning ordinance in the country—encourages large-lot assemblage that directly threatens the city's remaining landmarks. The "Chicago plan," an innovative proposal for zoning revisions which might save Chicago's landmarks through air rights transfers, is Chicago's single recent contribution to urban design theory. Though the proposal has not been implemented in Chicago, it has been, in principle, adopted in New York's Seaport district.

Population and geography
Chicago is an anglicized version of the Indian name for the river *she-kag-ong*, "wild onion place." But in place of the onions, it was the population that grew wild.

European settlement in Chicago began in 1779, while the American Revolution was being fought in the east. In the period of national expansion prior to the turn of the 20th century, growth in Chicago was spectacular. Between the time the city was formally chartered in 1837 and 1870, the population grew from 4,000 to 300,000. By 1910 it was over 2 million, having more than quadrupled in three decades. In 1970 the population of the 227-sq-mile (600-sq-km) city was leveling off at 3,400,000; but the 5,000-sq-mile (10,300-sq-km) region including Chicago was at 7 million—and still growing.

The central business district (107) is often referred to as "the Loop," a reference to the elevated rapid transit system that surrounds the old business center. Within the 100 square blocks of the Loop [an area of approximately 1 sq mile (2.6 sq km), which today extends beyond the elevated], 550,000 people work; 80 percent of them commute to work by public transportation.

Chicago's phenomenal growth is primarily attributable to Chicago's unique location in the heart of great mineral wealth and fertile agricultural lands, with the most extensive railroad network and the busiest airport in the world. The railroads, along with water transport, played an important part in Chicago's development, making it the great industrial center of the United States as well as the center of the movement westward in the 19th century.

Referring to the westward movement, Milton Rakove wrote in *Great Cities of the World*, "Geography decreed that most of them would go by way of Chicago, that they would be supplied through Chicago, and that their produce would find its way back east after being processed in Chicago."[1]

Historical development
As had London 200 years earlier, Chicago disregarded its opportunity, presented by the Great Fire of 1871, to rebuild itself according to plan. Instead, only the street grid, based upon the U.S. Government Rectangular Survey System, was reestablished (108). But by 1900, the physical growth of the city was clearly aligning itself to the emerging railroad patterns.

The neoclassical architecture of the 1893 World's Columbian Exposition in Chicago marked an unfortunate turning away from a

109

110

113

111

112

114

new generation of architects. But the fair itself, which was conceived, planned, and built under the direction of Daniel Burnham, stimulated public interest in civic beauty and marked the beginning of an effort to improve the urban scene in the U.S., giving life to the American planning movement (109).

After several years of negotiation, Chicago's Commercial Club agreed to sponsor Burnham and Edward Bennett to explore the possibilities for future comprehensive development of the Chicago area. The plan they proposed in 1909, and which the city adopted, has had a profound impact on Chicago's development (110). Unfortunately, despite the fact that the vast majority of people going downtown use public transportation, the city has converted Burnham's parkway drives along the Lakefront (111) and throughout the city into superhighways to serve the few who commute by automobile (112). Otherwise, Burnham's plan continues to influence the thought of the city's urban designers.

An erratic zoning history that began with Burnham's preference for the European approach of regulated cornice heights has culminated (since 1957) in a combination of a generous FAR and even more generous bonuses that encourages large lot assemblage and threatens the city's remaining landmarks.

Burnham recognized and utilized elevator technology and steel frame construction, but he preferred to constrain this technology to the European approach of regulated cornice heights (113). Individual pieces of architecture were viewed as facades which should defer to the larger plan with its attendant boulevards and public spaces. Therefore, in his plan, Burnham instituted a 14-story, 240-ft (73-m) height limitation on all new construction.

From 1923 until 1942 Chicago enjoyed a liberalized zoning policy which not only allowed buildings to be 264 ft (80 m) in height, but also permitted, *above* the main building, a tower, not to exceed 25 percent of the lot area, nor one-sixth of the volume of the main building below.

In 1942, after years of little new construction, the zoning was revised severely downward, limiting buildings to 144 ft (44 m) in height.

Prior to Chicago's next major zoning revision in 1957, planners in Chicago considered adopting a variation of New York's height and setback zoning, but in the end rejected this approach because they felt that the light gained due to the setbacks was more theoretical than real and that setbacks complicate design and increase construction costs (114). Furthermore, the so-called Chicago school of architects found the New York setbacks aesthetically appalling.

Mies van der Rohe was already leading the way toward establishing the steel-and-glass highrise as an integral part of Chicago's skyline, and his design for the Seagram Building in New York was under construction. As director of the architecture department at the Illinois Institute of Technology, Mies was training a whole generation of Chicago architects, a tradition in style that New York never possessed.

So instead of requiring setbacks, the city adopted a base FAR of 16 for the Loop and offered a series of bonuses tied to the provision of amenities such as plazas, arcades, and even setbacks if desired.

Since up until the mid- and even late-1950s, most new buildings in Chicago were on sites only one-quarter or even less of the total block, the typical new building under the 1957 zoning ordinance could take advantage of only about two of the zoning bonuses: one for a setback and perhaps another for an arcade. In this way, it was predicted, most buildings could reach an FAR of 20, close to that of the buildings built from 1923 to 1942 averaging FAR 19 to 22.

The development of full-block sites, which became very frequent in the 1960s, was not foreseen. On a full block site, by setting the building back on *all* four sides, by providing a continuous arcade at the base of the building, and by also providing building setbacks, the building could reach an FAR of at least 40, which would allow a developer to build a structurally sound 140-story building containing about 6 million sq ft (550,000 sq m) on each block in the central area. The bonuses were offered even

109   The 1893 Columbian Exposition was a major setback to architects in Chicago pushing for a new interpretation of modern construction technology. But the fair did spark an effort to make many American cities beautiful.

110   Burnham and Bennett's 1909 plan has had a profound influence on Chicago's development.

111   Chicago's lakefront as envisaged by Olmsted and Burnham. This 1900 photo is of Jackson Park.

112   Chicago's lakefront today contains a major highway, serving fewer than 20 percent of incoming commuters, which separates the lakefront from, and makes it inaccessible to, surrounding neighborhoods.

113   Much of the Burnham plan has been implemented over the years, but the plan's height limitations were short-lived.

114   Under the old zoning, a building could fill its site completely and go up to a certain height, after which a tower could be placed on the base (left). The 1957 zoning change allowed much bigger buildings (right) in exchange for arcades and plazas at the base.

115

116

117

118

119

120

115 The Standard Oil Building—80 stories, FAR 24.6.

116 The John Hancock Building—95 stories, FAR 26. Besides the space bonus they get for plazas and arcades, buildings in Chicago are bonused if they set back from the street as they go up. Theoretically, the Hancock Tower could have gone up until it reached a point!

117 The Sears Building—110 stories, FAR 36—took advantage of the zoning's incentives by providing an elevated plaza and a variety of setbacks. Though the setbacks allow the architects to arrive at a creative architectonic solution, it is difficult to determine what benefit the public derives from this supposed amenity as they stand in its shadow and ponder its height.

118 While the elevated plaza that surrounds the Sears Building is a more obvious amenity than are the building's setbacks, it is so poorly designed that it is almost impossible to use. It is a major step backward in plaza design from the elegant *and* useful Chase Manhattan Plaza Skidmore, Owings, & Merrill designed 15 years earlier (99).

119 Two of the four sides of the Sears Plaza base are blank walls that offer nothing to the average pedestrian, who is unlikely to even try to use the unusable plaza above.

120 This base of a building, a few short blocks from the Sears Building—and similar to the base of buildings across the street from the Sears Building—is of a vanishing breed in American cities. Yet, such shop fronts are animated, ever-changing museums of American culture and the world marketplace and serve to keep streets active and alive. The need for usable urban public space is not questioned. But urban space should not be randomly placed and arbitrarily designed.

though these huge buildings would probably need to provide the type of amenities that were bonused just to be able to function.

And developers flocked to take advantage of this "loophole" in the zoning. The 48-story Mid Continental Plaza Building is built at an FAR of approximately 24; the 74-story Water Tower Place is built at an FAR of 22.7; the 52-story IBM Building is built at an FAR of 24.5; the 80-story Standard Oil Building is built at an FAR of 24.6 (115); the 100-story John Hancock Building is built at an FAR of 26 (116); and the 110-story Sears Building is built at an FAR of 36 (117).

Scraping the clouds at 1,450 ft (440 m), the Sears Building came to an abrupt halt because it had reached the limit set by the Federal Aviation Administration. While the bonus system has allowed the architects to achieve by 100 ft (30 m) their admitted goal to surpass the height of Yamasaki's World Trade Center buildings (77) (making Sears "the tallest building in the world"), the bonus system does not sufficiently guarantee that the public will benefit from the so-called amenities (118, 119, 120).

Chicago's zoning is only symptomatic of the laissez faire attitude the city administrators have toward planning and urban design—a condition which has produced a startling set of contradictions in this remarkable city. Because of the lucrative zoning, Chicago's rich heritage of landmark buildings that symbolize its major role in the development of modern architecture is in serious jeopardy (121). The Rookery, for example, is one of three buildings left—out of a total of 27 that were in the Loop—designed by Burnham and Root (122). Louis Sullivan's Stock Exchange is only the most recent casualty. In this case the City Council, with a benign Mayor Daley looking on, refused to designate as a landmark the internationally renowned Stock Exchange.

Not for 20 years, until in 1974 the business community produced at its own expense the unofficial "Chicago 21," had the city had a plan for the development of its downtown. And with the exception of a small part of its riverfront, the city still has no formal urban design policies whatsoever to protect and enhance the center.

Chicago's fabled "Magnificent Mile" has suffered from a new wave of construction monitored by no urbanistic considerations beyond those of a particular owner, expressed in a "restrictive covenant," protecting that owner's interests, but without sufficient regard for civic amenity that would benefit the whole street.

In 1918 Mayor Bill (The Builder) Thompson opened the way for development on upper Michigan Avenue by having the city build a double-deck bridge over the Chicago River linking the Loop to the potentially valuable real estate to the north. The mayor's friend, William Wrigley, was the first to move his headquarters to a new building he had built across the river (123). Then the competition-winning scheme for the Chicago Tribune Building was built, along with several other buildings. Upper Michigan Avenue was to be a quality street, however, and the restrictive zoning reflected this intent (124). But only the Depression and World War II curbed uncontrollable speculation on the so-called Magnificent Mile. In the last few years, more than 10 new buildings have been built, as well as countless additions to existing buildings.

In a 1967 beautification study for the avenue, landscape architect Lawrence Halprin cautioned that the wave of new tall buildings ". . .will completely destroy what remains of the humane scale of the street."[2] Buildings like the John Hancock "should not ever be allowed to appear continuously along the street," but should instead be "regarded as landmarks."[3] Yet, built just across the street to the south from the 100-story John Hancock Building is the 74-story Water Tower Place (125), which cuts off much of the sun and view from the Hancock residents (poetic justice, perhaps, for the immense shadows the Hancock Building cast on Mies' 860–880 apartment building complex along the Lakefront).

Luckily for the Hancock, it owned a parcel of land the Water Tower people needed to complete their site. Hancock agreed to sell it if the developers of Water Tower Place would agree to sign a restrictive covenant guaranteeing that Water Tower Place would be located on its site in such a way that it would protect the views of Hancock's tenants. Such are restrictive covenants in

121

122

123

124

125

121 Though recently designated as a landmark, the Reliance Building (center) is illustrative of the speculative pressure on smaller historically significant buildings. Also zoning in Chicago is a regressive tool when it comes to landmarks: the larger the site, the more bonuses a developer can take advantage of.

122 Burnham and Root designed 27 buildings in downtown Chicago. The Rookery is one of only three that remain; its lobby gives some indication of the city's loss.

123-124 Upper Michigan Avenue has always been seen as a street of prestigious buildings, but speculative development since the middle 1960s may have been at the expense of the street's quality.

125 Water Tower Place—74 stories, FAR 22.7—was sited to "protect" the views of Hancock residents (116).

126

127

128

126-127 The Marina City complex has intelligently developed the potential of the riverfront for a variety of users. Unfortunately, every surface of this introverted city-within-a-city is either a blank wall or an open parking garage. Compare this approach of an urban building with the attitude of the European-style building at the corner of the site.

128 Except for the protection afforded by the river along one of its sides, Marina City could be surrounded by buildings the size of the IBM Building shown here.

Chicago. But despite certain urban design failings of the Hancock Building (caused in part because the sunken plaza in front of the Hancock lacks the enclosure that makes the plaza at Rockefeller Center (32) so successful and in part because the space itself has acerbated existing wind problems), the size and location of this live-in Eiffel Tower made it a handsome new symbol for Chicago—ephemeral as such symbols are in American cities. The presence of the Water Tower Place, in an urbanistic sense, offers the same insensitivity as the Pan Am Building built behind the old Grand Central Office Building at the foot of Park Avenue in New York.

Though as architecture it has many fine qualities, Marina City illustrates the urbanistic consequences of the lack of sound zoning, planning, and urban design policy in Chicago.

When it was built in 1964 in an undeveloped area at the periphery of the Loop, Marina City was widely praised by architects and planners for its innovative combination of housing, office space, commercial and community facilities, and parking. The first 19 stories of each of the 60-story apartment buildings are devoted to parking. Alongside the two apartment buildings stands a 16-story office building—of equal height to the parking—and a theater used as a television studio. A section through Marina City reveals docking facilities for 700 boats at the base of the building as it meets the river; a restaurant overlooking the river above the docks; and finally, a terrace level or platform above the restaurant, also overlooking the river, which provides a continuous—if awkward—pedestrian connection from Dearborn to Clark Street (126). Within the complex, there are numerous shopping and recreational facilities.

Promoters of Marina City have often described it as a city within a city—presumably because if offers little externally to the city that surrounds it. Virtually every major surface of Marina City that faces the street of this introverted scheme is a blank wall or parking (127). What little glass area there is at the base of the building is not for shops, and the railing makes it clear there is not meant to be a continuous connection between the building and the street. It is the antithesis of the 4-story building at the edge

of the Marina City site which is typical of many buildings in the center of European cities in terms of style, height, and use—where apartments and shops have an intimate relationship with the street.

Because Marina City was at variance with the existing zoning code, the city wrote and passed its Planned Unit Development (PUD) ordinance especially for the occasion. PUD allows the city's department of planning and development to waive such extraneous limitations as density when it is felt the overall project so warrants it. Normally, according to the ill-fated 1966 Comprehensive Plan, the density developed by Marina City would require a park of 8 acres (3.2 ha) for active recreation. The city provided none. Instead, it was deemed that the open space afforded by Marina City's location on the Chicago River was sufficient for this requirement. The Chicago River indeed! Not even fish would dare to swim in it, although it makes a fine view and does prohibit development immediately south of Marina City.

The final misfortune, however, was the location of the Mies van der Rohe–designed office building for IBM. Just to the east of Marina City and taller than the Marina City Towers, it cuts off view and a substantial amount of sun for probably 30 percent of the Marina City residents (128). Apartment dwellers in midtown Manhattan do not expect much sunlight for their money and most are happy to have an oblique view of a dying tree. But Chicago's high residential densities are by and large confined to the Lakefront and therefore have access to the sun and spectacular views.

Marina City illustrates the potential problem downtown dwellers will face without a modification of the zoning as higher density residential buildings are built farther inland.

Chicago 21, a master plan for center city sponsored by the business community, incorporates some ideas of its own and other ideas, proposed but not implemented over the last 10 years, into what amounts to a comprehensive plan (though without any official status) for an 11-sq-mile (28-sq-km) area including the Loop.

Chicago 21 was designed by the Chicago offices of the architectural firm of Skidmore

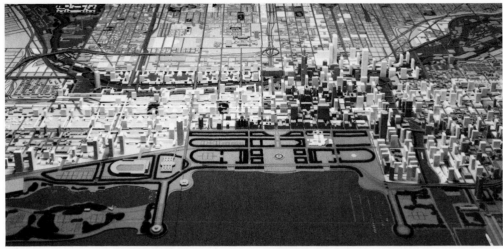

129

130

131

129 Chicago 21 is a plan for the Loop sponsored by the business community that was derived mostly from unimplemented planning concepts from the past, including a proposal to finish the lakefront park downtown in accordance with the Burnham plan.

130 Housing along the riverfront as proposed in the Chicago 21 plan would be in direct competition with the suburbs for buyers.

131 Chicago 21 recommends that State Street be converted into a pedestrian transitway. At present, there are no exclusive bus lanes in downtown Chicago.

Owings & Merrill (SOM), with the assistance of Real Estate Research Corporation, the transportation firm of Alan M. Voorhees and Associates, and University of Chicago sociologist Professor Morris Janowitz. Like the Burnham plan, it was sponsored by the business community. And like the comprehensive plan, which was never approved by the City Council, Chicago 21 has no official status.

Unlike the comprehensive plan, which was neither comprehensive nor even a plan, Chicago 21 does comprehensively plan for the center of the city, incorporating a variety of ideas that have been proposed in recent years, but, with or without official imprimatur, never implemented (129). To existing ideas, Chicago 21 has added some of its own, with a conscious attempt at an urban design structure to tie it together.

Whether it will have the impact of the Burnham plan, which did have the city's endorsement, is doubtful. The Burnham plan was produced at a time when the city's population was 2 million people and served as a guide while the city grew in the next four decades by an additional 1½ million people. But now, Chicago's population has been static for years, even though office space in the Loop has almost doubled since 1960. So the middle-income housing in the "new towns" Chicago 21 envisages at the edge of the Loop is admittedly in direct competition with the suburbs. And according to the plan, without developer interest in the areas peripheral to the center, the list of recommended improvements for the center will be difficult if not impossible to achieve. And there is much to do in the center.

Chicago 21 recommends that

–The city redevelop the river's edge for pedestrian use and housing. The city's 1975 report recommending this policy is based on recommendations made in 1969 by the landscape architects Johnson, Johnson, and Roy (130).

–The lakefront Grant Park be completed more or less in formal accordance with the Burnham plan, a recommendation architect Harry Weese made in a 1968 report.

–There be implementation of a mall on State Street, which the city is undertaking (131).

–The elevated rapid transit structure that encircles the Loop come down to be replaced by the city's proposed underground loop system following a similar configuration, a plan which has been stalled for years and which now the Chicago chapter of the American Institute of Architects (AIA) is against.

–The city continue its underground pedestrian circulation system which ties together some large buildings and the subway system, as well as establish a policy of constructing second-level bridges between major department stores as has been done in Minneapolis.

–The city designate 29 buildings as landmarks. The plan reiterates support of the concept of development-rights transfer as a method to save landmarks as recommended in the Chicago plan, which the city, by word and deed, has previously rejected.

The most encouraging element about Chicago 21 is that a privately financed development corporation has been established providing a structure for development to share the risk and cost of building the new town, which is considered of prime importance to the overall success of the plan. The most discouraging element, besides the plan's continued insistence on even more highways to serve the center, is that the city has ignored so many of the plans proposed in recent years by the architectural and business community.

And even if the city should decide to implement part or all of Chicago 21, Chicago is one of the few large American cities with no trained urban design staff to see to it that the goals and quality of the plan are adhered to.

The Chicago plan proposed the concept, since applied in New York City though not in Chicago, of "development rights" derived from allowable square footage *not* built on landmark sites, but "banked" for future purchase and use on other sites.

In the Chicago plan, lawyer John Costonis and real estate analyst Jared Shlaes proposed Chicago establish a development-rights "bank," much as New York City has since done in the Seaport District, to hold the square footage that exists when the bulk of a landmark building is subtracted from what the site could theoretically be developed to, including the bonuses offered by the zoning. This allowable square footage, although not built, is called "development rights." Costonis's book, *The Chicago Plan,* and several articles by Shlaes, elaborate on this concept.

The bank would receive development rights from three potential sources: (1) benevolent owners of existing or to-be-designated landmarks would contribute the excess development rights derived from the landmark structure to the bank; (2) less benevolent owners of a landmark or potential landmark may agree to have their building designated as a landmark and sell excess development rights to the bank; (3) the development rights of buildings whose owners remain adamant about designation, who prefer to retain the landmark for its speculative value vis-à-vis construction of a new office building in the future, would be condemned and the owners would receive compensation at fair market value. In order for this to work, the city must be willing to provide seed money so that the bank may buy rights associated with those landmarks immediately threatened by pressure of new construction until the bank can sell some of the development rights, provided there is a market for them.

In Chicago, unless the zoning is revised, the marketplace for the sale of development rights probably must be outside the downtown area. This is because with the existing zoning rules, most of the developers—especially those who own one-half or full block sites—can build much more than they would actually ever consider building downtown. To be politically manageable, the marketplace must be within the city limits.

As one example of this, Costonis suggests that a potential marketplace was the area surrounding O'Hare Airport—a huge tract of land within the city's jurisdiction. The city dramatically increased the zoning from farmland status to allow for office buildings, apartments, and hotels. The city was content to receive the increased tax revenues the new structures would provide. But Costonis argues that rather than automatically receiving an up-zoning, the developers could as easily have been required to buy the increased development rights they needed from the development-rights bank. But it's probably too late for the O'Hare area; and it is unlikely there will be a market for large-scale development of land zoned at low densities that could buy enough development rights to make the bank work—although Shlaes thinks Chicago's near north side is potentially one such area.[4]

Both Costonis and Shlaes recognize that the Chicago plan faces another problem. Suppose a landmark building is on a site of 32,000 sq ft (2,990 sq m) only 25 percent of a typical downtown block and suppose also that it is built to an FAR of 14, or 480,000 sq ft (45,500 sq m). The present zoning allows that site to be built up to an FAR of 16, and because of its location on the block, it can take advantage of probably only two of the zoning's bonus provisions—thereby reaching an FAR of 20 for a building of 640,000 sq ft (60,800 sq m). Greatly simplified, it can be said that landmark designation would deny the owner of the landmark economic potential equal to the difference between a building of 448,000 sq ft (42,560 sq m) and a building of 640,000 sq ft (60,800 sq m), or 192,000 sq ft (18,240 sq m). It would be expected then that the city would compensate the owner for the value of those development rights.

While it might be a manageable sum for the city to pay for 192,000 sq ft of development rights, the owner might very well own more than just that one building. He may, in fact, own many, if not all, of the buildings on the block, in anticipation of building an office building. This is not uncommon. Although many landmarks in the center of the Loop are viable pieces of real estate, returning 7 to 10 percent to investors, the developer, by owning the land around the landmark as well, can now take advantage of many more bonus items, increasing his potential FAR not just to 20, as permissible if he redevelops just the landmark site, but to 40. He could build his own Sears Tower and call it Montgomery Wards. For the sake of calculation, the entire block, 128,000 sq ft (30,340 sq m) built at FAR 40, would entitle the developer to build 5,120,000 sq ft (486,400 sq m). The city in this instance would have to compensate the owner for 4,672,000 sq ft (443,690 sq m), a far cry from the 192,000 sq ft (18,190 sq m) of excess development rights above just the landmark.

132

132   Had the Chicago plan been in effect and if Chicago's zoning were set at FAR 16, the Sears Building could have purchased the development rights from as many as 15 landmarks and still have been an economically viable development. If the allowable bulk of future buildings is strictly controlled, development rights above landmarks would then have a salable value. This photograph is only meant to illustrate the concept of available development rights that could be transferred to future buildings.

And as much as any factor, it is this exponential nature of zoning in Chicago— the larger the site, the more zoning bonuses there are to take advantage of—which is encouraging developers to assemble half and full-block sites and place landmarks in such trouble. And Costonis believes that, should the city contest compensation for any development rights other than those directly above the landmark itself, then the courts would probably agree with the owner that it would be an infringement of his right to develop the larger parcel to the higher density.[5]

Even if the city eliminated all the bonus provisions in the zoning—a necessary but unlikely action—the base FAR of 16 still allows for very big buildings and is close to New York's maximum FAR of 18. The 60-story First National Bank Building is built at an FAR of 17, and the 30-story Chicago Civic Center is built at an FAR of 12, both of which suggest that buildings on full-block sites built at an FAR close to the Chicago base of 16, or even less, are economically feasible. Without taking advantage of any of the many possible bonuses, these two buildings in particular have devoted half of their respective sites to well-landscaped plazas that contain expensive pieces of art work. These buildings and others indicate that it may not be unrealistic for the zoning in Chicago to mandate, without bonuses, certain amenities or, on occasion, that a particular development build around a certain landmark.

Are buildings constructed at FARs above 16 an unnecessary giveaway? What if the truly big buildings instead of automatically having the right to be big had to buy development rights from the bank of development rights derived from landmarks? Would they still be economically feasible?

The economics of big buildings are not always as straightforward as typical speculative buildings. A developer will lure a major tenant to a speculative building he intends to build by offering to name the building after that company. In many cases the major tenant may actually occupy only 25 percent of the building. Once the developer has secured a prestigious tenant it is generally easier to market the rest of the building and to get the necessary construction loans. Speculative buildings tend to be predictable. The development community has built

many buildings of a certain size and type of construction that have rented well and the economics of which are known.

A big building is more risky, with more variables, and often has many untested procedures. The developer of the John Hancock Building went bankrupt and had to pull out of the venture early on when troubles developed with the massive caissons, which had to be torn out and a fresh start made. At that point, believing, perhaps, that their prestige was on the line, the John Hancock Insurance Company, which had only intended to rent space in the building, took over as developer and owner.

The truly big buildings in Chicago are rarely speculative in the strict sense. Despite the inherent risks, the developers of these larger buildings are most often the major tenants themselves, who can afford to build corporate headquarters contrary to normal development procedures. When the head of Standard Oil's real estate section was asked at a conference why Standard Oil had built the building, knowing that they would occupy only 50 percent of that 80-story building, with most of the rest of the building remaining empty, perhaps for years because the office market was saturated, he replied something to the effect that that was not an overwhelming concern because one day Standard Oil would occupy it all. A normal developer would have gone bankrupt very quickly if half the building were unoccupied. Sears Roebuck, Standard Oil and John Hancock are not overly fettered by such problems.

Assume that the Sears Building could have built only to an FAR of 16 across the entire site. This would equal 2 million sq ft (190,000 sq m). As has been seen, this would have been an economically feasible building [the Civic Center is 1.5 million sq ft (142,500 sq m), and the First National Bank is 2.2 million sq ft (209,000 sq m), and both are on the same size sites as Sears], but far less than the size Sears wanted. The remaining 2.5 million sq ft (237,500 sq m) Sears needed could have been purchased from the development-rights bank and is the equivalent of buying the development rights derived from the most important landmarks in the center, which would have saved them from speculation (132). The difference between the existing size of 15 landmark buildings and what they could be if developed to an FAR of 20 equals approximately 2.4 million sq ft (228,000 sq m). The buildings are the Monadnock, Marquette, Reliance, Manhattan, Fisher, Chicago, Old Colony, Rookery, Gage, Railway Exchange, Champlian, Chapin and Gore, Fine Arts, Troescher, and Brooks. If the Reliance and the Rookery are now considered safe from speculation, then the Leiter II Building could be added to this list—although the very least Sears might do is sponsor a designation of the Leiter II Building as a gift to the city.

Land cost for the Sears site was $143 per sq ft, totalling an estimated $17 million; and building costs were $198 million. It is also estimated that "soft" costs, which include construction financing changes, developers fees, and leasing fees, amounted to at least $20 million. Therefore with land cost, construction costs, and carrying charges, total cost of the Sears Tower was at least $235 million. Theoretically, Sears would require an additional 156,250 sq ft (13,924 sq m) of land to build the additional 2.5 million sq ft (237,500 sq m) of space it desired [if on every square foot of land the zoning permits 16 sq ft (1.5 sq m) of building—FAR 16— then 16 X 156,250 = 2.5 million sq ft]. If the cost of a square foot of development rights is calculated from the cost of 1 sq ft (.09 sq m) of land at $143, then every square foot of development rights would cost approximately $9 ($143 ÷ 16). (Actually it can be expected that development rights would cost less than land because it might not be subject to the inflated prices often paid for hold-out parcels, especially now that large land assemblage is increasingly difficult in the Loop.) Therefore, the cost of the additional 2.5 million sq ft of development rights would be $22 million ($9 X 2.5 million sq ft), increasing the total development budget of the Sears Tower by only 9 percent. Jared Shlaes does not think an additional 9 percent cost would necessarily have deterred Sears from going ahead with their building.

Land values are based primarily on location, expectation, and market conditions. In general, it can be said that in the Loop land value is pegged to the typical new office tower, which is considerably smaller than the Sears Building. Land costs represent on the average between 15 to 30 percent of the total development costs of these buildings, but is substantially less a percentage of larger developments. In the case of Sears, the $17 million land cost of the original site is roughly 8 percent of the total cost. If Sears had to purchase development rights to increase its size, the land cost would have been 17 percent of total costs. But if the development rights were purchased at $4.50 per sq ft which Shlaes believes would have been possible, the total land cost including the development rights would have been only 12.5 percent of the total costs.

Among Sears, IBM, Marina City, Water Tower Place, John Hancock, and Standard Oil, all Chicago's landmarks might have been saved had the FAR been set at 16 and had the Chicago plan been in effect. But it is not too late to save the remaining landmarks.

Market analysts have estimated that Chicago has enough office space to last until 1980 before new construction is necessary. Thus the present weak market may minimize the immediate development threat to landmarks, although there will always be the possibility of some new construction of special buildings for corporate headquarters. It is entirely reasonable, in fact, to assume that within the next 10 to 15 years there will be at least five to seven buildings which will be developed the size of the IBM or Water Tower Place, or perhaps even larger.

If the city eliminates all zoning bonuses and firmly establishes an urban design plan for the Loop making mandatory a minimum amount of urban design features and amenities, the developer wishing to construct larger buildings would merely be obliged to buy development rights from the development-rights bank. If Chicago is to finally save its landmarks, it could utilize the inherent leverage of this technique to do so.

In 1973 the Department of the Interior joined the battle to save the Chicago landmarks by reissuing a 7-year-old study—the Chicago Theme—which called for a section of the downtown to be declared a "National Cultural Park." The Department of the Interior said it would provide the seed money necessary to get the plan started, provided the city would legislate the development-rights transfer system as outlined in the Chicago plan.

The lull in construction would seem like the ideal time for the city to take the following steps:

–Adopt the Chicago plan and thereby establish a development-rights transfer bank. This would make the city eligible for funds from the Department of the Interior with which the city could purchase—after condemnation if necessary—the development rights derived from any landmarks immediately threatened with demolition. As suggested by Costonis and Shlaes, the city could also donate the development rights from above City Hall and the Rookery (the city owns the land under the Rookery).

–Designate as landmarks at least the 29 buildings in particular, and the Loop area as a whole, as recommended in the Chicago 21 plan. These landmark buildings represent only 5 percent of the total buildings downtown.

–Remove all bonuses, leaving the base FAR in the Loop at 16. Additional FAR could be purchased from the development-rights bank. Should this be contested in court or in cloak rooms, as a taking of development-rights potential without compensation, the city should be able to argue persuasively that buildings constructed at greater densities than FAR 16 impose an extraordinary burden on the city's infrastructure and its cultural heritage and that through the Chicago plan, a formula has been established for developers wishing to build buildings larger than the base FAR of 16 to pay for this burden by buying the development rights from the bank. Should the developers persist in a court fight, then the city should be consoled to know that there is a growing body of planning law through recent court decisions which suggests that area-wide reduction in overall density for such public purposes without compensation would be held constitutional. Stated another way, in 1957 the city of Chicago "willed" the bonus structure above the base FAR of 16. After viewing the ill effects of the 20-year history of this policy, the city can now "unwill" the bonus structure.

–A special design review board of architects appointed by the Chicago chapter of the AIA should be established to review all new buildings built above FAR 16 to determine what urban design features should be included.

To date, the commissioner of development and planning in Chicago, Lewis W. Hill, said that the city's Planned Unit Development policy, always flexible, had been amended to encourage developers of superblock sites with bonuses, heretofore reserved for the provision of arcades and plazas, to build around landmarks. This seems to preclude the city's support of the Chicago plan, which alone stands as Chicago's main contribution to the evolution of contemporary urban design theory for expanding urban cores.

One other approach to saving Chicago landmarks that could work with the Chicago plan would be for the city to buy the truly threatened landmarks outright. To do this, Robert De Voy—who served as an economic consultant to the Chicago plan and was a Senior Vice President at the Real Estate Research Corporation—believes the city could probably borrow 100 percent of the purchase price of the landmark.[6] Or the city could even issue revenue bonds to raise the purchase price. In either case, the landmark would remain on the tax rolls, and its revenues would pay off the debt, since, according to Costonis, the majority of landmarks are—or with better management could be—revenue producing. Once the debt service and taxes are paid, remaining revenues—if any—could go into a revolving fund for renovation and purchase of other landmarks in and out of the Loop.

Transportation problems created by the city's permissive development policy have led the city to propose building new subway lines extending north and south from the Loop.

As the focus of its radiating transportation network, the Loop has always been a tightly organized business center which has slowly grown both outward circumferentially and inward by taking down smaller old buildings (often landmarks) in the center and rebuilding at greater densities.

The effect of allowing office construction on upper Michigan Avenue has apparently

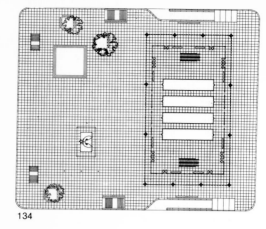

134

135

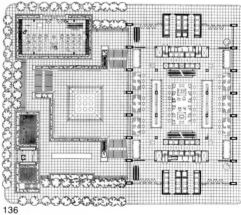

136

137

133

133   Many Chicago architects believe the elevated trains that encircle the Loop should remain and could be made quieter, safer, and more aesthetically pleasing.

134-135   By placing the Civic Center Building on the northern half of the site, a significant urban plaza with southern exposure has been created.

136-137   Conceptually similar to the Civic Center, the First National Bank Plaza is a more actively programmed space. One significant difference between the two projects is the amount of seating provided.

created an imbalance in the transportation system. To alleviate the congestion caused by this poorly planned policy on upper Michigan Avenue, the city is proposing to build a new subway line extending northward from the Loop, as part of a plan to remove the elevated lines and put them underground in a similar configuration.

Led by architects Harry Weese, Larry Booth, and Douglas Schroeder, the Chicago chapter of the American Institute of Architects now opposes taking down the El. The architects claim that the elevated structure is exciting and could be made quieter and more attractive at one-third the cost of putting it underground (133). Weese readily admits that this amounts to "architects dabbling in things beyond their traditional expertise," but "we put these ideas forth as hypotheses—the burden of proof is on them to prove us wrong."[7]

The new line will also run southward 2 miles (3.2 km) from the Loop to service the convention center, McCormick Place. In 1957 when the location of the convention center was being discussed, Harry Weese and other distinguished architects recommended in their own study that the city build the convention center on one of several available sites downtown in the midst of the hotels, restaurants, and not incidentally, good transportation. This, they argued, would leave the lake shore park alone as the Burnham plan recommended.

The policy, or nonpolicy, that has now necessitated the construction of the new subway lines north and south of the center contradicts a stated policy in the city's own guidelines for the development of the Illinois Center air rights site at the northeastern edge of the Loop: "public policy would not encourage types of uses and levels of intensity of development in any subarea which required major additional public expenditures to transportation while other suitable sites within the central area had unutilized access capacity."[8] Although there are vast areas at the periphery of the Loop, with direct access to existing subway lines, the Illinois Central air rights project allows a density many times greater than that recommended in the comprehensive plan. And the new subway lines will therefore have to go through and stop at the air rights site.

Because there is no urban design policy in Chicago, it is instructive to look at certain recent buildings which suggest what urban design policy might be and to look at other buildings which show precisely why urban design policies should be established, if for no other reason than to prevent such buildings from happening again.

Civic Center
The Chicago Civic Center, with its attendant plaza, opened in 1966 and became one of the first urban spaces in that dense downtown area. (C. F. Murphy Associates were the architects with SOM and Loebl, Schlossman, Bennett and Dart, associate architects.) The plaza is an important contribution to the downtown area because Grant Park at the edge of the Loop—similar to Central Park's relation to midtown Manhattan—is too far from the mass of workers to serve as an actively useful open space.

The 77,000-sq-ft (7,150-sq-m) space across the street from City Hall, however, is designed to serve the needs of the city's ceremonial functions rather than to be an active public space for daily use, for it contains only 18 benches, which, including a ledge around the Picasso sculpture, is enough to seat about 250 people (134, 135). If the standards William H. Whyte helped develop for New York's plaza legislation were applied to the Civic Center, its plaza would be able to seat an additional 1,000 people—equivalent to the seating density around Mies' Seagram Plaza, which is no less a dignified space as a result of its active use and which the Civic Center emulates.

One First National Plaza
Just two blocks south of the Civic Center, C. F. Murphy Associates, in a joint venture with the Perkins and Will Partnership, designed One First National Plaza. The immensely successful space in conjunction with the bank building is conceptually similar to the Civic Center, although here the plaza is sunken to provide good accessibility to the subway (136). The building is on the northern half of the site, therefore creating a plaza with southern exposure. A truly urbane space of the first order, it has ample seating, a fountain, a huge mosaic by Marc Chagall, a restaurant, and food kiosks (137). The programmed activities in the summer bring throngs of people to the

138

139

140

138   Treatment of the sidewalks around the First National Bank offers a superb example of what the rest of the downtown sidewalks could be like.

139   Street-level floors devoted to lobbies and banks are a recurrent problem in American downtowns. Banks believe they must have ground-level frontage to be competitive with other banks (although there are fine examples of second-level banking floors in downtown Chicago). Banks, in fact, are often either the major tenant or actually the developer of buildings in which they locate. And without a bank or other such prestigious uses, developers have for years believed a lobby trapped in travertine will enhance the building's prestige and marketability. However, neither banks nor lobbies add much to the life of the street, but merely force pedestrians into overcrowded and often overpriced restaurants and shops in older buildings that do not share these concerns about image. In the case of the Brunswick Building shown here, whose ground level is split between a lobby and a bank (with underground shopping and connections to the subway), not only are the excitement and activity of the street diminished, but so is the Civic Center Plaza across the street.

140   Lake Point Tower, with its 3-story brick wall surrounding a parking garage, exploits the lakefront park, segregates the building from potential users, and helps make surrounding streets both unsafe and uninteresting.

space. The treatment of the sidewalks at the edge of the space, with attractive paving, outdoor cafes, long low ledges used as benches, and dense planting of trees and flowers, is as refreshing as it is unusual in that area. It is an elegant model for what the sidewalks in the rest of the center could be like, if they were widened in conjunction with a reorganization of surface transit priorities (138).

Although The First National Bank goes a long way towards providing an active, usable urban space, it is only one of scores of banks and savings and loan institutions downtown. Until recently Chicago has had no branch banking. Most of the banks have evidently felt compelled to present a prestigious image at the ground level where they feel they are in direct competition with other banks for customers (139). This has helped to make most of downtown Chicago a ghost town at night.

In New York, which has had branch banking a long time, large institutional banks with branches in the business centers realize that 80 to 85 percent of the branches' business comes from the building in which it locates. In recent years, because of this fact, banks in New York have been slowly coming to accept what the zoning has increasingly been insisting they do—locate on the second level and keep the street level for shops and restaurants that serve the needs of shoppers, making for a more active street life both day and night.

It would probably be impossible to win support for a zoning amendment prohibiting ground-floor banking in Chicago. New York's Fifth Avenue zoning district might, however, offer a workable solution for Chicago: it permits banking uses to occupy no more than 15 percent of the ground floor of a building's frontage. Not enough room to cash a check in, but just enough to present the bank's stately image and provide escalators or elevators to below grade or second- and third-level banking floors.

Lake Point Tower
One major goal of the Burnham plan, largely implemented, was the creation of the lakefront park. There were to be no buildings, save perhaps a minimum number of public buildings—like bathhouses—as a

complement to the park. The area where the river meets the lake was the one major exception, where warehouses were a vital part of river commerce. But as the railroads and warehouses close to the mouth of the river have become obsolete, developers are seizing upon this as a vast area for redevelopment. The city has yielded to developer pressure to increase the zoning—through, of course, "planned" unit development. The Lake Point Tower apartment building is now one of three huge private apartment buildings constructed east of Lake Shore Drive. Alvin Boyarsky, for many years a member of the architecture faculty at the University of Illinois and now the head of London's Architectural Association, calls it "an hermetically sealed, heavily guarded, isolated monument to 'as is' taste, which exploits the 20-mile (32-km) long linear Lake Shore Park without offering any extension or amenity to the public"[19] (140).

Chicago River-edge Plan
The Burnham plan also recommended a two-level circulation system to separate the arrival and delivery of goods that arrived by river from the surface traffic. The idea of lower-level goods delivery systems was popular in Chicago. For over a decade an intricate system of tunnels 42 ft (13 m) connected every major railway terminal and had four public receiving depots outside the Loop. The tunnels actually contained small freight cars and delivered about 650,000 tons (585,000 metric tons) of package freight to these terminals in 1920 (141, 142). It was estimated at that time by the Tunnel Company that this operation saved 5,000 truck movements per day. Much of Burnham's lower-level service system, called Wacker Drive, was completed in 1926 and still serves today as a network of delivery routes for many buildings close to the river; however, its receiving function from river boats has largely dissipated, only to be replaced by strip parking lots (143).

A new city policy would convert these parking areas and other unused portions of the river's edge into strip parks. The SOM design for the plaza around its 1965 Equitable Building set the tone for the reclamation of the edge of the river for pedestrian activity. Even the city acknowledges it is "an example of quality design and orientation to the River" (144). Unfortunately, the city

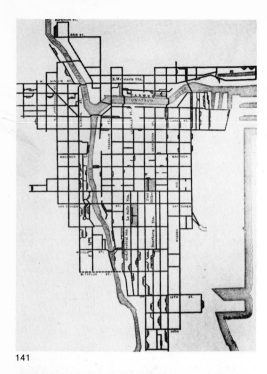

141

142

143

144

141-142   At one time Chicago had an underground delivery system connected to virtually every building downtown that saved an estimated 5,000 truck deliveries a day in the early 1920s. Today, these tunnels are used for co-axial cables.

143   Burnham's two-level street system with goods delivery at the lower level still makes sense; but many parts of the river's edge, no longer important as a connection to barges, have become strip parking lots.

144   The Equitable Building was the first major attempt of a new building along the river to devote the river's edge to public use.

145   Chicago's Department of Planning and Development designed one of the strips along the river as a prototype plaza for future development of the remaining strips. Unfortunately, the space has been French-curved to death with planters placed where pedestrians want to be.

146   In fear, perhaps, that the city would continue with its inappropriate design, the IBM Corporation along with other businesses paid to have three other river-edge plazas developed. The design they sponsored is a handsome, simple, and straightforward approach that allows access to the river's edge.

145

146

147 The internationally famous Stock Exchange Building did not make Mayor Daley's *personal* list of landmarks, and so it was razed. Architectural photographer Richard Nickel, who had permission to photograph the interior of the building while it was being demolished, was killed when the building fell on him.

148 Entrance detail of the Stock Exchange.

147

148

149

149 Entrance detail of the Heller International Building which replaced the Stock Exchange—a trade which might be likened to Chicago's Art Institute destroying one of its paintings by Renoir to allow room for a new poster by Peter Max! Less than 5 percent of Chicago's downtown buildings are landmarks. Surely there is sufficient imagination among people to find a way to save what precious few landmarks remain.

evidently felt it had to demonstrate its own design abilities on one section of the river. The design denies the pedestrian access to the river edge in large sections by planting several inappropriate "free-form" planting beds (145). Three other strip parks, however, designed by landscape architect Joe Karr, consulting with architects Harry Weese and Bruno Conterato, show it to be a sound policy and offer a more positive suggestion of how the river front in this urban setting should be treated (146).

It is sad that there are not concrete urban design plans to present here that will ensure that Chicago maintains its rapidly diminishing grace and beauty. One of the most important decisions the city has yet to make is whether its remaining landmarks will be an integral part of the city's future.

In perhaps one of their finer moments, it seems many architects in Chicago refused the commission to design the office building to be erected atop the grave site of Sullivan's Stock Exchange (147). The developers found willing accomplices in Texas, however, where if Houston is any indication of the status quo, discernment for the urban environment does not appear to be a high cultural value. The new building is pretty much boarded up because windows keep popping out. But no matter, there is no market for the new space anyhow. So the building sits empty where once stood the vibrantly active and elegant Stock Exchange (148, 149).

At the end of it all, the developers claimed bankruptcy—or to paraphrase William Zeckendorf, who was the developers' developer, "If I borrow $100 from a bank and can't pay the note when it comes due, I'm in big trouble. On the other hand, if I borrow $1 million from a bank, and can't pay the note when it comes due, then the bank's in big trouble." Meanwhile, back in Rome, the fellow who took a few hammer swings at Michelangelo's *Pieta* was arrested and sent to jail. Yet the developers who destroyed the Stock Exchange are free to destroy other masterpieces of architecture which stand in their way of trying to make a small fortune.

Philadelphia

The fourth largest city in the U.S., Philadelphia is the only American city whose development has been guided by comprehensive planning for close to 30 years. The "comprehensive plan" first formally issued in 1961 has often been amended to meet new economic and social conditions, and its impact has been significant. But the success of the plan is due more to architect/planner Edmund Bacon's long commitment to Philadelphia and to his creative guidance of the planning process, than to the plan itself.

Population and geography
Three hundred years after William Penn penned his 2-sq-mile (5-sq-km) plan, modern Philadelphia covers 130 sq miles (340 sq km) with a population of close to 2 million people, making it the fourth largest city in the United States. The surrounding eight-county region—including four New Jersey counties on the eastern side of the Delaware River—contains 3,350 sq miles (8,500 sq km) and a population of about 3 million people.

The central business district has grown about the axis of Penn's plan—primarily along Market Street. Altogether, 335,000 people work within the confines of the original plan (150). Of those who come to work in the center, more than 70 percent use the city's diverse public transportation system, which includes two subway lines and a radiating network of commuter railroads, trolleys, and buses. The rest come by automobile.

Historical development
Philadelphia sits on land deeded by Charles II to William Penn in 1681. The king had

owed Penn's father money; but young William took 40 sq miles (100 sq km) of land in the New World instead, with the vision of establishing a colony where his Quaker ideas would be free from English persecution (151). By 1682, Penn and his surveyor, Captain Thomas Holme, had drawn up a grid plan, with the lots to be sold primarily to Penn's followers. The town was sited on a 2-mile (3.2-km) stretch of land between the Delaware and Schuylkill rivers and was about 1 mile (1.6 km) wide from north to south (152).

Some denounced Penn's plan as monotonous; but Penn defended its uniformity, maintaining that it reflected God's order. From the very beginning he demonstrated the humane possibilities of such a layout by reserving in the center of the plan 10 acres (4 ha) of land for public buildings—where today stands the City Hall—and in each of the four quadrants of the city, a public space of 8 acres (3.2 ha). In Philadelphia's early days these public squares often contained gallows and, conveniently enough, graveyards. The misuse of these public squares may have been acceptable then because the houses were located far apart, leaving ample open space for gardens and orchards. Penn thought this configuration would reduce the chance of conflagration and plague—two catastrophes he had witnessed in the 1660s in London.

In the original plan High Street (today Market Street) was 100 ft (30 m) wide, dividing the city north and south. Broad Street, also 100 ft wide, divided the city east and west. All other streets were 50 ft (15 m) wide, and typical blocks were either 425 by 675 ft (130 by 200 m) or 425 by 500 ft (130 by 155 m).

151

152

150   It took 200 years before downtown Philadelphia filled out the original area of the plan by William Penn and Thomas Holme. Today, of the 355,000 people who work within the confines of the original plan, about 225,000 work in the downtown area; 70 percent of them come to work by public transportation.

151   Scull and Heap 1750 map of Philadelphia shows the 2-sq-mile (5-sq-km) plan sited between two rivers in the midst of Penn's 40-sq-mile (104-sq-km) holding.

152   Drawn up for William Penn by Thomas Holme in 1682, the Philadelphia plan was equivalent to the size of London at that time.

153　Clarkson and Biddle map of Philadelphia of 1762. Early growth of the city followed not the plan, but the major source of employment along the Delaware River, where blocks were continually subdivided to provide more housing.

154　Rittenhouse Square today, one of the four major green spaces created in the Penn plan.

155　Consistent with the idea of baroque planning, the Benjamin Franklin Parkway is a boulevard between two major public buildings. To achieve the views offered by this type of connection, it was spliced across the Philadalphia grid on a diagonal.

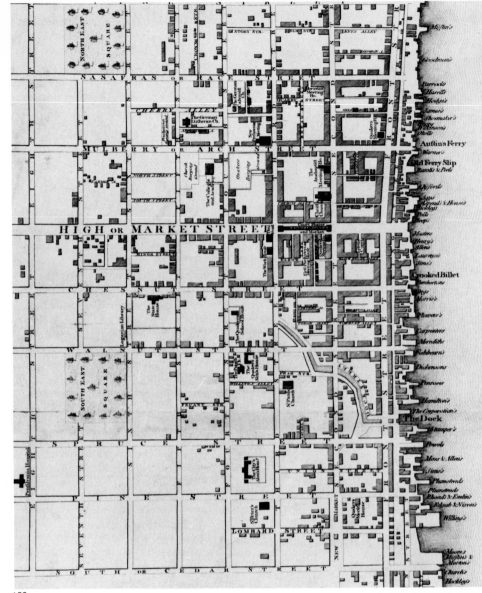

153

154

155

The growth of the city, however, centered not about the main square, but around the port on the Delaware River. Pressures for more housing close to the major source of employment led to construction of row houses in the open spaces between the earlier buildings. Later, the large city blocks were subdivided, with two, three, and sometimes even four, new and very narrow streets opening up the interior of the blocks for housing (153). These "new" streets are very much a part of the special character of Philadelphia today. And perhaps because of the increasing density, the four original squares eventually became the pleasant green spaces Penn intended with hardly a hint of past inglories (154).

The principle of grand vistas between significant public buildings that L'Enfant had perfected in his plan for Washington, D.C., influenced an 1892 proposal for a diagonal boulevard running northwest across the grid from city hall square through Logan Square (one of the four original squares) to the site of the Philadelphia Museum of Art and Fairmount Park beyond. In 1910, French landscape designer Jacques Greber was invited to produce a design based on the earlier proposal and "create a diagonal vista which would break the 'monotony' of the grid plan."[1] The Penn grid has nicely survived the Baroque imposition of the Benjamin Franklin Parkway (155).

As Philadelphia grew, the grid was extended. In later years geographical features had an increasing influence on the grid, which eventually gave way to Levittown-like cul-de-sacs. And—unlike Savannah, Georgia—Philadelphia did not maintain the same balance of public spaces to private ownership as it expanded.

From 1933 to 1960, zoning encouraged the setback system, but with an overall height limitation; 1960 revisions, intended to encourage more open space in the city center, set an FAR of 12, with generous bonuses for plazas and arcades and an extra bonus to encourage higher density where the street system was best able to handle it.

To conform with the regular street pattern, Penn insisted that "the houses built be in a line"[2] as often as possible. Not until 1933— some 250 years later—did the city set up new rules in the form of zoning. Passage of the zoning law was sparked by the increasing number of highrise buildings in the center of the city. However, concern about density did not lead to a direct limit on the amount of floor area that could be built on a parcel of land. Instead, above 200 ft (60 m), a building was required to conform to the familiar setback configuration popular at that time. But unlike the Chicago and New York ordinances, which allowed a tower to spring up to unlimited heights once the building set back a certain distance, the Philadelphia law did set an overall height limitation. The building could not pierce the top of the imaginary pyramid that was used to determine the setbacks.

In 1960, the zoning was revised to encourage more open space in the rapidly changing center. The setback system, which encouraged full lot coverage, was replaced by regulation of the floor area ratio. The base FAR was set at 12. Generous bonuses were included for the provision of plazas and arcades, and an extra bonus was available for buildings fronting on wide streets to encourage higher density where the street system was best able to handle it. Under this system, a building on a large site could conceivably reach an FAR of 25. Few buildings have even approached this size in Philadelphia because the city has ample development sites, and there is simply not sufficient market demand at any one time to pack all that density into one building.

Philadelphia's development since 1947 has been guided by comprehensive planning which involved the public in, and made implementation part of, the planning process.

Since World War II few American cities have consistently followed the guidelines of a comprehensive plan. Philadelphia may be the most important exception. Philadelphia-born architect Edmund Bacon has been the chief proponent of the comprehensive plan concept. Long before Bacon became the executive director of the city planning staff in 1949, he was active in numerous civic groups which succeeded in having the City Council create the Planning Commission; and he devoted his professional career, until he retired from the Planning Commission in 1970, to the design and implementation

156

157

159

158

of the evolving comprehensive plan of Philadelphia.

Set up in 1942, the commission had as one of its duties the annual preparation of a 6-year recommended program of public improvements. This planning tool, which incorporated budget commitments and authorization for implementation, eventually took much of the mystery out of the planning process, giving communities across the city a better chance to participate in the development of city projects affecting their neighborhoods.

The Better Philadelphia Exhibition of 1947—jointly sponsored by the business community and the city—was open to the public in Gimbels department store. And the public came—385,000 in all—to see what the Center City might be like in 30 years with careful planning. Architect Oskar Stonorov was the principal designer; Bacon was the co-designer. In addition, children from kindergarten to high school age, from a dozen schools across the city, were invited to prepare images of the city as they saw it and as they saw it could be. Bacon believes that the involvement of these children accounts for part of the success of the exhibit and, over the years, the plan: many could directly identify with the plan and were willing to support bond issues in later years to carry it out.[3]

Bacon's concept of creating garden settings open to the sky for subway arrivals in Center City and linking the city's varied movement systems with retail activity was distorted by the Pennsylvania Railroad and its developer, Robert Dowling, in the initial phase of Penn Center; but the most recent developments in and near Penn Center and along Market Street East have at last fully embraced Bacon's original concept.

One of the main eyesores in downtown Philadelphia in the late forties was the "Chinese Wall"—the Pennsylvania Railroad viaduct, which ran parallel to Market Street, 16 tracks wide, to a dead-end terminal building at the western side of City Hall (156, 157). The railroad no longer needed the structure. Trains running from Washington to New York and Boston could stop at the 30th Street Station near the edge of the city center, from which there were subway and bus

connections to the center. So urban designers began to think about the opportunities presented by demolition of the viaduct.

Conceptually, Bacon thought that rather than just clear the site, the railroad should actually excavate to one level below ground. A sunken garden with flowers and fountains could then let light and air down to commuters using the subway, trolley, and commuter rail complex located below grade at this spot, later to be called Penn Center.

Skyscrapers spaced far apart and oriented in the north-south direction would straddle the light well (158). Two stories of shops—on the garden and street levels—would provide needed retail space and keep both the streets and the mezzanine level alive with pedestrian activity. The wall of linear shops at the garden level would be interrupted in special locations to provide views of the garden from the incoming trains.

Rockefeller Center was admittedly a model for Bacon's Penn Center ideas. But the lower level concourse of Rockefeller Center disturbed Bacon because the shopping is completely cut off from the sunken garden, a situation which eliminates natural light and hinders orientation.

In 1953, when the railroad announced its plan to tear down the Chinese Wall and also to retain control over redevelopment of Penn Center, Bacon, by then executive director of the Department of City Planning, took the unconventional approach of presenting the railroad with his plan for its property.

Bacon had engaged Louis Kahn to help develop the proposal. Kahn had worked on the Market Street East part of the 1947 plan, and Bacon had great respect for him. But in Bacon's words, Kahn "personalized the design . . . when the need was to make the design acerbically clear—to communicate an idea that was so compelling, so self-evidently relevant, that they [the railroad] would support it."[4] Bacon felt that Kahn's "semicircles there played against this form over here"[5] camouflaged and endangered the basic urban design ideas. Professor Wilhelm von Moltke, who served from 1953 to 1961 as Bacon's chief designer on the

160

161

162

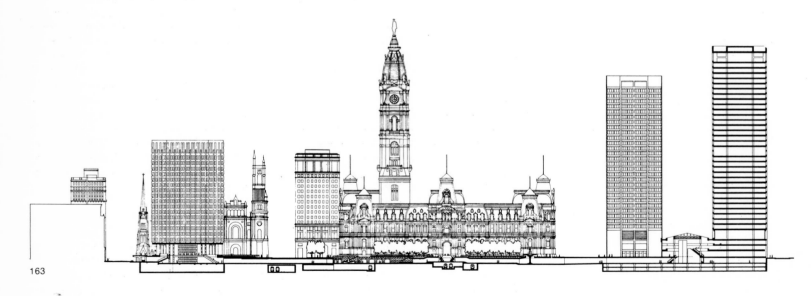

163

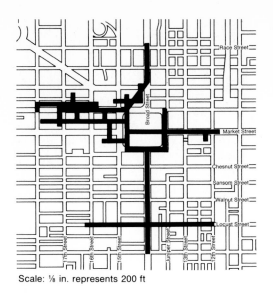

Scale: ⅛ in. represents 200 ft

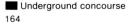 Underground concourse
164

160   The IBM Building provides an open connection to the below-grade shopping and transportation concourse.

161   The Center Square buildings provide exterior and interior connections to the below-grade concourse.

162   Center Square's 3-story interior space contains shopping and restaurants and connects the two office buildings.

163   This section looks east to City Hall and cuts across the Center Square buildings (right) and the Municipal Building (left) and shows the underground connections.

164   Downtown Philadelphia has an extensive underground pedestrian shopping concourse which connects to several major buildings and to all means of public transportation.

planning staff and later was the head of Harvard's urban design program, adds that although "Kahn was much admired by all' he was "a poet—the more mundane but fundamental problems of urban design didn't interest him."[6]

Giving up on Kahn, Bacon turned to Vincent Kling. This has proved fortunate for Kling since following that time his office has designed three of the six buildings in the 3-square-block Penn Center site; four of the buildings immediately around Penn Center; two of the three sunken plazas in Penn Center; and the two major public spaces adjacent to it.

The railroad rejected the Bacon plan and began working instead with Robert Dowling of the City Investing Company of New York. Dowling thought Bacon's proposal to connect the subway, commuter rail, bus terminal, and parking with a shopping concourse a good idea. He thought it all being open to the sky a bad idea.

Fancying himself an "architect"—and perhaps just to be contrary—Dowling proposed the concourse be covered with a concrete deck that would serve as a plaza at grade level for the office buildings, which he "placed" in an east-west orientation—the opposite of Bacon's well-thought-out proposal. Says Bacon, "It is difficult to convey the pain this caused us."[7]

Nevertheless, Bacon had won a significant battle just by getting the railroad to engage in a dialogue. He even got the railroad to agree to set up a board of design, which included himself, Dowling, and architect George Howe. Then he suggested that the Dowling "concrete deck" be cut open in three select locations, letting at least some light and air down to the lower level. Bacon knew that light and air were the key to the success of that level. This scheme eventually was agreed to and carried out (159).

As built, the original 3-block area of Penn Center falls far short of Rockefeller Center. The shortcomings are due to the railroad's deviations from the original Bacon solution. There are not enough light openings into the shopping concourse. The railroad decided to run the shopping concourse itself, even though Bacon had persuaded James

Rouse, the shopping center developer, to take the lower level. And finally, the street level along Market Street, where Bacon knew shops would be an important stimulus to pedestrian activity, has been devoted mostly to lobbies and institutional uses.

Still, Bacon's basic idea has survived all the distillment and has evolved over the last 30 years to a point where the most recent buildings in and across from Penn Center and those along Market Street East have come full circle—embracing Bacon's original concept. Vincent Kling's IBM Building, for example, has an open garden-like connection to the Penn Center concourse (160). More recently, Kling's solution for the twin-tower Centre Square complex, across the street from the first of the Penn Center buildings, includes both an outdoor and an indoor lower-level concourse, as well as a subway connection (161). The indoor connection is actually a huge glass-domed room which joins the two office buildings (162). It contains three interconnected levels of shops, plus escalators to the concourse level below, which runs under the street to the subway (163, 164).

A principle established by Bacon as policy, without the weight of law behind it, has kept the statue of William Penn atop City Hall symbolically above the city's tallest buildings which are expected to rise no higher than the base of the statue.

Neither the 43-story building in Centre Square, nor any other existing or planned building in the city, is taller than the base of the statue of William Penn that stands atop City Hall tower (165). [From the street to the top of Penn's hat is 548 ft (220 m).] Strangely enough, there are no height limitations in Philadelphia. Bacon says legal restrictions were politically impossible, but he has achieved the moral equivalent: "I established, as a matter of policy, the principle that it was totally wrong to build above the statue—I would have put the maximum height limitation for a new building at City Hall clock if I had had my way. The whole concept of the plan is the crossing of two great axes, which was reinforced by the position of the underground subway. . . . And the significance of the City Hall tower is the lifting into the third dimension of the assertion of the centrality of the crossing of those

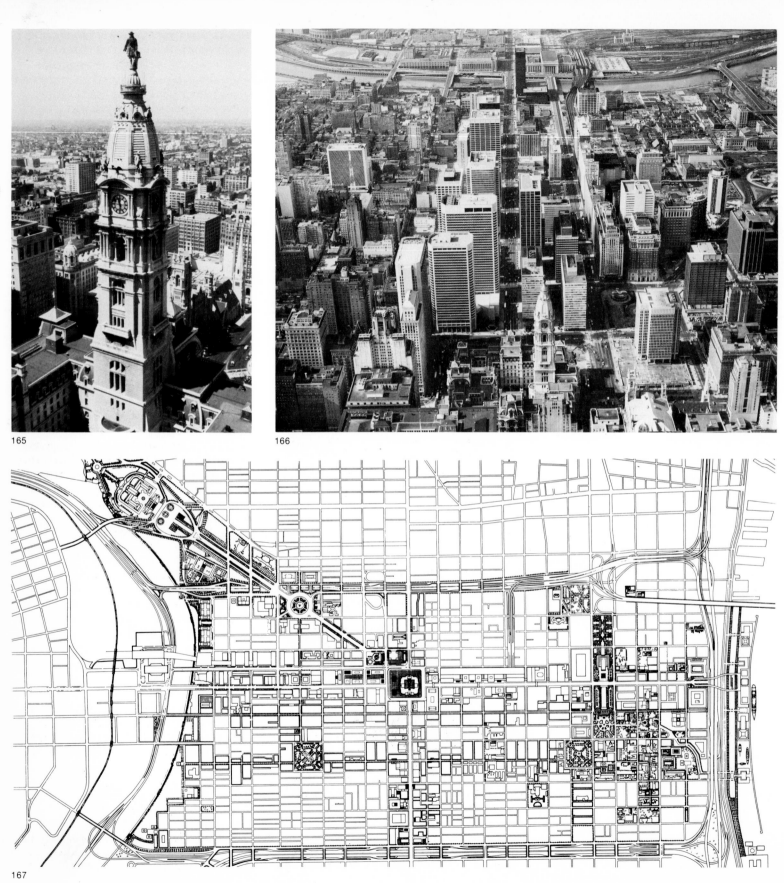

165

166

167

165 City Hall, topped by a statue of William Penn, is taller than any other building in Philadelphia.

166 Market Street is conceived as a linear spine, accommodating the city's tallest buildings and served primarily by public transportation.

167 The 1961 comprehensive plan had been at the center of the city's development long before it was formally drawn up and adopted.

two axes. There's no reason to go above the height of the city hall. There is plenty of room along the Market Street spine to build efficiently. For symbolic reasons and reasons of clarity of the whole structure, it is wrong to go above the statue of William Penn. And I waged this as a lonely moral battle. I used to say to developers who came in with tall proposals, there's a gentlemen's agreement that nobody will go above the statue. The issue is whether or not you are a gentleman."[8]

In an earlier scheme for Centre Square, some not-quite-so-gentle men from SOM's New York office proposed a building 20 stories higher than the statue. Incensed, Bacon went to the mayor and said: "I put my neck on the block. It's my dead body or this . . . I will absolutely resign."[9] The building was not built, and today Philadelphia is one of the few large American cities that has a piece of civic architecture as a dominant regional symbol and focal point.

Market Street was long viewed by Bacon as a linear spine, with the subway providing excellent access all along the street; the zoning has succeeded in encouraging a very high FAR for two or three blocks on either side of Market Street and then a dramatic drop to three-story buildings.

Bacon has long favored Market Street as a linear spine, with tall buildings flanking the east-west subway line there and profiting from the large numbers of people the subway can move. In fact, the 1960 zoning change reflected Bacon's view that the FAR should be very high for two or three blocks on each side of Market Street and should then drop dramatically—as it does—to three-story buildings within four blocks of Market Street (166). Broad Street is a counter-axis, but it is not intended to have the same density as Market Street.

Bacon's Market Street ideas have obviously benefited from various proposals for linear cities, the first of which is generally credited to Spanish businessman Arturo Soria y Mata, who put his proposal forward in the late 1880s. Mata's *ciudad lineal* was designed as a new town around and away from Madrid, following the streetcar line which he was (conveniently) promoting. Bacon's approach is also simply logical. The subway provides excellent access

along Market Street, and accessibility to good transportation has often been the most important part of the decision on where to locate a building. When the developer ignores accessibility, the city usually winds up investing heavily in new transportation facilities.

When Bacon had built support for the idea of an ongoing comprehensive planning process and the city's 1961 comprehensive plan came out, it proposed the regeneration of Market Street East as a city and regional shopping center and envisioned it as a pedestrian link between Penn Center to the west and the Independence Hall and Society Hill areas to the east.

Bacon and his group did not actually formalize all the things they had been working on and thinking about sincg 1947 until the city came out with its 1961 comprehensive plan (167). The 1947 exhibit was more a three-dimensional sketch of what could be; but rather than elaborate on it, Bacon, once he became executive director of the Department of City Planning, chose instead to win support for the idea of an on-going comprehensive planning process. First, however, he brought a number of excellent urban designers—like Wilhelm von Moltke—onto the planning commission's staff. Next, Bacon used the legally mandated 6-year public improvement program to deal with what he calls the city's "explicit and tangible" urban design problems.

The 1961 plan devoted much attention to the eastern portion of Market Street. With four department stores along it, Market Street East from 7th Street to the face of City Hall at 12th Street was the traditional shopping center for the city, but it had become rundown in recent years. The 1961 plan proposed that it become, through urban renewal, a regenerated city and regional shopping center. It could then also serve as an enclosed pedestrian link between Penn Center to the west and the Independence Mall and Society Hill area to the east.

Beginning in 1958 with urban design sketches by Von Moltke—a three-level shopping system connecting to subway, buses, commuter trains, and parking, with office buildings above—the ideas evolved through many architects and many stages

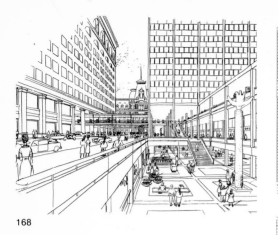

168

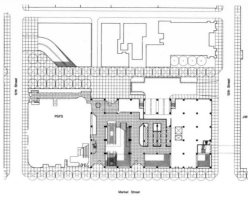

169

170

171

168 Drawing by Wilhelm von Moltke shows an early proposal for Market Street East. Many of the basic principles shown here have not changed over the years.

169 Plan of 1234 Market Street shows public space, connection to the PSFS Building, and the bridge connection (shown with dotted lines) to Wanamaker's.

170 Section through 1234 Market Street shows public space and connections to the subway and Market Street East project.

171 Interior of 1234 Market Street: subway riders can see directly into the naturally lit space.

(168). Architect Romaldo Guirgola advanced the Von Moltke scheme to include a 6-story-high glass-enclosed pedestrian arcade, but with shopping at only the lowest level in accordance with reduced estimates of shopping needs. The Philadelphia Redevelopment Authority then invited the Chicago office of SOM to synthesize the urban design features of the Guirgola proposal into a buildable set of urban design specifications. The complexity of these mixed-use structures, coupled with a lack of public funds to build the enclosed public space, forced interested developers to back away.

Despite all the changes in project architects over the years, the concept of Market Street East remained the same: to reinforce Market as a linear shopping street, with emphasis on the pedestrian at a lower shopping concourse level and with connections to subway and commuter trains.

On the north side of Market Street lies the Vine Street highway. The urban designers proposed a spur for this road, connecting to a 5,000-car parking area—primarily for shoppers—with special lanes for commuter buses.

Also to the north of Market lies the elevated Reading Railroad viaduct and terminal, a sentimental favorite in Philadelphia and now on the National Register of Historic Landmarks. The Reading enters the city from the north; the viaduct is perpendicular to Market Street, and the terminal fronts on the north side of Market between 11th and 12th Streets. The viaduct and the terminal were to be demolished so that the Reading could be rerouted underground, turning west (a block north of Market) and extending into the suburban station at Penn Center. This would give the incoming commuter the opportunity to stop at either the eastern or the western part of downtown. Pressure to save the old station is mounting, and plans have been developed showing that it would be possible to underpin the old viaduct, putting the tracks beneath it and using the elevated structure as the bus route off the highway and the station as the bus terminal.

Meanwhile, on the south side of Market Street East, another urban renewal site was being developed between Wanamaker's

department store—designed by Daniel Burnham—and the landmark Philadelphia Savings Fund Society (PSFS)—designed by George Howe and William Lescase and built in 1930. Although it was not part of the Market Street spine across the street, SOM had also established urban design guidelines for this particular site. The requirements called for a park along the west wall of the PSFS, with an office building along Market Street between the open space and 13th Street. The developer's architects—Bower and Fradley—convinced the Redevelopment Authority that an open space at that location on a shopping street was incorrect.[10] They pointed out that an interior public space connecting to the subway was a more useful and important space, and also noted that the west wall of the PSFS was intentionally designed to be built against.

1234 Market Street
The finished building is an exceptional piece of urban design: two-thirds of the area of the lower level, grade level, and upper mezzanine level of the building is devoted to a glass-enclosed public space lined with shops (169). Clear glass distinguishes this public space of the building (which was made possible by the urban renewal program) from the upper office floors which have dark glass. The clear glass also makes the public space visible, open, and inviting. At the lower level a glass wall makes the subway visible, and an underpass provides access to the westbound subway platform (170). (It will also connect to the Market Street East spine when the spine reaches this far.) Although the public space is enclosed, it comes the closest of anything yet built to Bacon's vision 30 years before of the experience the subway rider should have entering the center city along Market Street (171).

The building butts up against the PSFS, preserving the individuality of both buildings while maintaining the continuity of the street wall. The building also provides a plaza behind both 1234 Market and the PSFS; a connection from the first and second floors of the PSFS to 1234 Market; and a bridge from 1234 Market across 13th Street to Wanamaker's (172, 173). It should be noted that the PSFS has endured as a model building in terms of urban design

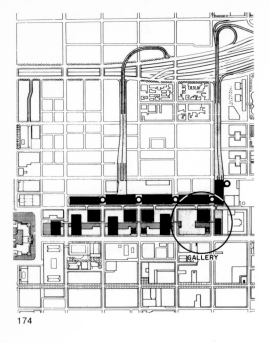

174

172-173 The exterior of 1234 Market Street maintains the street wall, appropriately butts up against the PSFS Building, and bridges over the street to Wanamaker's.

174 Site plan of Market Street East project.

175 Exterior of the Gallery.

176 A multilevel space, as shown here, will be a requirement for all future buildings in the Market Street East development.

172

173

175

176

considerations it recognized. Besides designing the PSFS building to be built against in the future, for "design reasons," the architects convinced the bank to place the 2-story banking floor of PSFS at the second level with escalator access from Market Street, as this solution left the street level for more active—and revenue-producing—retail space. The building also provided for a future below-grade shopping concourse to connect to the subway.

The Gallery
Viewing the success of 1234 Market Street, the Philadelphia Development Authority hired Bower and Fradley to update the plans for the Market Street East spine. In the 15-year history of the previous design proposals for the spine, economic projects for office space had tripled, which meant that retail space needed to be increased too. Therefore, the entire urban design plan had to be redone.

Two blocks of the 6-block scheme are now completed (174). These two blocks include a major new store for Gimbels designed by the Ballinger Company and the Gallery designed by Bower and Fradley (175). Developed by Rouse and Company, the Gallery is 200,000 sq ft (19,000 sq m) of retail space that can accommodate 125 shops and restaurants. The Gallery occupies the western third of the block between 8th and 9th Streets, abutting the Strawbridge and Clothier department store, to which it is connected at three levels. The Gallery then crosses both under and over 9th Street by way of a multilevel shopping bridge and tunnel, which leads to a four-level major public space surrounded with shopping and adjoining the new Gimbels.

Passing through the entire two-block project is the pedestrian space designed by Bower and Fradley. It has three levels and is glass-enclosed, skylighted, and air-conditioned (176). In the future, the Redevelopment Authority will expand the pedestrian space incrementally as the rest of the 6-block area is rebuilt. New private structures in the area must align with the pedestrian space, and structural systems and facing materials must correspond to the design established by Bower and Fradley. Office buildings may straddle the public space, but they must line the pedestrian space with lower buildings containing shops.

Because of the increased size of anticipated office buildings, elevator banks are expected to take up a large area. The elevator lobbies must therefore be located at the upper level of the three-level pedestrian spine so as not to take away space from the enclosed shopping street.

To the north of the first phase of this 6-block area the Parking Authority has constructed an 800-car parking garage. Space is planned to park an eventual total of 5,000 cars behind Market Street East.

Until the market for office space picks up, the rest of the plan may have a little wait. But considering the remarkable history of planning in this city, there is much optimism that, given time, the plan will be completely implemented. Money to build the public portion of the development comes from the city and HUD.

The Market Street East project is a good example of the complex design—both in process and in result—that cities must be prepared to engage in if the urban center is to become anything more than a mere collection of architectonic cubes on deserted plazas. Every agency of the city, state, and federal governments must be willing to work as one with each other and in partnership with private developers toward a common goal that is responsive to the needs and desires of the city.

The 20-year history of Society Hill is a lesson in the use of urban renewal to preserve and renew the prevailing character of a historic area.

The Philadelphia Historical Commission has been extremely busy since it was established in 1955. To date, the commission has designated nearly 5,000 buildings in the city as historic landmarks. About 2,000 of these lie within the area of the original Penn plan. In the Society Hill area alone, there are 700.

Twenty years ago in the Society Hill area, in addition to dilapidated 18th- and 19th-century row houses, there were old warehouses, a few colonial churches that had seen better days, and the wholesale produce market. Urban renewal funds were to be used for redevelopment of the area, but Bacon fought against the mass clearance traditions of urban renewal. He felt that the

177

178

179

177 I. M. Pei's three apartment towers are an integral part of the overall restoration of Society Hill.

178 The selective clearance of irretrievable buildings has enabled the creation of a system of greenways and small parks.

179 The east/west Chestnut Street transit-mall is based on recommendations of the 1961 comprehensive plan.

prevailing character of the area had to be preserved and that only selective clearance of irretrievable structures should occur. This selective clearance would provide space for a system of greenways, small parks, new town houses (which would pick up the scale of the older ones), and a few carefully placed highrise apartment buildings (177, 178).

The 20-year history of Society Hill is a model of urban renewal. Many middle- and upper-income families were attracted to the city, increasing the population in the center of the city by 13 percent—to 50,000 people—between 1960 and 1970. It is true that most of the lower-income residents who relocated during the renovation of the district cannot afford to move back. But because of the success of Society Hill, the idea of rehabilitation has become very popular in Philadelphia, and the policy of the redevelopment authority remains renovation rather than mass clearance. Because large sections of Philadelphia have much the same possibilities as Society Hill, it is likely that lower-income residents will ultimately benefit from this approach.

Two of the three major highways envisioned in the 1961 comprehensive plan are almost complete—and among the most sensitively designed of inner-city highways; the 10-block-long Chestnut Street Mall and Transit Way, slightly altered from the original intent, began operation late in 1975.

The 1961 comprehensive plan envisioned the Center City as surrounded by highways with limited access points connected primarily to parking garages.

The highway along South Street will not be built because of community opposition, which had the benefit of support from architects Venturi and Rauch and from the non-profit Architect's Workshop. The architects and the community worked together to develop alternatives to the highway.

However, the highway running east-west on Vine Street north of the city center and the Delaware River highway to the east of downtown are almost complete. Among the few Center City highways still being worked on, they are among the most sensitively de-

signed. The Vine Street section is being depressed and designed to fit within the city grid, and the section of the Delaware River highway adjacent to Society Hill has also been depressed (150), providing a pedestrian connection at grade between Society Hill and the new recreational facilities and proposed housing of the Penn's Landing development.

In the 1961 comprehensive plan, Chestnut Street—running one block south of and parallel to Market Street—was envisioned as a transit way that would provide bus connections to the center from the parking garages at the two river highways. The shift away from parking at the rivers in favor of recreation has slightly altered the original intent of the now constructed Chestnut Street Mall. But two-way bus service still made sense for shoppers and workers wishing to traverse the linear shopping area. So the part of the plan that made the most sense has been implemented.

Designed by architects Ueland and Junker, the 10-block mall goes from 8th Street to 18th Street. The normal three lanes of traffic on Chestnut Street narrow down to two lanes, exclusively for the use of buses in the mall area. The narrower roadbed allows for wider sidewalks, and all-new street furniture and graphics have been installed (179). Total cost of the mall was $7.4 million, with funds coming from the U.S. Urban Mass Transportation Administration, the state, and the city.

The merchants were against the mall at first, but now they are happy. The mall began operation late in 1975, and Christmas sales that year jumped 12 to 14 percent.

The open spaces of Penn's original plan have been complemented by others as the city grew; and in the heart of Center City, three separate projects, next to each other, now provide three new and actively used public spaces.

William Penn's original plan has in general proven to be exceedingly good at fulfilling the needs for more open space as the city has grown. Although all four quadrants of the old plan were provided with public squares (Rittenhouse, Logan, Washington, Franklin), the city grew to a size beyond the

180

180 The plaza of the Municipal Building provided needed public space in the rapidly expanding downtown.

181-182 Dead-ending the Benjamin Franklin Parkway one block sooner allowed traffic problems to be eliminated and a large public space to be created.

181

182

183

183   Dilworth Plaza, along the western face of City Hall, is interconnected to all surrounding buildings by the underground concourse.

imagination of anyone in the 17th century and Penn's open spaces eventually proved insufficient. The problem was particularly acute in the center, because the main square there was devoted to public buildings and because, as the city grew in the 20th century, it grew dead center on the plan.

To a large extent, three separate projects—all next to one another, all in the center, and all designed by Vincent Kling's office—have helped to solve the problem. The projects are the Municipal Services Building, JFK plaza, and Dilworth plaza.

Municipal Services Building Plaza
Completed in 1965, the 16-story Municipal Services Building is set on only 25 percent of its site, leaving a large civic plaza as an important urban space in what was before a very cramped area (180). Beneath the plaza are municipal offices and connections to City Hall and to all the transportation facilities in Penn Center (see 163).

JFK Plaza
Originally, the diagonal Benjamin Franklin Parkway cut its way across the grid and ended at City Hall, where it caused a traffic bottleneck. The parkway itself divided each of the city blocks it crossed into two triangular sites. JFK plaza was created when Bacon's group suggested to the mayor that the parkway be terminated one block sooner and that the roadbed be filled in to get back the complete block. It is a well-designed, comfortable, and actively used public space (181, 182).

Dilworth Plaza
Dilworth plaza sits adjacent to the western edge of city hall. Before the city intervened, Market Street came right up to city hall, dividing two very narrow blocks of land just to the west of city hall. One of the blocks—the Old Broad Street Station site—was vacant and owned by the railroad. The other had an old building on it which the owner was about to tear down.

In this case, the Planning Commission recommended that the city purchase both sites for use as a park. The plaza now provides a major open space for the area and is connected to every major building in and around Penn Center and City Hall by the underground shopping concourse (183).

Philadelphia, like all American cities, has serious urban problems. Few large cities in this country, however, have dealt with their downtown problems as successfully as Philadelphia has over the last 30 years.

This remarkable achievement is due on one hand to the capabilities of reform mayors Joseph Clark (1952–1956) and Richardson Dilworth (1956–1960) and on the other to the persistence of Edmund Bacon and the urban designers he attracted to Philadelphia to work on these problems. As Wilhelm von Moltke puts it, ''Bacon could understand politicians and could deal with them. He was energetic, dedicated, and believed in Philadelphia. And he was a very good salesman.''[11]

Specifically, the key, besides Bacon's ability, was his perseverance. Many architects seek work anywhere they can get it, and as a result they can rarely point to any significant contribution they've made to the environment in which they live. Bacon, however, made a 30-year personal commitment to Philadelphia, and he spent 21 of those years in a position of considerable authority. Bacon became a city bureaucrat, he endured the frustrations of city government, he spent decades nursing problems that wouldn't go away. He did all this because he keenly understood that it is the city government which makes the vital decisions that determine the quality of life in a city, its neighborhoods, and its business districts and that there are no instant solutions for the complex problems of the design of cities.

Houston

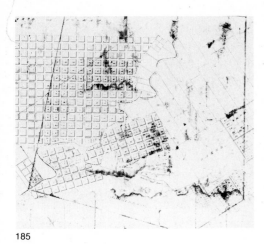

185

Houston is the only large U.S. city without zoning controls. Planners there argue that government nonintervention makes it easier for the private sector to perform effectively and that, even with this freedom, the city is not significantly different in appearance and development from other large American cities which *have* zoning controls. The argument may be specious, but it is not easy to refute by visual observation and comparison.

Population and geography

With reservations, *New York Times* architecture critic Ada Louise Huxtable says "Houston is the city of the second half of the 20th century."[1] From the time it was founded in 1836, Houston has grown steadily and since the Second World War, dramatically. In 1940 the city covered an area of only 73 sq miles (190 sq km) and had a population of 385,000. By 1976, the city covered an area of 509 sq miles (1,300 sq km) with a population of 1,500,000, making it the fifth largest city in the United States. But that is only a small part of what Houston will one day be. For through annexation powers, the city can grow annually by 10 percent of its own size, reaching an ultimate area of approximately 2,000 sq miles (5,000 sq km), an area covering all of Harris County over which, except for a few incorporated municipalities therein, Houston already has "extraterritorial" control, an area 6 times the size of New York City! The surrounding 7,000-mile (11,000-km) region, including what is left of Harris County when Houston is subtracted, contains an additional 1 million people, making a total population for Houston and its surrounding region of 2,500,000 (that is, as of the latest estimates, for the region is growing by 1,000 people a week). The best guess is that 120,000 people work in downtown Houston, of which 86 percent come by automobile and the remaining 14 percent by bus—almost exactly the reverse of how people come to work in downtown Chicago (184).

Historical development

Houston's development was, and is still, primarily based on real estate speculation. It all began in the 1820s when Mexico started granting permits to various entrepreneurs to settle between 100 to 300 families within its Texas territory. The Galveston Bay and Texas Land Company—one such entrepreneurial enterprise—was selling both stock in their newly formed company and land script in Texas. Few realized that script merely offered the right of the bearer to settle on a prescribed piece of land in Texas, but did not confer ownership.

With the settlers in residence, Mexico not only started to impose religious doctrine, but import duties on all the essential goods these new communities needed for survival.

Numerous conflicts arose between the Texans and their Mexican landlords. Resolute in their determination for an independent state, folk heroes Bill Travis, Davy Crockett, Jim Bowie, and 200 countrymen defended the Alamo in March 1836—against Mexican President Santa Anna and an army of 5,000. Six weeks after the fall of the Alamo, Sam Houston felled Santa Anna's army on the plains of the San Jacinto bayou.

Victory over Mexico assured Texas its independence, albeit tenuous. Capitalizing on Sam Houston's popularity, Augustus and John Allen named the large landholding

184 Downtown Houston is very much a drive-in office center. Of the roughly 120,000 people who work there, 86 percent come by automobile.

185 In 1836, Gail Borden drew up the original grid plan of 62 blocks over the flat planes of the new city. By 1839 it was already being extended to serve as the organizing framework for the growing city.

186

188

187

186 Bird's-eye view in 1893 by Augustus Koch.

187 Houston's central business district is comprised of 337 blocks within the inner highway ring. Most buildings, however, are contained on only about 40 blocks, with a great many of the remaining blocks devoted to parking.

188 The "magic circle" is 5 miles (8 km) west of downtown and is typical of the sprawling city. Even within the shopping center, patrons often must drive to the different shops.

they had bought in 1832 from The Galveston Bay and Texas Land Company the "Town of Houston" and touted it as a perfect site for the capital of the newly formed government of the republic. While in his lifetime George Washington refused to call the nation's capital "Washington" (instead he always referred to it as the "Federal City") Sam Houston apparently had no such modesty. As president of the Republic of Texas, he used his influence to assure that his friends could go ahead with their new town plan. The only problem was that the Allen brothers *had* no plan for the new town. For this they turned to friend, editor, and engineer Gail Borden. Borden surveyed the Allen holdings and divided a tract of 128 acres (51.2 ha) into 62 blocks (185, 186).

The plan was set by mid-1836 and the August 30, 1836 issue of *The Telegraph and Texas Register* noted: "We call the attention of our readers to the advertisement of the town of Houston, by Messrs. A. C. & J. K. Allen, who are well known in this country for their persevering enterprise as business men. From all we can learn, the location they have selected possesses as many advantages as any other interior town in Texas, and on account of the easy access to Galveston and the facility for procuring timber, as well as its central location, this town, no doubt, will be a rival for the present seat of Government of Texas."[2] (Laying out Houston was no small deed, but condensing milk became Borden's true calling and his source of much wealth.)

Much of Houston's wealth was pumped from the subsoil all about the eastern and central Texas region, and it was oily. Along with the oil came another break for Houston, compliments of the U.S. Army Corps of Engineers. The Corps dredged the Buffalo Bayou from Houston to the Gulf of Mexico, giving Houston an inland deepwater port that was safe from the ravages of hurricanes (such as the one in 1900 that flattened Galveston) and from which all that oil could be processed. Finished in 1914, the Houston Ship Channel has enabled Houston to become the third busiest port in the country.

Borden's original orthogonal network of 62 blocks 250 ft (75 m) square with street right-of-ways of 80 ft (24 m) has been

greatly expanded, and today 337 of these blocks are within the inner highway ring and constitute the central business district. The vast majority of downtown buildings, however, are contained within less than 40 square blocks. Many remaining blocks are open parking lots awaiting development (187).

The focus of a series of radial and concentric highways, it would seem that downtown Houston will remain important as the city continues to grow. But the competition has begun; and it was inevitable that the city, as it spread over such a vast amount of land, would—like its mentor Los Angeles—develop subcenters.

Five miles (8 km) west of downtown Houston on the West Loop freeway begins an area known as "the magic circle": a spreadout series of shopping centers, hotels, and office buildings, including the Galleria and Greenway Plaza (188). Neiman Marcus, in fact, closed its downtown store to move to the Galleria to be near other prestigious merchants. In all, it is estimated that 60,000 people work in the magic circle.

Houston has never had zoning, relying on restrictive covenants in individual deeds—some 10,000 of them—to protect residential areas from noncompatible uses; and it is not easy to refute the local argument that development and appearance differ very little from those of cities that *do* use zoning as a planning tool.

To describe Houston's zoning policies would seem easy for there are none. Zoning is a taboo word in this fiercely individualistic city. Put to the vote twice, in both cases—1948 and 1962—the electorate resoundingly defeated proposals for citywide zoning. It is argued by many in Houston, including Roscoe Jones, the director of planning, that there is little difference between Houston's development and "appearance" and the development and appearance of those cities that *do* actively use zoning as a planning tool. But the argument against zoning is even more complex. For many people in Houston, approval of zoning now may deny them what they feel is an inherent right to sell their property for a use which might maximize their property value but which the imposition of zoning might preclude.

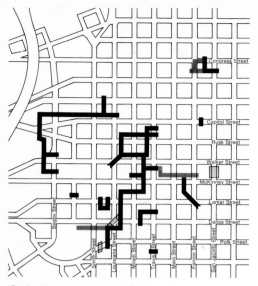

Scale: ⅛ in. represents 200 ft

▨ Proposed tunnel
▮ Underground tunnel
▨ Overhead concourse

189

190

191

However, what about those in residential areas who might fear just such a conversion of a lot now containing a house to one containing a factory? While this has been one of the oldest precepts of zoning—to separate noxious uses from residential districts and thereby also protect property values and the right of expectation—there are at least 10,000 restrictive covenants in Houston that effectively do protect most residential districts from the incursion of such "non-compatible" uses.

In fact, it would be far more difficult to change a restrictive covenant, which would require the approval of every home owner within the subdivision, than it would be to change a zoning resolution, which would only require a public hearing. And even if the public were heard to be against a zoning change or the granting of a variance from the intent of the zoning, the zoning board would not be obliged to vote accordingly. Political and economic pressures may resolve conflicts of conscience against the will of the community.

But restrictive covenants went beyond preventing factories from moving in. They also prevented factory workers from moving in—black *and* white alike! (In northern cities, large-lot zoning—so-called exclusionary zoning—has had, and still does have, precisely the same effect.)

Restrictive covenants only affect the land area within a particular development, and therefore, the perimeter of a subdivision, unless butted by another subdivision with similar covenants, may find an unwelcome factory as a neighbor. Indeed, Houston's planning director says that "industrial areas may also be found close to older residential areas," and "while some of these industries may produce obnoxious effects upon the adjacent residential areas, it should also be pointed out that most do not have a deteriorating effect on the area and, in fact, provide job opportunities for low to moderate income groups conveniently located near their homes."[3]

In considering this position, remember that 38 percent of a dangerous pollutant in Manhattan's air comes from New Jersey. Jurisdictional disputes would prevent New York from zoning away New Jersey. Also, having a General Electric factory 100 miles (160 km) north of New York City zoned in an industrial area doesn't prevent the fish New Yorkers eat from containing dangerous levels of a cancer-producing chemical released into the Hudson River by the faraway plant. And think too about cities like Gary, Indiana. If zoning seriously created a buffer zone around the steel mills, a developer could probably not build housing until he got to South Bend.

In Houston, the city argues that laws on the books against pollution and nuisances are sufficient to deal with problems of absolutely incompatible uses. It is only a question of enforcement of those laws.

That zoning is a weak tool—some would say flexible—in the face of development pressures in all parts of the country can be seen in an analysis of the percentage of variances granted based on requests. In Professor Charles Haar's book, *Land Use Planning: A Casebook on the Use, Misuse and Re-use of Urban Land*, he indicates in a study of three cities (Cincinnati, Philadelphia, and Cambridge) that between 77 to 86 percent of the applications for variances from the zoning were granted.[4] And during Mayor Daley's epic tenure in Chicago, an average of over 95 percent of the variance requests were granted.[5]

There are certainly limits to what zoning can and cannot do. Chicago lawyer Bernard Siegan, with an analysis of some issues raised here as well as other factors, makes a persuasive argument for nonzoning, using Houston as an example—especially when Houston is compared with similar automobile-oriented cities that have zoning.

A policy of nonzoning is not meant to imply that Houston does not have planning as an integral function of city government. As Siegan points out, Houston's "subdivision regulations contain controls over land development generally common elsewhere in the country."[6] And close to three-quarters of built-up Houston has been subject to these controls. Also, says Siegan, the city planning department "makes studies and recommendations for the location of streets, parks, public buildings, public utilities, waterways, examines plots of subdivision, etc."[7]

189 Over 40 buildings in the downtown are connected by tunnels, although it is not always possible to go directly from one building to the next, partly because some developers don't want to connect to their neighbors!

190-191 Because so much of the street level is devoted to the automobile, much of the shopping and many of the restaurants are underground.

Compared with visual observations of several dozen U.S. cities, it is difficult not to agree with Siegan and Jones that Houston does not "appear" visually very different from most of the zoned cities. But whether or not the end product is something to brag about in either case is debatable. More specifically though, is it true that downtown Houston is no different from the downtown areas of other U.S. cities? The difference between the nine cities surveyed here in terms of climate, location, and history would make that an unrealistic comparison. Still there are remarkable similarities between Houston, with *no* zoning, and the most comparable of the other cities, Minneapolis, *with* zoning, which are worth exploring.

Comparison of Houston and Minneapolis reveals more similarities than differences; and the distinctions there are—in Houston, enclosed connections above ground are only between buildings of common ownership, leaving most connections between buildings underground; in Minneapolis, enclosed connections between most major downtown buildings of whatever ownership are mainly at the second-story level— stem from developer choice in both cities rather than from nonzoning in Houston and zoning in Minneapolis.

The population of the Houston and Minneapolis regions is about the same. Both have similar low-residential densities. Both downtowns are major employment centers within their respective regions. While it may be said that development in downtown Houston is in competition with subcenters like the Galleria and Greenway Plaza, it is also true that downtown Minneapolis is in direct competition with downtown St. Paul, plus numerous regional shopping centers.

Workers in both downtowns depend heavily on the automobile to get to work; downtown Houston—86 percent—downtown Minneapolis—50 percent. This might indicate the potential for greater bus service in the future for Houston, but may also indicate that the population of Minneapolis and St. Paul, more or less evenly distributed about their respective centers, is more easily served by bus than Houston, which is still the major focus of its much vaster region.

In Minneapolis, where the climate seems to be cold continuously, a series of enclosed second-level bridges over streets and a few connections under streets tie most of the major downtown buildings together (324). In Houston where it is hot a lot, a series of underground connections and a few enclosed second-level bridges tie most of the major downtown buildings together (189, 190, 191). Both the Minneapolis second-level system and the Houston underground system contain shopping and restaurants. In both cities all construction of bridges and tunnels was done privately.

In both cities property ownership extends to the center line of the street. Both cities have easement rights for streets and sidewalks and in turn grant easement rights back to property owners for projects above or below the streets. Both cities have a main shopping street which has in each case remained viable despite the extremes in weather conditions and the expansion of internal shopping environments. The possibility of converting Houston's Main Street to a shopping mall has been discussed. Minneapolis discussed it and did it on Nicollet Street, and it offers an exciting model for Main Street in Houston (322, 323).

Beyond the functional aspects of connecting buildings, private developers in both cities have experimented with building large enclosed public spaces, although in this case Minneapolis has far excelled Houston. Besides numerous smaller enclosed spaces in buildings, Minneapolis has architects Philip Johnson and John Burgee's IDS Crystal Court (331). The Pennsoil Building in Houston, also by Johnson and Burgee, creates a large enclosed space (192, 193, 194). But apparently the Houston site was too small to allow the space to be large enough to contain benches and cafes which in part make the IDS space in Minneapolis so successful. And the IDS Building is right on the major shopping street, which increases its usability. This is not the case with Pennsoil. But the Pennsoil Building does have an opening that lets light from its glass-enclosed space down to the lower shopping level.

With the exception of Peavey Park in Minneapolis, which was built in conjunction with Orchestra Hall (350), and a similar but

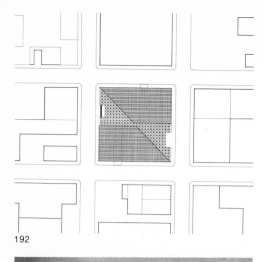

192

193

194

192-193-194   The Pennzoil complex is one of the few buildings in downtown Houston that has tried to create an interior urban space. But it is not as large, nor as actively programmed, as the IDS space in Minneapolis (331).

less successful effort in Houston built in conjunction with its theater complex, the development of exterior plaza space, whether created with a bonus as in Minneapolis or without a bonus as in Houston, is dismal in both cities. The effect of open parking surrounding the downtown area is bleak in both cities, but worse in Houston simply because there is so much of it. Both Houston and Minneapolis have examples of buildings that provide internal parking lots that avoid access to the parking across sidewalks. Still, there are too many automobile-pedestrian conflicts related to parking lot accessibility in both cities.

The comparison between these two cities ends with a comment about the final built form. They are still remarkably similar—though subtly different. As is pointed out in the Minneapolis chapter, there is little correlation between what a developer in that city is encouraged to do through zoning incentives and what he usually does do. Most of the time this is because the developer rarely needs to construct the huge buildings the zoning in Minneapolis allows. In fact, most of the time new developments are built at or below the level where the city offers bonuses for larger buildings in exchange for amenities such as plazas or arcades. Furthermore, the success of the first—and especially the second—level shopping system implicitly encourages developers to build to the property line to maximize the amount of retail space available.

In Houston, without bonuses, developers have been providing strip plazas around buildings not so much for their use as a public amenity, for it is impossible to conceive how the public could enjoy these benchless behemoths, but rather because the space provided is more the result of siting the building in such a way as to allow it room to distinguish itself from its indistinguishable neighbors—to be seen as the prestigious object it is intended to be. Not incidentally, though, siting a building this way also maximizes the light on it and the view from it. SOM, among other architectural firms, has been providing corporations in Houston with such buildings: One Shell Plaza (195, 196) and Two Shell Plaza (Chicago office) and the Tennecco Building (San Francisco office) are illustrations of this trend. Besides the fact that shopping at grade level would interfere with the desired image of these buildings, after the plazas and the automobile are accommodated, there is little room for shopping anyway. Many downtown buildings have drive-in banking at the ground level and almost all have access to a parking garage (197). The result is that most downtown blocks in Houston have at least one and often as many as three or four driveways crossing the sidewalk—and lots of flashing danger signs (198). There may be little hope in Houston where "the car is king" of ever recapturing the street life and quality of urban buildings as suggested in the Humble Building built in 1921 (199), with its canopied shopping streets and large trees. It was and still is a practical solution to the climate of Houston, protecting people against the rain and sun.

Some distinctions, however, must be made between Houston and Minneapolis. A second-level shopping system has ample natural light and views and is a far more pleasant environment than an underground shopping level, not only for those who shop there, but especially for those who must work there 8 to 10 hours a day. In Minneapolis, most of the bridges are between substantially older buildings, built in an era when less attention was paid to the image of a building as developers today perceive it to be. Though constructed with private funds, the bridges in Minneapolis had city endorsement. In Houston, what second-level bridges there are, connect only between buildings of common ownership. No doubt developers feel that a bridge to another building under different ownership would detract not only from the appearance, but also the marketability of their new building. Developers in Houston have therefore been in favor of the more expensive, less pleasant, but also less visual underground system. In addition, in the recent past, the Mayor of Houston was against overhead bridges. But this may have been more a reaction to the massive Houston Center and Hyatt Regency air rights developments over streets. And, anyhow, the Mayor's position, unless sustained in the courts, has little bearing on what developers believe to be their inherent right to construct buildings over streets.

Even with the innocuous tunnels, there are no assurances of cooperation among major landowners in Houston. The developers of

195

197

196

198

195-196 Typical of most corporate buildings in the downtown, the solution for One Shell Plaza was to surround the building with a useless plaza and parking ramps.

197-198 Drive-in banking and entrances to parking lots are a more common feature of downtown Houston than of other, older American cities.

199 The Humble Building is a fine urban solution to the problems of sun and rain.

199

201

202

200 1100 Milam is surrounded by a glass-enclosed arcade with shopping at the ground level and the office lobby at the second level.

201 Below-grade restaurant at 1100 Milam has an opening to the glass arcade above and is similar to the solution for the Pennzoil Building.

202 A second-level bridge connects 1100 Milam to the Hyatt Regency Hotel, which is part of the same development.

the Hyatt Regency and the 1100 Milam Building have for years refused to allow the large new adjacent Allen Center complex of buildings to connect to their tunnel system. "We do not consider it to be in the best interests of the venture to have additional tunnel connections into our tunnel system at this time"[8] was the way they didn't mince words.

The New York experience has conclusively demonstrated that zoning can make bridge and/or tunnel connections mandatory in new construction without relegating the public interest to the whim of developers. In the absence of zoning, a clear analysis of the success of the Minneapolis second-level system by Houston business executives may persuade them to initiate more bridges and second-level shopping. Sufficient evidence shows that at the current density of downtown Houston two or even three levels of shopping facilities, including banks and restaurants, could be sustained.

Beyond the analogies between Houston and Minneapolis, it is also true that too often the major public spaces in many cities were built with private money. As Shadrach Woods said of Paley Park (41): "Paley of CBS [was] doing what the Mayor of New York should have been doing."[9] It is not that large U.S. urban centers lack vision, for almost all have impressive master plans produced at considerable expense that they can point to. The problem is that in too few cities is there any evidence of the vision becoming reality. It is true that the city of Minneapolis did build Nicollet Mall along nine blocks. But that was in 1967, and what of the other 95 downtown block frontages in downtown Minneapolis? San Francisco has made a spectacular effort along Market Street, but that too is only one part of a much larger problem. New York did try, but failed to close one small section of one major street.

None of these examples are meant to offer solace to Houston. If not exactly suggesting on the part of these other cities a commitment equal to the problems they confront, they do at least suggest the semblance of concern. Ada Louise Huxtable aptly described Houston's situation: "No one seems to feel the need for the public vision that older cities have of a hierarchy of

places and buildings, an organized concept of function and form. Houston has a downtown singularly without amenities."[10]

Major examples of urban design in Houston reflect the initiative of private developers, and some raise fundamental questions about the future of the downtown area.

1100 Milam
If we assume for a moment that totally climate-controlled environments are essential to survival in Houston, then the 1100 Milam Building (designed by Joint Venture architects: Koetter Tharp Cowell and Bartlett; Caudill Rowlett Scott; Neuhaus and Taylor) may be the best example of what is possible in that city, relying solely on the initiative of private developers.

To explain how the building works urbanistically, it may be useful to trace the journey of a typical worker. Arriving downtown by automobile, the worker drops friends off at the main entrance and then proceeds down a ramp to three levels of parking (600 spaces) below grade. In much the same solution as One Shell Plaza, the ramp is at the edge of the site, so the pedestrian does not cross the driveway. (In Houston a pedestrian is a person temporarily between automobiles.) The first-level below grade, above the three parking levels, is reserved for shopping and restaurants. The project has four tunnels from this first underground level that connects 1100 Milam to four surrounding blocks. Escalators are provided to the ground level within the building. At the ground level there is also a shopping area, which is protected by a 30-ft (9-m) wide glass-enclosed sloping arcade that wraps around the building (200). A large area of this ground level is cut away as in the Pennsoil Building to let light into the restaurant below (201). There are escalators from the ground level up one level to the main elevator lobby. Here, too, there is retail space (mostly for airline ticket offices), and there is to be a restaurant on the mezzanine level above. From the second level there is a bridge diagonally across Louisiana Street connecting 1100 Milam to the Hyatt Regency Hotel, part of the same development and designed by the same architects (202).

The 1100 Milam Building is the most successful new downtown building in terms of

203

204

accommodating the automobile but still preserving the street level for pedestrians. If the glass-enclosed arcade is not as open and easily accessible as the arcade at the Humble Building, which tried in pre-air-conditioned days to solve the same problem, 1100 Milam is superior to the mass of corporate headquarters in its immediate vicinity with their drive-in banks and bleak underground systems, which are more a token gesture towards the thousands of people who work in any one of these buildings than honest attempts to provide an enjoyable, useful urban building.

Hyatt Regency Hotel
The Hyatt Regency Hotel complex spans a two-block site—one of the blocks is devoted to a 15-story public parking garage, the other to the 30-story hotel (203). In the tradition of John Portman's hotels, this hotel has created a 30-story skylighted lobby shape, well designed, impressive, with restaurants everywhere (204). Japanese architect Fumiko Maki suggests that churches and hotel lobbies should be thought of as public "city rooms"—churches more for solitude and quiet, hotel lobbies as city "living rooms." The problem with this idea is that while churches can function, as Maki suggests, for the religiously indifferent or tolerant, most hotel lobbies are designed to intimidate the nonhotel client and casual would-be user. This has certainly happened in the Hyatt Regency. In the center of this 30-story "living room" is a generous seating area, seemingly unrestricted. But access to it has been limited from the intention of the original design and a bar has been placed at a control point. It takes a quick survey of all those sitting in the vicinity to determine whether a drink is the price of admission or whether the seat is "rent free."

More than 1100 Milam, the exterior treatment of the Hyatt Regency project may signify the appearance and "attitude" future large-scale developments have towards the street. The 15-story garage portion of the site actually covers 65 percent of Polk Street as well. Polk is the street that "divides" the two-block site. This almost fully takes advantage of the view that the land to the middle of the street absolutely belongs to the adjacent property owner and that all the city requires is a 20-foot high by 80-foot (6- by 24-m) wide right-of-way for the street.

Except for the main entrance to the hotel, the remaining seven ground floor exterior sides of this 2-square-block site are brick walls, occasionally pierced by service entrances. It is a fully internalized, controlled environment and an ominous note for lovers of street life.

Houston Center
Nowhere can the drive-in city be seen better than in the Houston Center project, developed by the Texas Eastern Transmission Corporation (205). The company wholly owns a 33-square-block site approximately 4 blocks wide and 8 blocks long for a total of 46 acres (18.4 ha). But with air rights over streets, which the master plan has indicated will be used intensively, the site increases to 74 acres (29.6 ha). The site is equal to the functional area of the existing downtown and commences at its eastern edge.

The first building, Two Houston Center, is complete (206). A second, almost identical, structure is nearing completion; and a 1,300-car parking garage is on a third block. The three blocks are meant to serve as a model for the basic principles of the remaining site.

The futuristic-appearing master plan and the first building in the plan's image are by William Pereira Associates, the architects from "Outer Los Angeles" who gave San Francisco the Transamerica Pyramid (264). The plan is meant to give the Houston Center project a competitive advantage with other speculative development for the annual demand for downtown office space, currently estimated at 1 million sq ft (95,000 sq m). There are to be escalators, elevators, "people-movers," and elevated highways at the site's perimeter. The pedestrian walking between these moving conveyances will be treated to glass-covered and air-conditioned walkways.

The goal of the overall project is to provide space for offices, hotels, apartments, shops, entertainment, and convention facilities. The basic design calls for two levels of parking below ground level and three levels of parking above ground. The upper parking levels will deck over all street right-of-ways on the 33-square-block site. A lightwell will pierce the deck at most, but not all, of the street intersections within the project

205

206

205 The futuristic proposal for Houston Center poses difficult questions about the unrestricted use of air rights above streets and how a pedestrian would traverse the completed development.

206 Three buildings within the Houston Center have been completed; they have been built more or less in the plan's image.

area. The roof of the highest parking level becomes the major pedestrian level and the elevator access point to all buildings. The pedestrian level offers shopping and east-west and north-south connections throughout the development. There will also be a variety of outdoor spaces, both at this and ground level.

The first two buildings are no larger than recent office buildings in New York or Chicago. What is different is the "sense" or "perception" of the project because of the air rights development over the streets. The two major buildings in the Houston Center, for example, are connected by a 6-story structure which completely spans San Jacinto Street (207). Sam Houston would be mortified, as evidently are many contemporary Houstonians who have filed suit against the city, protesting that city officials do not have the right to give up complete air space above the public street easements. They are arguing in effect that the public easement includes the right to sun and view up to the sky. In these first two buildings, then, the future has been seen and some don't like it!

These first two buildings and the Regency-Hyatt hotel raise some fundamental questions about the future of the downtown area. If Houston Center is developed according to plan, it will mean that the pedestrian at street level wishing to hoof it north across the center will either have to pass through a 4-block long traffic tunnel—an 8-block tunnel should this lonely person be headed easterly toward the freeway—or the pedestrian would travel up an escalator to the fourth level to cross the project (208). But will the escalators be running at 10 P.M. or 12 P.M. or even 3 A.M. if our friend has been out on another part of the town? In fact, will the nonresident pedestrian even be allowed up there at those hours? These are potentially serious problems with this scheme, and most certainly will arise should this development be built as planned.

With the exception of the built areas over the street, Houston Center can be viewed as conventional for Houston; that is, most likely the major office or apartment buildings will be constructed within the block itself, as opposed to over the streets. However, if it is found that the principle of a

"walkable" center, which downtown Houston still is, makes much of the Houston Center project too far away from the existing downtown area, the developers may intensify the basically unrestricted use of air rights over the streets closest to the center.

The Houston Center project raises another major issue: can the streets and highways bring all these future workers downtown via the automobile? If 86 percent of the workers continue to rely on the automobile, the answer would seem to be no. Unless, that is, some changes in how people come to work are forthcoming—which does appear to be the case.

The Federal Environmental Protection Agency (EPA) has become involved in Houston's future (and for that matter the future of most other parts of Texas). After years of court fights between the Texas Air Control Board (TACB), EPA, and environmental groups, there seems to be some agreement about what Houston must do to comply with the constantly changing federal standards.

Originally the EPA standard as it applied to Houston meant that the city would have to reduce the pollution caused by hydrocarbon emissions from all stationary and mobile (vehicles) sources by 75 percent. While the stationary sources might be easily identifiable as several dozen major industrial polluters, the mandated reduction for vehicles—which roughly translated meant a 75 percent reduction of the vehicle miles traveled (VMT)—would have affected literally hundreds of thousands of drivers in the Houston area. By law, the EPA had to make the proposal. And even though the EPA knew enforcement would be impossible, it was a way of alerting the city to the problem.

The EPA's data, which led to requiring the 75 percent reduction in VMTs, evidently came from their analysis of air pollution in Los Angeles, where the pollution problem is 80 percent attributable to auto emissions and 20 percent to industrial sources. The TACB argued that the pollution mix is the opposite in Houston, where 80 percent is attributable to industry and the remaining 20 percent to automobiles, trucks, and buses. Therefore, TACB proposed instead a 7.5 percent annual reduction in the VMTs. The

207

208

138

207-208 Spanning the streets with buildings of unrestricted dimensions, as developers in Houston believe to be their inherent right, Houston Center holds an alarming prospect of the future street-level pedestrians will have to contend with.

7.5 percent figure was apparently arbitrary, but nonetheless has been accepted by the EPA.

To achieve what appears to be a modest reduction of dependence upon the automobile actually requires an extraordinary and complementary set of programs, not the least important of which is improved bus service. In 1974, with city and federal funds, Houston purchased the privately run bus system. Since that time, the older buses have been replaced, and 75 new buses have been added to the fleet, bringing it up to 450 buses. More buses will be purchased as soon as the city improves its maintenance and storage capabilities. To improve the competitive stance of buses with automobiles, a series of 500-car parking lots are being built at convenient points along the freeway system. From those points buses will have access to exclusive freeway lanes shared only with car-poolers.

Car-pooling is potentially one of the most important components of the Houston system. The city's CAR-Share program uses a computer to match those interested in car pools by their home and work locations and their hours of employment. The city's pitch is the sheer economy of the program. It is estimated that the average driver in Houston spends over $1,200 per year getting to and from work. To share the drive with three other passengers saves each one in the car pool over $900 a year. As of mid-1976 over 7,000 people were reasonably convinced and had enrolled in the program. Staggered work hours are also being used as a way to maximize the usability of the freeway network.

A great deal of leverage to make these programs work can be, and is being in many cases, asserted by major downtown employers. The United Gas Pipeline Company's efforts are a good example of what can be accomplished. The company has approximately 800 employees downtown. It offered them a variety of inducements to use more efficient transit modes, including free bus passes, which 53 percent of its employees have taken advantage of; free parking for those in a car pool with a minimum of four people, which 21.5 percent have taken advantage of; the company pays two-thirds of parking costs for car pools with three

people, which 2.7 percent have taken advantage of; and, finally, it pays one-third of the parking costs for car pools of two people, which slightly less than 1 percent have taken advantage of. In total, the program affects 77 percent of the company's employees.

Other programs by other companies also include the use of vans, which the company has purchased. A volunteer gets the van nights and weekends for personal use in exchange for the chauffeuring and collection of fares which cover the van's depreciation and operating expenses. By mid-1976, 16 percent of Continental Oil Company's employees were van-pooling and 36 percent were car-pooling.

Such programs by these and other companies are certainly in the interests of downtown workers and the community at large. But they are also in the clear interests of the large companies. First, in keeping the center an attractive, accessible location, the work force is less tempted to look elsewhere for employment, and the company thereby protects its downtown investment. Often the investment goes beyond the rental of office space and may include actual ownership of the building and interest in other buildings as well. Texas Eastern, for example, offers inducements for car-pooling and bus-ridership similar to those mentioned above. They certainly must realize better than most that their plans for Houston Center can never be realized without a dramatic shift to efficient means of transportation, for office space in downtown Houston cannot increase 1 sq ft without the effective use of all these programs. And this is where there is an ironic twist in the EPA standards: as the VMT is decreased by 7.5 percent, more office space is constructed which immediately fills the vacuum. In the long run, the only thing that will make Houston's air, and the air of most U.S. cities, breathable again without danger to health will be automobiles (and trucks and buses and trains and planes) that do not pollute—at all.

Washington, D.C.

210

Downtown Washington is the third largest employment center in the U.S. Its zoning is the most restrictive in the country, deliberately producing uniform building solutions so that private buildings defer to the grandeur of the L'Enfant plan and of the public buildings. But L'Enfant's plan devoted so much land to streets that it has been natural for Washingtonians to rely primarily on the auto to get to work—with great sacrifice to the beauty of the plan, destroying, among other things, many of the urban spaces at the plan's key intersections in order to increase traffic flow.

Population and geography
Of the original 100 sq miles (260 sq km) of the District of Columbia, the 30.75-sq-mile (78-sq-km) parcel on the west side of the Potomac River was returned to the state of Virginia in 1846, as the government could not foresee any future need for the land. Today, within the remaining 69.25 sq miles (180 sq km) of Washington, D.C., live about 722,000 people. The surrounding 2,733-sq-mile (6,885-sq-km) region houses an additional population of close to 2,300,000 people. Within the very dispersed, ever-expanding downtown area of Washington, work an estimated 350,000 people, making it the third largest employment center in the United States (209). Only 35 percent of those who work in the center come by public transportation. Almost all these people ride buses, although this will change now that the new subway, the Metro, is partially open. The other 65 percent of the commuters rely on cars, although this too will change when the Metro is completed.

Historical development
From the moment the original 13 American

colonies declared independence from the British Empire in 1776 until the hostilities were officially ended with the Treaty of Paris in 1783, the Continental Congress moved around the eastern part of the United States like a band of nomadic tribesmen. During those seven hectic years, the Congress kept a safe distance from the British army, moving from Philadelphia to Baltimore, then back to Philadelphia, then to Lancaster, York, Philadelphia again, Princeton, and Annapolis. After the war, this band of gypsies settled in Trenton for a month in late 1784 before arriving in New York for a 4-year stint. In New York, George Washington took the oath of office in 1789 as the first President of the United States of America.

There was general agreement in Congress that the government of the federated states should have a permanent home located in a territory controlled by the Congress. Several state governments realized that close proximity to the new capital would still have economic benefits. In fact, New York, New Jersey, Maryland, Virginia, and Pennsylvania all offered land deemed sufficient for the national government free of charge.

There was also a general feeling in the Congress that the new capital should be free from local interests, that for symbolic purposes it should be located at the center of the colonies and that the site selected should be on navigable waters, yet should be as impervious to attack as possible.

But where was the center of the United States? The southern states argued that it was in the geographical center between Georgia and New Hampshire—conveniently

209 Zoning restrictions in Washington, D.C., have forced the downtown business district, including federal agencies, to spread over a vast amount of land. Of the approximately 350,000 people who work in the center, 65 percent drive there.

210 In 1790, Congress authorized a plan to locate the Federal City somewhere along a stretch of the Potomac River. The city itself was to be 10 miles (16 km) wide by 10 miles long.

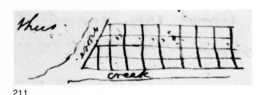

211

south of the Mason-Dixon Line. Northern states argued that the capital should be located at the center of the population, somewhere in Pennsylvania.

Washington, Jefferson, and Madison, all Virginians, favored a site along the Potomac River. Washington stressed the fact that a site along the Potomac would be 200 miles (320 km) away from the sea with good access to the expanding western territories.

At one point in October 1783, Congress decided to locate the government along the Delaware River, only to change its mind 10 days later, stipulating that the capital should be built at Georgetown below the lower falls of the Potomac. To end the conflict, it was proposed that the Congress should alternate meetings between Trenton and Annapolis. This prompted Francis Hopkinson to suggest—200 years before the English pop-architecture group, Archigram—that the federal buildings ought to be upon a wheeled platform, so they could move easily between the two sites. But Hopkinson's proposal never got rolling.

A location close to the present site of Washington, D.C., was settled on when Hamilton—then Secretary of the Treasury—agreed to support a southern capital if Jefferson—then Secretary of State—could convince Virginia and Maryland Congressmen to vote for a revenue bill to pay off the national debt, including all state debts incurred during the Revolution. The bill also provided money for an Executive Department and a judicial system.

This agreed to, Congress passed a residence bill in 1790, giving Washington authority to select a square site 10 miles long by 10 miles wide (16 by 16 km) somewhere along an 80-mile (130-km) stretch of the Potomac (210). Congress would reside in Philadelphia from 1790 to 1800 while the new capital was being planned and built. Virginia and Maryland offered to cede whatever portion of the 10-mile square federal capital might fall within their respective states. They also chipped in $200,000 towards the construction of public buildings.

Several disputes among landowners prompted Jefferson to propose a site that would avoid these problems, although it was somewhat smaller in area than Washington thought necessary. The first sketch of Jefferson's plan for the district appears in a letter to Washington in September 1790 (211). Jefferson thought Philadelphia an ideal model for the new capital and proposed a similar grid system of streets. Later, Jefferson shifted the site slightly and enlarged it considerably.

Although Jefferson adopted Penn's grid, he opposed Penn's requirement that all houses should be built in a row, thinking it too restrictive. But he did favor height limitations, as in Paris, to keep the streets "light and airy."[1]

In 1791, Washington appointed three commissioners to oversee work on the federal district. To solve the major disputes among landowners, a formula was established whereby the original owners would retain title to half the lots in the new city. Approximately $67 per acre was to be paid for all land occupied by government buildings, and no compensation would be paid for land designated as streets or alleys. The government was to sell the 10,000 lots in the subdivision plan, which was expected to produce a revenue of $850,000. This money, plus that already donated by Virginia and Maryland, was to pay for public buildings. That things didn't work out quite so smoothly as planned is another story.

A brilliant plan by Major Pierre Charles L'Enfant, commissioned by President Washington, evoked the goals of the young republic and became a permanent framework for the development of the nation's capital.

Andrew Ellicott was appointed to make surveys of the areas under consideration. Shortly thereafter, Washington hired Major Pierre Charles L'Enfant to join Ellicott in preparing the surveys and to begin plans for the city once the final location was selected. Washington sent Jefferson's ideas to L'Enfant, who had ideas of his own.

L'Enfant had come to America to fight in the war. He came from a family of artists and was educated in the engineering sciences of the day. He was familiar with the work of the famous French landscape planner Le

211 Once the site for the new capital was selected, Jefferson wrote President Washington: "Will it not be best to lay out the long streets parallel with the creek, and the other crossing them at right angles, so as to leave no oblique angled lots but the single row which shall be on the river? Thus. . . ."

Nôtre, had probably visited Versailles, and saw the Baroque transformation of Paris. So although Jefferson loaned L'Enfant the plans of several major European cities, L'Enfant was already knowledgeable on the subject of Baroque planning.

L'Enfant rejected Jefferson's grid ideas as totally unrelated to the features of the site—especially the hills. Instead, once the precise boundaries of the District of Columbia were established, he set out to interpret the goals of the young republic in his plan. The Capitol Building housing the Congress would go on the high point of the city—Jenkins Hill. In the spirit of separation of the branches of government, the President's House was 1½ miles (2.4 km) away on the second-most prominent site (212, 213). A great mall was laid out in front of the Capitol—a feature Jefferson had also suggested in his plan (214). On the mall where the axis through the White House crossed the axis through the Capitol, an equestrian statue of George Washington was to be placed. The statue later turned into a 555-ft (170-m) high obelisk that, although placed off the axis, would have warmed the heart of Sixtus V. From each of these foci, the White House and the Capitol, a series of radial avenues was laid out—each avenue bearing the name of the state. The principal radial—Pennsylvania Avenue—was 160 ft (48 m) wide and connected the Capitol with the White House. Other radials were established from other major points, and where radials intersected each other, 15 public spaces were formed in the shape of either circles or squares. Then L'Enfant superimposed a grid system for the minor streets. The end result, according to one critic, was a "short order European capital with quick plazas and a side order of statues to go."[2]

L'Enfant's temperament put him in constant trouble with the commissioners. He believed he was responsible only to the President. When he had a new house torn down because it encroached a few feet upon one of his proposed radials—the house of the nephew of one of the commissioners—Washington, who had always been a great admirer of L'Enfant, felt he had no choice but to discharge the Frenchman. By 1792, however, L'Enfant's work was largely done, and since then the capital has developed pretty much according to the L'Enfant plan.

Washington's zoning has limited building heights and bulk since 1910 and offers no amenity bonuses; but many developers have recently been providing arcades with shopping at ground level. A city with as much public open space as the L'Enfant plan provided for Washington hardly needs to encourage any more plazas.

Although downtown Washington is large, its stature is not reflected in the height of its buildings. Washington has the most restrictive bulk zoning ordinance of any large American city. The 1920 and 1958 zoning ordinances did not alter the basic concept of rules laid down in "An Act to Regulate the Height of Buildings in the District of Columbia." More frequently called "The Act of 1910," this law was passed by Congress when highrise technology was beginning to change the face of downtown America.

The Act of 1910 set the maximum height of buildings at 130 ft (40 m) on avenues 110 ft (34 m) wide, and 110 ft (34 m) high on streets 90 ft (27 m) wide. The north side of Pennsylvania Avenue was the exception to the rule in the downtown area, and buildings there could be 160 ft (48 m) high. Although it has generally been assumed that the controls were intended to ensure the dominance of the Capitol dome (215), which rises to 315 ft (95 m), it is also apparent that the Congress was imitating the height controls of Boston [125 ft (38 m)] and Chicago [130 ft (40 m)]. These early height regulations seem to have been tied directly to the fire-fighting capabilities of the day.

For all sorts of reasons—from urban design considerations to the need for increased jobs and tax revenues—the zoning commission has been pushing for a major revamping of the zoning ordinance. The main objective of this zoning revision is a selective increase in the height limitation to 250 ft (75 m). This increase would be limited to areas in the city that do not interfere with prominent views of symbolic government buildings.

At present, the highest FAR in the downtown area is 10, which means theoretically that a developer can erect a 10-story building across the entire site. But since the zoning forces him to provide a rear yard so that the back portion of the building and abut-

212   L'Enfant's initial conception of Washington, D.C., was on a much grander scale than Jefferson's vision. Jefferson's suggestion that there be ''no oblique lots'' was in immediate jeopardy when L'Enfant proposed that radial streets connect significant points in the city. This version of L'Enfant's plan was drawn up by Andrew Ellicott.

213

213 Despite numerous buildings over the years which have violated L'Enfant's plan, the reality almost 200 years later is remarkably close to the original conception.

214

adopted Statue, by Crawford

215

216

ting buildings will have some light and air, the developer must build a few floors higher to take full advantage of the allowable square feet. At this point, however, he runs into the height limitation. As the maximum height along the widest avenue is 130 ft—with the exception of Pennsylvania Avenue—if the average floor-to-floor dimension of an office building is 11 ft (3.3 m), then the maximum number of stories a developer can possibly build is 12, just about the height of every building along K Street and Connecticut Avenue (216). Because these regulations are so constraining, there is little or no flexibility in placing the building on the site differently, possibly to provide some amenities or perhaps just to vary what some consider the monotony produced by the uniform height. This makes the open space provided in the L'Enfant plan, including the boulevards and the streets, doubly important.

Although in cities outside the United States, it was not uncommon for one building type to prevail for hundreds of years, architects today prefer more flexibility than the Washington zoning gives them. And in many other cities they get it. In New York and Chicago, as has been seen, a developer could take an FAR 10 limitation and build a 20-story building on half the site, leaving the other half for a plaza. Indeed, developers in those cities are encouraged to do so, and they are allowed to build a few extra floors in addition to the basic 20 stories in exchange for the amenity of the plaza.

There is at present no plaza bonus in Washington. In fact, there are no amenity bonuses at all. But is this so bad? Many of the new 8- and 12-story buildings have provided arcades at the ground floor. There is no incentive to provide what might be considered a non-revenue-producing area; but neither is there a penalty, for the area of the arcade does not count against the maximum allowable square footage of the building. Developers evidently provide the arcade because they feel it is an amenity which is nominal in terms of cost and enhances the building's attractiveness and therefore its competitiveness. Arcades or no arcades, the ground floors of buildings in Washington are often lined with retail shops simply because retail space pays higher rents than office space. It would not

seem to be too difficult, therefore, to take the provision of these two basic elements of an urban building—an arcade with shopping—away from chance and simply make them mandatory. It is clearly not a hardship to do so, but rather would appear to be in the economic interests of the developer.

As to the flexibility that would enable a developer to build a taller building in exchange for a plaza, that is plainly absurd in Washington. The L'Enfant plan has provided more public space in the city center than can be found in any other large American city. Washington is literally peppered with parks, some huge like the Mall, and others smaller, like Lafayette Square north of the White House. While some of these spaces have been raped to accommodate the automobile, that can be rectified (217).

If L'Enfant's vision of the streets as linear parks, densely planted with trees and defined by continuous rows of buildings, were carried out as it still could be, the needed relief from the uniformity of building mass imposed by the zoning would soon be obtained.

The wide avenues L'Enfant provided were meant to be treated as boulevards, densely planted with trees and defined by continuous rows of buildings. That the trees don't grow very well in the midst of all the automobile pollution is another problem. If trees were at least planted along the many streets and avenues where they could be and are not and if they were well maintained (which even the lonely trees that are there are not), these trees would be the basic elements of linear parks—common in Paris and possible in Washington (218).

This approach could within a few short years provide the needed relief from the monotony of the buildings. In a city as grand as Washington, with a bold urban design infrastructure established by its brilliant plan, it is foolish to look to developers to provide amenities on their sites by shifting the building mass around. New York, Chicago, Philadelphia, and San Francisco are very different from Washington, and it is a mistake to use their zoning approach, which encourages developers to provide open space, as a model for Washington. In all those cities, urban designers

214   L'Enfant sited the Capitol Building on the highest point in the city and placed an expansive mall in front of it—not dissimilar to an earlier idea of Jefferson's.

215   It is not clear whether the initial purpose of Washington's height limitations was related to protecting the dominance of the Capitol dome or the ability to fight fires.

216   Between zoning restrictions and height limitations, architects have little left to design, externally at least, but the building's facade.

217

217 Logan Circle has been dissected to accommodate
highway engineers' interpretation of efficient traffic flow.

218

218 Ideally, streets in Washington would be planted
and maintained as well as Paris boulevards.

faced a desperate need to provide more open space in dense downtowns. The cities could not afford to condemn land for this purpose, so they turned to the developers. Sometimes this approach has worked wonderfully, as in the First National Bank plaza in Chicago. More often it has failed dismally, as in the CBS and GM plazas in New York. But whatever the strengths or shortcomings of incentive zoning, it does not seem to be the correct approach for downtown Washington. Buildings constructed to the lot line along the street, with shopping arcades on the ground floor, would be just fine in Washington, especially if more attention were paid to L'Enfant's vision of the streets as linear parks.

The zoning commission has been pushing for a major revision of the zoning ordinance which would provide a selective increase in the height limitation to 250 ft (75 m), but the usual arguments for bigger buildings seem academic in the special circumstances of downtown Washington.

Beyond the need to allow larger buildings in exchange for public space, there are at least two more arguments in favor of bigger buildings. First, in theory, a dense, compact downtown area is easier to serve in terms of transportation. Because the downtown is in a specific spot, roads and railroads can be aimed at that place, rather than scattered all over the landscape. Also movement within the center can be primarily on foot.

Washington, however, is anything but compact. Its downtown has one-third the number of workers located in Midtown Manhattan, but covers an area at least 5 times as great as that of Midtown. (This calculation excludes significant government subcenters like the Pentagon and other areas at Roslyn and Crystal City, all just a few miles away in Virginia.) By necessity, movement within the downtown area of Washington often means relying on buses and taxis because walking is so prohibitive in terms of distance and time.

A second factor in such a spread-out center is the pressure of the downtown on surrounding neighborhoods. In Washington, many 2-, 3-, and 4-story landmark structures have already been razed as the center has expanded. Surprisingly, Washington's

landmarks legislation is very weak. Although the sanctity of important government buildings is not usually an issue, many buildings—in this, one of the oldest and most important U.S. cities—are in private ownership and subject to intense speculative pressures. Obviously, a contained central business district would lift much of this pressure on residential areas.

There are many distinct disadvantages to bigger buildings as well. The effects of too much density relying on 70-year-old subway systems is well known in New York and Chicago. And downtown workers in those cities must think that the only people who have sun during the day are sunbathers in Miami. These negative aspects of increased building heights, when coupled with increased density, are among the reasons there is so much anti-highrise sentiment in San Francisco.

Either way, what advantages there may be in even modest height and density increases as proposed for Washington may be academic as far as the downtown is concerned. In those areas of Washington that could sustain more construction, especially in the old downtown section, the zoning commission says the prevailing 110- and 130-ft (34- and 40-m) limitations would remain in effect because of the proximity to important federal buildings. Even with these limitations, thousands of cubic feet of office buildings could be built in the old downtown. Architect Chloethiel Smith has proposed that there be an increase in height limitations the further away from the center the development is, forming nodes at Metro stations, but making sure that significant long views are protected. Given the constraints, this may be the appropriate solution.

John Carl Warnecke's simple, humane solution for Lafayette Square indicates that urban design innovation in Washington is possible even with the inhibitions of the L'Enfant plan and of the city's rigid zoning rules.

The strong L'Enfant plan and the rigid zoning rules have combined to inhibit innovations in the theory and practice of urban design in Washington. One outstanding exception is John Carl Warnecke's solution

219

219   By placing required new offices behind, not in place of, early 19th-century townhouses (which were then renovated), the historic character of Lafayette Square has been preserved.

for the east and west blocks fronting on Lafayette Square north of the White House.

On the advice of some Boston architects who should have known better, the General Services Administration (GSA) had been about to tear down several historic houses that flank this elegant square to build a new executive office building on one of the blocks and a federal court building on the other.

Newly elected, President Kennedy directed that efforts be made instead to preserve the past while accommodating present and future needs. The Warnecke scheme has remodeled the best of the historic houses and replaced others with facsimiles of what was there, so that the character and quality of part of the center of Washington as it was in 1800 can still be seen and appreciated today. As for the larger office structures that were needed, Warnecke tucked them in behind the houses at the centers of the blocks—a sensitive, simple, humane solution (219).

Washington's older downtown has been in decline, largely because federal policy has been dispersing federal offices across the Potomac to the Virginia suburbs; now there is a new policy which calls for renting in depressed areas of center city if social and economic improvements may result.

Most of the building activity in central Washington has been in an area slightly northwest of the old downtown. The new area is being called "Connecticut Avenue West" or "K Street West," and many people see it as the new downtown. There seem to be many reasons why developers have shifted their attention away from the old core, including lower land costs and easier assemblage of land, but one reason stands out: the steady deterioration of the old downtown, culminating in the 1968 riots.

The old downtown stretches for a dozen blocks or so between the White House and Union Station, and F and G are its principal commercial streets. A 1975 *New York Times* article reported that the old downtown "is a hodgepodge of long-standing tenants—credit clothiers, credit furniture dealers, auto parts suppliers, low-rent offices, sagging hotels and barred-window liquor

stores—and a new crop of go-go parlors and pornography shops. The city blocks are indented by vacant lots, cleared of burned out hulks and refilled with litter."[3]

The federal government, through its real estate policies, bears a major part of the responsibility for the decline of the old downtown. The General Services Administration, which is responsible for both the leasing or design and construction of all federal buildings, has been moving the government's offices across the Potomac, to the Virginia suburbs. The zoning is more lenient there; but the major factor is land costs, which are one-tenth of those in the most expensive parts of Washington. Cheap land means cheap rents, and since GSA policy insists on renting space $2 to $3 below market costs in Washington, the agency has gone shopping for bargains in the suburbs. The real cost of this policy is incalculable. The national capital has lost jobs, taxable income, retail sales, and sales taxes. The national government has saved a few dollars in rent, but how many has it lost in higher welfare and unemployment insurance disbursements and in urban renewal programs made necessary by the government's flight to the suburbs? Furthermore, the energy crisis has pointed out the energy-efficient nature of downtowns easily accessible by public transportation.

Things may be getting better for the old downtown. All this decay is just a few short blocks from the Capitol and the White House; and there are indications that the federal government has been feeling an uncharacteristic embarrassment at the results of its policies, perhaps because the results are so close to home. At any rate, the GSA now has a policy to rent in depressed areas of the city if to do so will lead to social and economic improvements. There are to be urban renewal programs in the northern section of the old downtown, the closing of streets for pedestrian use in the center, and the opening of several Metro stops, which may generate new development. The renovation of Union Station to the east is now complete.

F Street Plaza, the remodeling of two blocks of F Street between 12th and 14th Streets, was a first attempt to stem the deterioration of the old downtown.

220

222

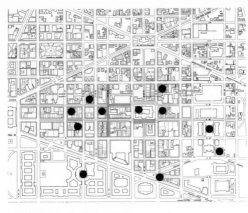

● Entrance to Metro stations
▨ Streets for People area
▧ Streets for People initial improvements

220 The F Street Plaza is actually a linear park in the center of the street. It was built in an effort to reverse the deteriorating trend of the old downtown.

221 The map illustrates the first streets in Washington to be entirely closed to traffic in favor of pedestrians.

222 Detail of pedestrian street at Gallery Place.

Originally, plans for a change in F Street were supported and partly sponsored by the business community. The Washington office of Doxiadis Associates prepared a design in 1963 that would have widened sidewalks by 10 ft (3 m) each, planted trees, and all the rest. The street was to be left open to automobiles, but its narrower width would have discouraged heavy traffic use. The general design was straightforward and more or less what many other large cities have adopted. Unfortunately, closer analysis showed vaults under most of the sidewalks and utilities under the street near the curbs. These obstacles prevented the planting of trees.

The design was then changed by architect Chloethiel Smith in 1965 to provide a brick-paved, tree-lined median strip 20 ft (6 m) wide in the center of the street with benches and new lighting (220). If it is not the ideal arrangement, nonetheless the results have been encouraging. The trees have greatly improved the appearance of the street, pedestrian activity and retail sales are up, and automobile traffic is down.

The "Streets for People" project has engaged in the planning process a wide variety of interested citizens in order to incorporate their suggestions in street improvements, ranging from putting backs on benches to construction of a 4-story, glass-enclosed Metro Center Galleria over G Street between 11th and 13th Streets.

The success of the F Street Plaza has led to a more ambitious program of street improvements in the downtown area of F and G Streets. It is known as the "Streets for People" project. The Cambridge architectural firm of Ashley, Myer, Smith (now Arrowstreet) was hired to propose a plan to promote the revitalization of downtown through reorganization and redesign of the major streets in the old center.

The architects tried to identify and engage in the planning process a wide variety of interested people. All the potentially affected businesses were consulted. More than 1,500 individuals and 60 affinity groups were asked for their views. Then a representative group was brought together for a 10-week consultation period, during which the participants were paid. Out of this proc-ess grew a consensus of which area should be improved during the first phase, as well as a number of design suggestions that were incorporated into the final proposal. The suggestions ranged from simple features like benches *with* backs to a large fountain in front of the Portrait Gallery. As recommended, there will be an information center and provisions for street vendors on 8th Street. The first phase, opened in early 1977, has entirely closed G Street between 9th and 10th Streets, F Street between 7th and 9th Streets, and 8th Street between E and F Streets (221, 222). These improvements are at the very center of the old downtown, and a lot of people are watching them carefully to see what effect they will have on surrounding properties.

Some other parts of the overall Streets for People plan may seem overly ambitious—such as the 4-story, glass-enclosed Metro Center Galleria over G Street between 11th and 13th Streets. Still, the design is an accurate reflection of the desires of the people in the community. They want a downtown environment equal to the best that is found in other cities. Given a real voice in community affairs, they have opposed the all-too-typical downtown environment in this country, which is often a by-product of speculative development.

If carried to completion, the Streets for People project—funded under the federal urban renewal program—will cost at least $50 million. The first phase, which cost $6.3 million, was carried out by the District of Columbia Redevelopment Land Agency.

Pennsylvania Avenue, the nation's main ceremonial street, was long neglected and badly rundown when President John F. Kennedy in 1962 established the Pennsylvania Avenue Redevelopment Commission. After some false starts, a new Pennsylvania Avenue Redevelopment Corporation is working towards a combination of restoration and redevelopment in the "lively, friendly and inviting"[4] spirit President Kennedy had in mind when he initiated the effort in 1962.

Precisely as L'Enfant planned, Pennsylvania Avenue—Washington's widest avenue—is the city's and the nation's main ceremonial street. What L'Enfant did not plan is that

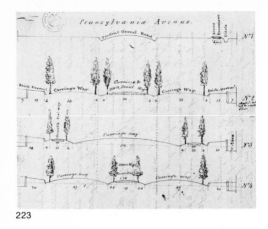

223

225

226

224

223   As President, Jefferson, now able to exercise more control over the design of the capital, had Pennsylvania Avenue lined with trees.

224   The largest courtyard of the Federal Triangle was always meant to be a park, not a parking lot!

225   In the first test of new urban design controls for Pennsylvania Avenue, J. Edgar Hoover insisted that to avoid the problem of purse-snatchers there be a brick wall instead of a shopping arcade at the base of the new FBI Building.

226   The Presidential Building has followed the new urban design controls for Pennsylvania Avenue.

Pennsylvania Avenue would become one of the most rundown streets in Washington.

In 1803, Jefferson, then President, had Pennsylvania Avenue lined with four rows of Lombardy poplars in keeping with the grandeur of the Avenue (223). But its grandeur in scale did not deter it from being the liveliest street in town, with "boarding houses, hotels, saloons, and shops."[5]

As the international importance of the United States increased at the beginning of the 20th century, renewed interest was placed on the symbolic appearance of Pennsylvania Avenue. A commission was set up in 1901 bearing the name of its chairman, Senator James McMillan. Consultants to the commission were Charles McKim, Daniel Burnham, Frederick Law Olmsted, Jr., and Augustus St. Gaudens, men who were, respectively, among the outstanding architects, planners, landscape architects, and sculptors of the day. The commissioners developed a plan based on the Beaux Arts principles of the 1893 Columbian Exposition in Chicago. Out of this plan grew the Federal Triangle. This triangular grouping of massive federal buildings, constructed between 1920 and 1930, houses many of the prominent functons of the national government. The Federal Triangle covers 23 blocks of the L'Enfant plan, and it lines the south side of Pennsylvania Avenue, between the Capitol and the White House, with buildings that can only be described as *governmental*.

In 1962, a Presidential Commission was appointed to produce more recommendations about the future of the Avenue. Nathaniel Owings (the O in SOM) was its chairman. The commission saw little merit in any of the buildings along the avenue's northern edge, and it proposed that everything be cleared. All new buildings were to be 50 ft (15 m) further back from the existing building line, enabling the creation of a broad sidewalk with three rows of trees. Buildings were planned to be 110 ft (34 m) tall, the height of those in the Federal Triangle across the street, and they were to have an arcade, with shops at its base, running along Pennsylvania Avenue.

As for the south side of Pennsylvania Avenue, the commission wanted to build upon the few remaining sites in and around the Federal Triangle. It also suggested that the large courtyards between the government buildings, which had become parking lots, be converted to public parks (224).

The FBI Building was to be the first test of the quality and feasibility of the plan. The GSA agreed to the recommended 50-ft setback, the planting of the three rows of trees, and the maximum height of 110 ft. But J. Edgar Hoover insisted the proposed shopping arcade be replaced by a brick wall 16 ft (4.9 m) high (225). The reason? Good old J. Edgar was afraid the FBI's office girls might be raped if there were arcades. And then there were the muggers and purse-snatchers, all operating with impunity right at the FBI's front door. And retail? "What if there is a Commie working in the tie shop?" Mr. Hoover wanted to know. In his 40-year reign, few challenged Mr. Hoover. Moreover, at that time, as *Washington Post* architecture critic Wolf Van Eckardt noted, "The very idea of the stores and restaurants on the street floor of a Federal office building seems outrageous and un-American to the General Services Administration."[6]

The commission had better luck with the Presidential Building, a private office building located at 12th Street and Pennsylvania Avenue. It has a setback and provides a shopping arcade on both its Pennsylvania Avenue and 12th Street frontages (226).

Over time, reaction to the goals of the commission's plan for Pennsylvania Avenue grew more and more unfavorable. Critics questioned the need for a modern monumentality that was insensitive to the many fine old buildings on the north side of the avenue, buildings which, in addition to their own merit, are symbolic of the diversity of the American architectural tradition.

In 1972, the Pennsylvania Avenue Development Corporation was established with a broad set of powers that were tempered by a fresh set of more socially conscious goals. The corporation began with a block-by-block analysis of what was there; working closely with preservation groups, it then identified important buildings that were to remain. Famous old hotels are to be renovated, as are various landmark buildings.

227

The corporation has also established urban design guidelines for each block. Where there is to be new construction, the emphasis remains on setting the buildings back 50 ft and providing a shopping arcade. In general, there will be a blend of hotels, housing, office space, cultural facilities, and shopping in new and old buildings, and the corporation will be responsible for planting trees and repaving the sidewalks. This most recent design concept is more in keeping with the "lively, friendly, and inviting" spirit President John F. Kennedy had in mind when he initiated the 1962 effort.

With 60 percent of the land area of central Washington allocated by the L'Enfant plan to streets, Washington has 182,000 automobiles (including taxis) headed downtown during morning rush hours with 65 percent of incoming commuters; the other 35 percent come by bus. The new Metro, which got started in 1968 after 50 years or so of talking about it, is expected to reduce the proportion of auto commuters from 65 to 40 percent.

Major L'Enfant more than adequately anticipated General Motor's utmost needs, allocating 60 percent of the land area of central Washington for streets. With the possible exceptions of Los Angeles and Houston, Washington has probably the highest proportion of downtown land devoted to the automobile of any city in the country. And it hasn't ended there. A look at the Washington region shows a vast network of highways, many unfinished but almost all headed in the general direction of downtown.

Highway engineers were in the midst of cooking several more fresh batches of spaghetti when emphasis shifted to mass transportation and the new Metro. Still, the highway advocates managed to get a couple of fairly *al dente* pieces in place, and arteriosclerosis was already setting in before they were stopped.

Some sort of subway for Washington has been in the talking stages for at least 50 years, but no one has ever accused Washington bureaucrats of being in a hurry to get to tomorrow. Tomorrow, however, had to come. Incredibly, in the morning rush hours more than 182,000 automobiles (including

some taxis) are headed downtown, carrying 65 percent of incoming commuters. Autos and taxis account for about 80 percent of the city's air pollution. Only 2,600 buses—less than 2 percent of the total number of vehicles during rush hours—are all that is required to carry the remaining 35 percent of the incoming commuters.

The Metro finally got rolling in 1968 (after a few years of congressionally funded studies), when the region's eight political jurisdictions committed themselves to the 100 miles (160 km) of track. The original $2.98 billion cost estimate has since risen to $5 billion.

The design of all the stations was by architect Harry Weese and Associates. The stations are high, vaulted rooms—free of New York's peristyle platforms (227). There is indirect lighting, and the stations are climate controlled. The technology used for all operational aspects of the system is the same as that developed for BART in San Francisco.

The Metro system may go a long way towards fulfilling a major regional planning goal. Washington's Year 2000 plan is predicated on fingers of development running along highways radiating from the core. The Metro lines do not exactly follow the highways; but they are consistent with the goals of the plan, and the Metro will be watched closely to see if moderate- to high-density suburban development occurs along its route and especially at Metro stops.

The Metro will also be watched to see how many automobile drivers stop fighting and start switching to the new subway. It is estimated that the average driver spends $2 to $3 per day in operating expenses for his automobile, plus an average of $3 in daily parking fees. A round trip on the Metro costs $1.10. It is anticipated that the cost and convenience of the Metro will reduce automobile use from 65 percent to 40 percent—still a sizable number of vehicles for the center of Washington to contend with.

The government itself could induce a great deal of new ridership for the Metro. Currently there are close to 7,000 free parking spaces in downtown Washington reserved

227 Stricter control over parking in the downtown area may be the key to make Metro—Washington's new subway—work.

for congressional staff members, and the Department of Transportation offers very inexpensive parking in its three buildings. Dependence upon the automobile has obviously gotten way out of hand in Washington.

If the Metro is as successful as it should be, perhaps Congress, seeing its advantages first-hand, will tip the national funding balance away from highways and towards mass transit. Then maybe New York and Chicago and other cities will be provided with the resources necessary to renovate their subways and in general improve public transportation in accordance with the high standards established by the Metro.

An innovative proposal for a comprehensive strategy for surface transportation would reorganize all the avenues in central Washington in a selective transportation network that would resolve conflicts between modes while continuing to allow automobile access to most of the grid network.

As important as the Metro is to the future of Washington, it is only one part of what must be a comprehensive transportation strategy that deals as effectively with surface transportation. One of the most exciting and imaginative proposals to be found for Washington comes from a feasibility study for the D.C. Department of Transportation and the D.C. Municipal Planning Office by Joseph Passonneau and Partners.

Passonneau, former dean of the School of Architecture at Washington University in St. Louis, has proposed in an elaborate study that all avenues in central Washington—as opposed to the narrower streets—be reorganized. Passonneau has shown that, with from 110 to 160 ft (34 to 48 m) between buildings, the avenues are wide enough to have exclusive bus lanes, bike lanes, widened tree-lined sidewalks, and lay-bys for deliveries (228, 229). Automobiles would still be permitted on most of the avenues; but buses would no longer be in competition with them.

The city has been experimenting during rush hours with lanes marked for buses, taxis, and bikes only. The problem of surface movement, however, is an all-day

problem. Buses will most likely remain more important than the Metro in moving people back and forth during the day across the vast central employment and shopping area. Buses, bikes, and basic services, not to mention the pedestrian, must have priority over the automobile.

Passonneau's selective network resolves conflicts between modes and still allows the automobiles access to most of the grid network.

Preliminary redesign on two avenues has begun. These proposals, which tie together and expand on street changes already under way, could give Washington this country's first truly 20th-century city distribution system.

Getting something built is a key problem in Washington where a maze of overlapping jurisdictions complicates every project and where, even though "home rule" now allows the local government to set priorities, budgetary control still rests with the congressional appropriations committees.

Although the design work on the two avenues is an encouraging beginning to an exceptionally intelligent and long overdue plan for the city, Washington is, unfortunately, one of the toughest cities in the United States in which to get something built. One of the primary reasons is the maze of overlapping jurisdictions that has resulted from a series of partial reorganizations of the local government.

Until 1965, Congress was exclusively responsible for all legislation concerning the District of Columbia. The President had some administrative power because he got to appoint the three members of the Board of Commissioners. One of the commissioners, however, had to come from the Army Corps of Engineers. Both the House and Senate had and still have a District Committee and District Appropriations Committee.

In 1965, President Johnson changed this system by appointing a mayor, deputy mayor, and city council—people who were supposed to act in the interests of a non-voting constituency. In 1972, there was a change again—home rule. Now Wash-

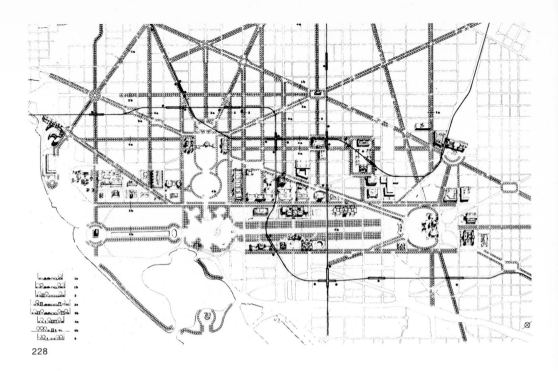

228

229

228 The Passonneau plan would restrict the use of the radial streets in the Washington plan to give priority to pedestrians, bicyclists, bus riders, and service vehicles.

229 Sketch by Passonneau shows 19th Street north from K Street as part of a proposed reorganization of the radial street network in the Washington plan.

ingtonians could actually vote for and elect the Mayor, City Council, and one nonvoting member of Congress.

With home rule came the right for the District government to engage in municipal planning. But the National Capital Planning Commission, a federal agency largely responsible for planning prior to home rule, remains strong, as it is now charged with watching over all planning decisions which might affect the nation's interest in its capital. Then there is the powerful Fine Arts Commission. The commission serves as the guardian of public taste and aesthetics by having design review powers over all private buildings to be constructed in the vicinity of a federal structure or park, if the building can be construed to influence the quality of the setting of the federal holdings. Then there is the Architect of the Capitol, whose famous former resident nonarchitect, J. George Stewart, remodeled the East Front of the Capitol ''over the collective dead body of the American architectural profession.''[7] And then there is the GSA and the Redevelopment Land Agency for urban renewal. It is a system that has worn down the pencils and patience of many architects.

Most important, home rule, while allowing the District to establish its own priorities, does not allow it the budgetary control which would enable the city to convert priorities into realities. This ultimate tool still rests with the congressional appropriations committees, the House committee in particular. Congressmen from Virginia and Maryland have found it useful to sit on the House committee to ensure that their suburban constituents are not adversely affected by District decisions. Those who live in Washington, then, remain subject to devastation without representation.

San Francisco

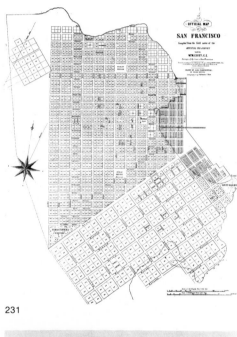

231

232

230   Of the 175,000 people who work in San Francisco's downtown, 46 percent come by public transportation and a similar percentage drive; the rest walk to work.

231   The blocks south of Market Street, and at right angles to it, were laid out in 1845 by Jasper O'Farrell.

232   Burnham and Bennett's plan for San Francisco was finished just months before the 1906 earthquake leveled the city. Nonetheless, the plan was not adopted.

San Francisco has adopted the most comprehensive urban design controls in the U.S., which for new construction include height, width and color limitations, *and* the protection of major public views. Furthermore, the city can exercise "discretionary design review" on all new construction that would have an impact on major streets and urban spaces.

Population and geography
Situated on a peninsula, somewhat akin to the shape of Cyrano's famous protrusion, the city is replete with hills; it has the Pacific Ocean to the west and the bay to the north and east. Discovery of gold in those hills put San Francisco on just about everyone's travel plans the summer of 1849 and for the next ten as well. But when the gold stopped panning out, it was the protected bay that sustained San Francisco as a significant international port city.

During the years of the gold rush, the population rose from 20,000 to 50,000 people by 1855 and grew steadily thereafter, reaching 715,000 people in 1970 within the 177-sq-mile (460-sq-km) city. The eight-county, 2,800-sq-mile (7,300-sq-km) region—exclusive of San Francisco—has a population of 3,800,000.

San Francisco's downtown is an area of approximately 400 acres (160 ha) with a working population estimated at 175,000 people (230). About 47 percent of these people drive to work, 46 percent use public transportation, and the remaining 7 percent walk. Ridership on BART (Bay Area Rapid Transit), San Francisco's new commuter train system, has (ironically) come from commuter buses which were, and still are,

faster and cheaper than BART. It has only reduced dependency upon the automobile by 3 percent on the Oakland side of the bay, although it is thought this figure will increase when BART is 100 percent in operation. (Before BART, 44 percent of those crossing the bay in the morning peak came by bus and 56 percent came by automobile; after BART, 24 percent came by BART, 24 percent by bus, and 53 percent by automobile.)

Historical development
The first plan of San Francisco in 1839 was a slightly askew grid. In 1845, Jasper O'Farrell made a second plan; and although it appears he tried to regulate it to fit the city's unique topography, landowners exerted sufficient pressure to force O'Farrell to continue the established pattern which they thought allowed for the convenient subdivision of lots. Market Street, however, was laid out as a diagonal which followed an old road leading to a mission. Blocks south of Market Street were laid out at right angles to it and were four times as large as the blocks to the north of Market Street (231).

In 1904, Daniel Burnham and Edward Bennett took their compasses and adjustable triangles to San Francisco. The plan they were commissioned to make—largely the work of Bennett—was presented to the Board of Supervisors in September 1905 (232). Burnham said the plan "shall interfere as little as possible with the rectangular street system in the city."[1] In April 1906, an earthquake cleared 30 percent of the built-up city, including the entire center. Fortunately for the surviving citizenry, most of the buildings in the city were heavily insured—

233

insurance being a major industry in the city—so that money was there to rebuild quickly. Unfortunately for Burnham and Bennett, the rebuilding outpaced the politics of decision making; and San Francisco, despite Burnham's optimism for the city, rebuilt more or less according to the framework of the razed city.

Burnham had envisioned diagonal streets intersecting concentric rings radiating from a small central loop or " 'perimeter of distribution' as in Paris, Berlin, Vienna, Moscow, and London"[2]: what modern highway engineers have come to see as the gospel. Many of the highways in San Francisco today, in fact, correspond roughly to the Burnham plan, but with total disregard of the scale, grace, and finesse with which Burnham had sought to integrate his new street network into the city fabric.

San Francisco's zoning, as amended in 1966, seeks to encourage mixed use and provides generous floor area allowances in return for urban amenities which, it is argued, ameliorate the impact of the increased density.

In 1921, San Francisco enacted its first zoning ordinance. Standard for the time, it zoned noxious uses away from residential areas and the expanding downtown. No restrictions were placed on the ultimate size of a building.

In 1960, a new citywide zoning ordinance was adopted because the federal government cautioned the city that without effective bulk controls redevelopment funds would not be forthcoming. In response, the Board of Supervisors—intending to be crafty—adopted an FAR of 20, which could increase to FAR 25 on corner lots. They thought that, essentially, these new controls were no controls at all, as there were no buildings in the city at that time which even came close to approaching that bulk. It took the construction of such buildings as the Wells Fargo Building and later the Hartford Building to make the Board of Supervisors realize that buildings constructed at FAR 25 were very big indeed.

With this new knowledge, the board lowered the permissible FAR to 16, but allowed FAR 20 on corner sites. This action was

made subject to change, however, based on a new study the City Planning Commission was directed to make for the downtown area, which was completed in 1966.

The 1966 zoning change was in recognition of the impact BART would have on the area to the south of Market Street and therefore included all sites up to three blocks south of Market Street within its designation of downtown uses. It divided the downtown into four categories—office, retail, general commercial, and support. All areas could build mixed-use buildings which could include apartments if a satisfactory case were made to the Planning Commission.

The base FAR was set at 14 for office, 10 for retail and general commercial, and 7 for support facilities. A set of 10 bonus items was introduced which could increase the FAR of office buildings to 25 on certain sites, retail and general buildings to 18, and support facilities to 12.

The Planning Commission argued that the difference between these generous floor area allowances and earlier generous floor allowances was that now buildings built above FAR 14 were subject to providing amenities plus other features which would ameliorate the impact of the increased density. The bonus provisions include: direct access from a building to rapid transit; proximity to rapid transit; direct access to parking; multiple building entries; sidewalk widening; shortened walking distances, usually by providing a through-block connection; a plaza; a setback on the sides of the building; low coverage at upper floors; and observation deck with free admission.

To date, several apartment buildings have been built adjacent to downtown office sites, especially the Gateway Center project. But only Fox Plaza has integrated the office, apartments, and ground floor retail uses into a single structure (233). Designed by Victor Gruen Associates in 1966, the 29-story building contains 60,000 sq ft (5,500 sq m) of commercial space at the first two levels, 10 floors—totaling 150,000 sq ft (14,200 sq m)—of office space, and 448 apartments.

Urban design controls for the entire city, including the downtown, were established in

234

235

233　Although mixed-use buildings are allowed in the center of San Francisco, Fox Plaza is the only building of this type.

234　As a way of maximizing views, urban design regulations allow taller buildings on the city's hills, but require low buildings at the waterfront.

235　Urban designers view the development of the center as one of the city's hills. It should have a high point and should step down as it approaches the waterfront.

1971 as one section of the city's overall master plan, with those policies that could be written into zoning law automatically enforceable and others—more subjective—to be monitored through the discretionary design review powers of the City Planning Department.

Alan Jacobs, who headed the City Planning Department from 1967 to 1977, set up an urban design team which in 1971 produced an urban design plan as one section in the city's overall master plan. A series of urban design policies were established for the entire city including the downtown. Those policies that could be written into zoning law were automatically enforceable. For other more subjective policies, the City Planning Department said it would use its discretionary design review powers to insure that buildings meet the intent of the policies. Two prime areas where the city's urban design staff said they would review every new building were those located on Market Street and those located on Union Square.

The urban design plan supersedes the 1966 zoning ordinance only when that ordinance goes beyond the following controls:

–Height. Three criteria were established for the overall height and bulk regulations which blanket the downtown area: where a prevailing height exists around major public spaces provided that height is consistent with allowing adequate sunlight upon those spaces; where new public spaces have been created, as along Market Street, to insure adequate sunlight in the future; and to reinforce the center somewhat in accordance with the city's topography—primarily its hills—and its historic growth (234). This last requirement is to be accomplished by allowing the center to have a high point, but mandating through a gradual reduction in allowable height that buildings become lower as they approach the waterfront. This will protect views of the bay from the many high points in the city (235, 236).

–Bulk. Another technique to reduce the general obtrusiveness of new construction is to regulate the width and diagonal dimensions of buildings so that they will be thin and graceful and in this way not impede views of the city from other points, which is a negative effect of fatter buildings.

–Color. New buildings are to be light in color to be in general keeping with the character of the city and to help reflect light and brighten the city, which has few days of direct sun during the year due to the constant fog.

–View corridors. Certain views down particular streets, especially views of the bay and the Bay Bridge, are to be protected by restricting the heights of buildings that might otherwise be built and block these views.

Height controls have been an integral part of San Francisco's zoning laws for decades. The city recognizes the special quality of its hills and splendid views. But the overall urban design changes reflect a view that San Francisco's zoning, as had been written, was piecemeal at best, ascribing to no overall urban design principles as to the "look" of the downtown area or its long-range quality. In particular the new urban design policies are a reaction to the Bank of America Building (Wurster, Bernardi and Emmons with SOM) which the planners saw as too high, too fat, and too dark, although this very distinction has made the building one of the more prominent symbols of the city (237).

Despite what planners have seen as the negative aspects of the Bank of America Building, it was carefully sited to provide a well-defined and rather elegant urban space. The siting of the building allows surrounding buildings access to light, sun, and a view of the plaza. Unfortunately, to accomplish all of this, the Bank of America plaza had to be positioned where it would receive the least amount of direct sun (238). It is obvious, when studying the placement of highrise buildings in downtown San Francisco, that developers have been extremely cautious to date in siting new buildings, especially the bigger ones, to provide sun and view, which is an important expectation of those who work and live in this city.

The building at One Market Plaza designed by Welton Becket and Associates incorporates all the major objectives of the new urban design controls.

The Southern Pacific Transportation Company owned a large block located on the south side of Market Street. Realizing that

236

237

238

the Department of City Planning would exercise its discretionary design review powers, Southern Pacific asked the department to outline its urban design criteria for the site, including the specific regulations of the zoning, before design of the building began.

The most difficult and probably the most important requirement was for the new building to respect the view corridors. Because Market Street divides two grid systems, views from both upper California and Pine Streets actually run across the Southern Pacific site and other sites, to the Bay Bridge and the Oakland hills beyond (239). The old Southern Pacific Building along Market Street is about 12 stories high and does not obstruct these long views (of the bridge with the hills beyond) from the top of California Street; but if it were torn down and replaced by a 40-story office building, one of San Francisco's most fabulous views would be lost forever (240).

Evidently Gertrude Stein had Oakland in mind when she said "sometimes when you get there there is no there there." But the hills are unmistakably there. And from Pine Street atop Nob Hill is a view of the Oakland hills. And Southern Pacific had to protect that view as well.

A building constructed within the remaining area of the site would still be quite large, and thus would become a bulky mass upon the skyline intruding upon other views from other directions. And it was for this precise reason that the zoning laws' new bulk requirements prohibit such a "fat" building. Only two separate buildings would meet this requirement. The two buildings were then staggered on the site to provide adequate light and view while respecting the established view corridors (241).

But now a third issue of the zoning had to be dealt with: a recognition that new construction must step down as it approached the bay. The two buildings offered an ideal opportunity to express this principle. The taller of the two buildings is 43 stories, and the other one, closest to the bay, is 28 stories (242, 243). The height of the two towers includes the 6-story base from which they rise. The base helps tie the new buildings to

the existing Southern Pacific Building, and the roof of this base structure is landscaped for use of the buildings' occupants.

The complex also provides a through-block shopping galleria to connect Market and Mission Streets. The galleria is skylighted and, along with the shops that front it, is also a cafe. The brick paving throughout the complex is the same color and pattern the city has used along Market Street. Finally, the new buildings are light in color.

The complete project represents one of the most compelling arguments that could be put forward for the value of urban design controls that can integrate the growth of downtown areas with the best features of its past developments. The buildings may not be a triumph of architectural design, according to conventional aesthetic criteria; but this is more a problem with the state of architectural criticism than it is a problem with this particular building. The urban design controls have prevented a building that, if built conventionally, would have been conspicuous and brutal on San Francisco's delicate landscape, no matter how sophisticated in traditional design terms. By conforming to the urban design controls, the building has become a piece of "background" architecture that functions as well as any new office building but maintains a respect for more important surrounding environmental qualities.

In meeting all these requirements, the entire project has not exceeded the base FAR of 14. In fact, it is built only to an FAR of 13.1. It has provided every imaginable public amenity without needing to take advantage of the bonuses allowable for the provision of such amenities. This points once again to the need for cities to reexamine bonus items that developers more often than not provide because it is good business or even necessary for the building to function well. As city planners and urban designers have become less timid and more knowledgeable about the real economics behind large-scale urban development, they are beginning to insist that these new buildings relax the burden they place on the city infrastructure by providing, for the right to build at all, plazas, arcades, shopping facilities, or whatever is deemed correct for that particular section of the city.

236 Urban design regulations now forbid tall buildings along the waterfront; such buildings block far more views than they create.

237 Bank of America is viewed by San Francisco's urban designers as too tall, too "fat," and too dark.

238 The Bank of America Plaza was sited so surrounding buildings could provide definition for the plaza and enjoy it as well. The best location for those purposes, however, does not afford the space much direct sun.

239

240

241

242

243

239   View corridors established in the zoning's urban design regulations prohibit a building from being taller than the 12-story building seen at the foot of Market Street. The view is looking from atop Nob Hill, down California Street to the Bay Bridge.

240   Had the views down California and Pine Streets not been protected, they would have been lost forever with new development, as has been the case on many parallel streets.

241   To meet the zoning's strict urban design regulations and the city's discretionary design review, two separate office towers were built behind the old Southern Pacific Building. The towers were staggered on the site to protect the views down California and Pine Streets.

242-243   In accordance with the principle that buildings step down as they approach the waterfront, the tower closest to the waterfront at 28 stories is considerably shorter than the other 43-story tower.

244 New buildings on Union Square must locate along the street line. There are also height limitations to ensure that the square always has sun. For this reason the tower portion of the Hyatt Regency Hotel is set back behind a lower building that fronts directly on Union Square.

New development in Union Square has respected the most formal and elegant of downtown San Francisco's three major open spaces, with sensitive design solutions by the San Francisco office of SOM responding to the urban design framework established by the City Planning Department.

Until the reconstruction of Market Street as a pedestrian transit way—with several attendant plazas connecting to BART stations—Union Square was one of three open spaces in all downtown San Francisco. Of the three, it is the most elegant and the most formal (244). Naturally, when there is any hint of new development, there are many backseat architects. When the San Francisco office of Skidmore Owings and Merrill received a commission to design an office building for Qantas Airlines, right next to the renaissance-style Fitzhugh Building, which was being considered for designation as a landmark, SOM chose to respect both Union Square and the Fitzhugh with a rather understated building that matches the height of the Fitzhugh—by the laws protecting Union Square, it could not be taller—matches the color and material of the Fitzhugh, and lines its facade up with the Fitzhugh (245).

Ironically, a battle is now raging in San Francisco because the specialty store, Saks Fifth Avenue, owns the Fitzhugh—as it does a similarly elegant landmark building on New York's Fifth Avenue—and seeks to raze the building and in its stead build an almost windowless 5-story structure. Members of the Foundation for San Francisco's Architectural Heritage produced an alternative design which showed how Saks could maintain the Fitzhugh and build an addition to it on the remaining back portion of the site it owned. The Heritage scheme provides virtually the same floor space as the Saks proposal while also providing for the possibility of renting out several floors of the Fitzhugh (246). Cost estimates that include the necessary changes to the older building so that it conforms to the building code show that this proposal would cost substantially less than an all-new structure. It is tragic that a similar effort to save Chicago's Stock Exchange failed, and it would even be more tragic to lose the Fitzhugh after all that has been learned about urban preservation.

On the same side of the square, another site has been developed as a Regency Hyatt Hotel. Once again, through the use of discretionary design review, the Department of City Planning established an urban design framework for the site, and SOM again provided a sensitive solution that met and added to the requirements. The building had to line up with the facade along Post Street and could not be taller than 135 ft (41 m), the prevailing height of the square. Instead of building that high, though, SOM chose to match the cornice line of a lower building that was tucked in between the Qantas and Hyatt Regency rather than leave it as an anomaly. In terms of height, it was felt that an especially tall building would detract from the skyline as established primarily in the financial district and Nob Hill, both some blocks away. If there were to be a tower, it should be no higher than neighboring ones. The 35-story hotel tower behind the lower building along Post Street is in keeping with these considerations. The complex was, of course, to be light in color and to contain retail frontage along the ground levels (247).

The base FAR in the Union Square area is 10. In this case, to build the size hotel needed, the architects took advantage of several zoning bonuses including multiple building entrances, a sidewalk widening, a plaza (which could not be along Post Street), a through-block connection between Post and Sutter Streets, low-building coverage at upper floors, and an observation deck.

The plaza is situated along the through-block connection and has a fountain, outdoor cafe, and a restaurant overlooking it.

The permitted FAR was thus raised to 14 out of a maximum FAR of 15 for the district.

A pioneering approach to urban design through urban renewal made urban design quality the key to developer selection and gave San Francisco its notable mixed-use development, Golden Gateway, which led to two other notable developments adjoining it to the south—the Alcoa Building, with a 2-acre (.8-ha) park surrounding it, and Embarcadero Center, which includes a 5-acre (2-ha) park.

Prior to the urban design controls, which in one form or another now affect all buildings

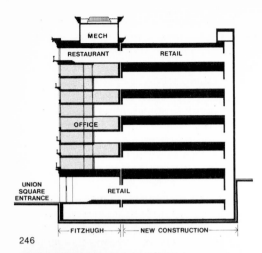

246

247

245

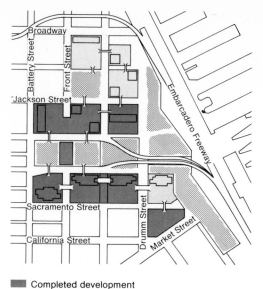

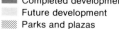
Completed development
Future development
Parks and plazas

248

245 A restrained piece of architecture, the Qantas Building matches the color, height, and roughly the proportions of the Fitzhugh Building seen on the left. The solution for the Hyatt Regency Hotel lines up the front portion with the height of the 3-story building that is likely to remain.

246 This section produced by the Foundation for San Francisco's Architectural Heritage shows how the Fitzhugh Building could remain, fronting on Union Square, with a newer building attuned to modern merchandising techniques built on the back portion of the site Saks owns.

247 The combination of straightforward urban design controls, discretionary design review, and conscientious architects has produced new buildings that fit well into the existing urban fabric. Compare these two buildings by Skidmore, Owings & Merrill where urban design controls were in place with the Grace Building in New York (40), also by SOM, where there were no urban design controls.

248 The Golden Gateway–Embarcadero Center urban renewal area is a 15-block development which contains office, hotel, residential, commercial, and entertainment facilities—all connected by an upper-level pedestrian system.

in San Francisco, urban renewal—thanks to the pioneering work of Justin Herman as director of the San Francisco Redevelopment Authority—was the main vehicle for achieving design controls. One of the largest urban renewal projects undertaken in San Francisco is the Golden Gateway Center—a 51-acre (20.4-ha), 15-block development nestled between the financial center and the Embarcadero Freeway. Ten blocks have thus far been developed. It is already possible to walk throughout the entire area on an upper pedestrian level which, via open bridges, connects apartments, offices, shopping and entertainment facilities, parks, and plazas.

Of the 15 blocks, architects Wurster, Bernardi and Emmons (WBE) designed the master plan for a 10-block area north of Clay Street (248). For it, they also designed 1,254 apartment units in a combination of highrise and town house structures that locate on three of the six blocks being devoted to housing. Many of the blocks have ground-level shopping, which helps keep the streets active and interesting (249). There is also open space at the pedestrian level, which is above two levels of parking, and one block in the center of the housing area developed as a 2-acre (.8-ha) grade-level park designed by Sasaki-Walker and Associates. The park has connections over the streets to the major pedestrian level in the housing complex (250).

On a two-block site north of the housing complex, the Alcoa Building (SOM) straddles Front Street, which no longer goes through at grade level (251). This would not have been allowed under San Francisco's new urban design rules. When John Portman proposed an even larger version of the same idea—a building over a street—on a two-block site south of the Alcoa Building, the plan was denied. Surrounding the Alcoa Building at the pedestrian level is a 2-acre (.8-ha) park.

The five blocks immediately south of the Alcoa Building are known as Embarcadero Center. Four of the blocks are now developed and contain three office buildings, ranging between 34 and 46 stories (252), and a Hyatt Regency Hotel all designed by John Portman (253, 254). Parking for the Portman complex is below grade, so the

two levels below the upper pedestrian level are devoted primarily to shopping and restaurants. With the completion of the fourth office building, there will be a pedestrian connection to the 18-story atrium space of the hotel and the 5-acre (2-ha) Justin Herman Park. The hotel itself has provided a sidewalk cafe along Market Street.

Urbanistically, Portman's Embarcadero Center is an improvement over his earlier Peachtree Center in Atlanta (301, 302), with more respect for street life and a clearer relationship between the buildings. In all, the total project, combining the talent of three forceful groups of architects—Wurster, Bernardi and Emmons; Skidmore, Owings and Merrill; and John Portman—is a far more appealing image for what Houston Center should be, instead of the heavy-handed antiurban development it is becoming (205–208).

A newer building by Anshen and Allen enhances the prestige of the old Bank of California Building by accepting its own role as a background building.

So much of old San Francisco was destroyed in the 1906 earthquake that San Francisco is a relatively new city and therefore preservationists look twice at a good eclectic building. The "old" Bank of California, designed by Bliss and Faville and built just after the disaster, is such a building. When the bank decided to expand its facilities, demolition of this prestigious landmark building was not a consideration.

Architects Anshen and Allen designed the new building which was completed in 1967. Although it has never won any architectural design awards, it is an excellent urban building, especially considering that great pains were taken to preserve the integrity of the older bank by its being subdued and reserved (255).

Because the new building is on a small site, it was necessary to slightly cantilever it over the older existing bank. Mechanical equipment has been removed from the roof of the old bank, which has been converted into a garden for bank employees and which surrounding buildings can enjoy visually.

San Francisco has made the construction of its rapid transit system an opportunity

249

251

250

252

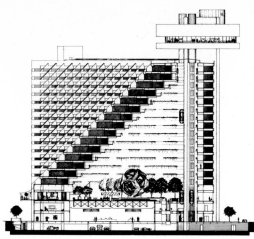

253

249　With the exception of Washington and Clay Streets, the street level has mostly been reserved for shopping.

250　One complete block within the urban renewal area has been developed as a park with a connection over the street so children can use it safely.

251　The Alcoa Building has a large pedestrian area above the parking platform. The mostly concrete wall surrounding the parking was built because Clay Street is a major artery to the Embarcadero Freeway.

252　Portman's 5-block parcel of the total Golden Gateway urban renewal development is known as Embarcadero Center. It is more clearly organized than Peachtree Center in Atlanta (see 301, 302) and devotes much of the street-level frontage to active pedestrian use.

253-254　The atrium space of the Hyatt Regency Hotel will have a bridge connection to the rest of the Golden Gateway–Embarcadero Center complex when Portman's fourth office tower is developed to the north of the hotel.

254

255

256

257

255 The addition to the landmark Bank of California is extremely sensitive to the older building.

256 By the 1960s, Market Street was no longer a prestigious address, and developers and architects did their best to avoid fronting buildings along it.

257 This section through Market Street shows BART at the lowest level, below the trolley cars. Environmentalists won a battle to keep electric buses (and their overhead cables) on the street level instead of diesel- or gas-driven buses with their attendant fumes.

for rehabilitating and beautifying its noisy and polluted old Market Street, long the central spine for buses and trolleys and now a major route for the new subway.

Market Street is the seam that divides warehousing, industrial, and service functions to the south of it from the business and entertainment sections to the north of it. The street itself is the focus of the city's retail shopping and a variety of amusement activities. As a main thoroughfare through the center of the city, it is the central spine for buses and trolleys. The street was noisy and the source of much pollution. And it was in such decay for so many years that when major new development began in the 1960s, buildings—such as the Crown-Zellerback—virtually turned their backs on Market Street (256). The nature of the street created many triangular sites along its northern edge, which are awkward to design for, and when redeveloped, unlike older buildings that were constructed right up to the face of Market Street, the newer ones took an ambivalent position about their location. BART changed all this, refocusing attention back to Market Street.

Because the street would be cut open for the construction of the subway, many saw it as the opportunity to finally do something with the street when it was rebuilt. In 1968 the voters of San Francisco approved a $24 million bond issue to pay for the street's improvement. An additional $10.4 million came from a combination of federal urban renewal grants and BART's obligation to reconstruct the torn-up street. The funds to refurbish the 2.2-mile (3.3-km) section of the street in the downtown area have been used in part to construct a tunnel level, above the BART tunnel, for the city's trolley cars, which run along Market Street and gradually fan out to many sections of the city (257, 258).

The pollution-free trolley cars are an integral part of the city's varied transit system and a key to the goal of many in the city of creating a completely nonpolluting public transportation system. At the street level, the funds were used for a major beautification program and a reworking of traffic.

The design team consisted of architects Mario J. Ciampi and Associates and John

Carl Warnecke and landscape architects Lawrence Halprin and Associates.

By dead-ending some nonessential streets that flow into the northern edge of Market Street, three main plazas were created which in themselves represent a 100 percent increase in the number of downtown open spaces. Two of the plazas are located at BART stops. The third, Justin Herman Plaza, is at the very northeastern edge of Market Street and is a focus for the Ferry Terminal and developments to the north, including Gateway Center and Embarcadero Center.

To ensure that these plazas always have sunlight, the urban design controls have placed the appropriate height restrictions on future developments on the south side of Market, across from the plazas (259).

Numerous smaller plazas also have been created along the north side of Market Street by closing at least one of the two streets that intersect with Market in every block. Besides creating greatly needed public space in just the right places, these traffic changes greatly reduce the automobile and pedestrian conflicts at these previously awkward intersections (260, 261).

Market Street, from building line to building line, is 120 ft (36 m) wide. The sidewalks were 22 ft (6.5 m) wide, leaving six lanes for surface vehicles, of which the center two lanes were reserved for trolleys and some buses. The new alignment of the street allows 35 ft (11 m) for sidewalks, although this dimension narrows slightly when lay-bys are provided for service vehicles. The street now has four lanes of traffic for most of its length, with buses given priority in the curb lane.

The private automobile is still permitted to drive on Market Street, but its negative impact should be lessened by the exclusivity of the public transit right-of-ways and the dead-ending for the plazas of many streets that previously led into Market Street.

The street received very careful attention to every detail (262). Commercial establishments must respect a new ordinance which restricts flashing signs and limits all overhanging signs and marquees to 6-ft

258

259

262

260

261

258 Ironically, most of BART's ridership has come from commuter buses. Although commuter buses are more convenient in the suburbs, BART offers better downtown service. That BART hasn't attracted motorists may mean that the system is poorly conceived, poorly planned (too few stops), or too expensive, with infrequent service. But it may also reflect insufficient penalties for those who drive.

259 Halladie Plaza was developed as both an entrance to BART and a major open space. There are height limitations on surrounding properties so that new construction—normally spurred by new transportation facilities—will not block direct sunlight to the plaza.

260-261 Instead of connecting directly with Market Street as it used to, Powell Street (260) and several other streets on the north side of Market have been dead-ended (261) to create pedestrian areas and frustrate automobile use.

262 Planned with careful attention to urban furniture, Market Street has been converted into an enormously pleasant and useful urban street.

263

263 The Embarcadero Freeway at the foot of Market Street and in front of the landmark Ferry Terminal Building was brought to an abrupt halt by angry citizens once its environmental damage became apparent.

(1.8-m) projections. The sidewalks, plazas, and crosswalks are brick, with granite trim at the border. Six hundred trees were planted, mostly in double rows. The graphics are all new, as are the benches, bus shelters, drinking fountains, and trash receptacles. The beautiful old "Path of Gold" street fixtures—similar to the original quality of such fixtures in so many American cities that have been replaced by the "gooseneck" monstrosities—have been retained and recast.

The unfinished Embarcadero Freeway is an unhappy legacy of the years before the "Freeway Revolt," when irate citizens stopped the powerful State Division of Highways from completing its plans for an extensive network of eight-lane, double-decked highways through the heart of the city.

The new Embarcadero Plaza at the foot of Market Street, coupled with the Portman-designed Hyatt Regency Hotel, has once again focused controversy on the elevated Embarcadero Freeway, which has freely scarred the old Ferry Terminal as it marches to an abrupt halt at the precise location where angry citizens' groups overtook this monster creation of the Division of Highways (263).

One part of an extensive plan for a freeway system that—luckily—never fully materialized, the Embarcadero Freeway looms like an albatross over this now very pleasant and continuously improving area.

In the original 1951 Traffic Ways Plan, these highways were envisioned as six-lane parkways with frequent access, scenic views, gentle curves, and speeds of no more than 40 to 45 miles per hour. Nonetheless, one by one, opposed neighborhoods blocked them in their respective areas of the city. With community opposition built up to a fervor, the Board of Supervisors was forced to delete large sections of the proposed highway system. By 1956 the federal government stepped into the picture with the Federal Highway Act, which upped the ante, offering to pay 90 percent of the highway costs.

The warehousing districts on the city's eastern edge made an easy target for highway engineers. But with federal funds come long strings. There would now have to be eight lanes of traffic with shoulders for emergencies and curves which trucks could easily negotiate at 65 miles per hour. And access onto the highway would not be very frequent. All of this made it a highway for out-of-towners. And the last straw, which enabled in-towners to stop all further highway construction, was the double-decking of the highways to avoid paying high land costs for the otherwise extremely wide right-of-ways. The stretch that passes in front of the Ferry Terminal originally was planned to run underground, but the additional cost of $15 million made this gesture to aesthetic sensitivity short-lived. If these highways could have been uglier, it was not for want of trying. Over the years, the public has been so incensed that it is a popular issue to discuss the highway's removal, for which many plans have been put forward.

The Freeway Revolt, as it has been called, led to renewed interest in public transportation; and BART is an outcome of this change in priorities. San Francisco's surface system of buses and trolleys has always served the city well. New regulations effecting exclusive bus lanes and priority treatment of buses at bus stops are also a manifestation of this new thinking. Now in some parts of the city, the bus-loading area is an extension of the sidewalk, and the bus merely stops in its tracks—in its lane—avoiding the lengthy fight to get back into traffic.

Concern with the special quality of San Francisco has led citizens to focus more seriously than in any other major American city on the question of height limitations which would prohibit all future construction of highrise buildings, with 43 percent of voters supporting a referendum that proposed a downtown height limit of 160 ft (49 m), or about 12 stories, and a 40-ft (12-m) limit in the rest of the city.

Before leaving San Francisco it is important to discuss briefly the highrise controversy that is more prevalent here than in any other downtown area of an American city. Indeed, unless the recently adapted urban design controls ameliorate the negative impact of highrise buildings as perceived by a growing number of San Franciscans, then San Francisco's highrise days may be num-

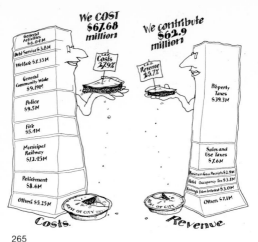

264 The Transamerica Building, though built prior to the enactment of urban design controls, does not violate the city's basic urban design principles; but it does violate the basic sensitivities of many who believe highrises ought to be banned altogether. The original Transamerica Building is the 3-story white triangular structure to the left of the pyramid.

265 In *The Ultimate Highrise,* it is argued that taller buildings downtown cost more in city services than they contribute in taxes. This, however, may be attributed to the fact that new construction is often underaccessed—sometimes because a developer is on good terms with the accessor's office or, better yet, the mayor and sometimes because politicians genuinely feel it is necessary to spark new construction and thereby create jobs and new taxes.

bered. And there is already some doubt as to whether or not the urban design controls can accomplish what may be impossible. For example, even though the Transamerica Building does fit within the urban design controls, its reception on the urban scene has been mixed: "Dropped here by some invaders from Outer Los Angeles, it may not go away . . .," states the AIA guidebook to San Francisco. Almost everybody in San Francisco probably wishes the Transamerica company could have stayed in its old headquarters (264).

In fact, it was the Transamerica Building that brought to a head sufficient sentiment against highrise buildings ("Manhattanization") to force a referendum on the November 1971 ballot which proposed that "no building could be higher than the lesser of 6 stories or 72 ft (22 m)." Voters would be able to permit higher buildings, if merited, in future elections. Thirty-eight percent of the 225,000 voters opted for the adoption of this resolution. In June 1972 an amended version of this referendum was presented to the voters, limiting the height of downtown buildings to 160 ft—about 12 stories—and 40 ft in all other parts of the city. This proposal won the support of 43 percent of the voters.

A report entitled "Impact of Intensive High-Rise Development on San Francisco" by the San Francisco Planning and Urban Renewal Association (SPUR), a privately funded citizens' planning group, tried to assess the impact of highrise development in San Francisco. Four alternate growth patterns considered to be the high and low range of future demand were analyzed: (1) an increase of 10 million sq ft (950,000 sq m) without height limitations; (2) an increase of 10 million sq ft with a 160-ft height limitation; (3) an increase of 30 million sq ft (2,850,000 sq m) without height limitations; and (4) an increase of 30 million sq ft with a 160-ft height limitation.

In contrast to one of the main premises of the anti-highrise book produced by the Bay Guardian, *The Ultimate Highrise* (edited by Bruce Brugmann and Greggar Sletteland), that highrises cost the city more in services than they actually pay in taxes (265), SPUR concluded that with either the maximum anticipated growth or the least amount of an-

ticipated growth, these buildings would produce a sizable tax surplus. SPUR claims this is so because new construction does not need proportional increases in police and fire protection, and the new water and sewerage lines the city is building are adequate to handle the maximum amount of anticipated growth. The report does suggest that low buildings may be less a burden on the general environment than taller ones, but takes the position that with stricter enforcement of environmental standards and plaza design, these problems of highrises could be overcome.

SPUR concluded that with stricter transit policies that discourage the use of the private automobile in favor of car-pooling, increased bus service, and staggered working hours, the city's transportation facilities could then accommodate the maximum anticipated growth.

If the city is to continue to allow growth in downtown San Francisco, then it may be forced to adopt many of the policies outlined by SPUR. In the interim, California's tough environmental review process may assure that new buildings are not disruptive. Under this state law, every new building, whether public *or* private, must submit an Environmental Impact Statement that precisely establishes its affect on the environment, transportation, nearby parks, sidewalks, and so on. In the near future this law may significantly alter many proposed buildings and may in fact completely prohibit certain buildings from locating in particular dense areas of the center.

At present, 94 percent of the buildings over 15 stories high are located in the downtown area, which represents only 3.4 percent of the city's developed land. From 1960 to 1975, 44 buildings have been built in that area containing a total of 22 million sq ft (2,090,000 sq m). *The Ultimate Highrise* argues that this tiny percentage of the land receives an inordinate amount of city services and is actually subsidized by the city at large. If SPUR is correct, this area produces a revenue surplus and may be able to achieve growth in an efficient manner to the economic benefit of the city consistent with environmental goals.

Boston

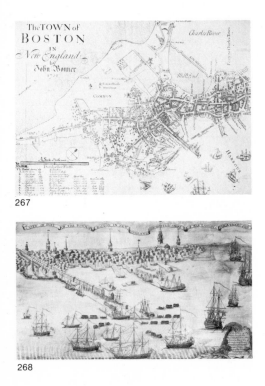

The greatest impact on the center of Boston has been from urban renewal, which at first placed too much emphasis on "new": to build the mediocre plan for the West End a whole neighborhood was razed. The urban design framework of the Government Center, which corrected some of the early wrongs, is excellent (although the quality of the individual buildings within the plan is not always as good as the plan itself). With urban renewal less and less a factor in many American cities, it is significant that most new construction in downtown Boston continues to adhere to urban design guidelines. This is a direct reflection of the downtown's low FAR and the city's willingness to exchange significant increases in FAR for buildings that adopt a prescribed set of urban design considerations.

Population and geography
Boston has grown considerably from the tiny peninsula that was virtually an island—connected to the mainland by a narrow causeway that was underwater during high tide. Beginning with an area of slightly more than 1 sq mile (2.6 sq km), Boston added over 5 sq miles (10.6 sq km) of landfill, and with annexation it has reached its present size of about 50 sq miles (130 sq km), with a population of 620,000. The four-county, 940-sq-mile (2,400-sq-km) region that surrounds Boston has a population of 2,780,000. Boston's importance is enhanced by virtue of its being the capital of the Commonwealth of Massachusetts and the major commercial and cultural center for New England. Of the estimated 225,000 workers in the downtown, 65 percent arrive by a combination of public transportation facilities, and 35 percent come by automobile (266).

Historical development
In the spring of 1630, Governor John W. Winthrop and Puritans from England landed in Charlestown to establish a new colony under a land grant from the king of England. Lack of fresh water caused the first settlement to wither. Undaunted, the colonists packed their bags and set sail on a modest voyage to the other side of the Charles River, where they reached a hilly peninsula the local Indians called Shawmut. There, too, they were disappointed, because the river was not the great inland route they thought it would be. But they stayed. And as good Colonialists, one of their first acts was to change the name Shawmut to the familiar sounding Boston, the name of the town in England from which they had set out on their transoceanic mission.

Although the streets of the new settlement did not adhere to the popular grid plan of that time, they were not atypical of the layout of many English towns, and they appear to have followed quite logically both the undulating contours of the landscape and the irregular pattern of the shore line (267). The streets also radiated from the early town center, where the focus of the town, the Old State House, was located only a block from the harbor (268).

As Boston grew, the three large hills on the peninsula forced settlement into what little flat land there was at the edge of the water and between the hills. In 1743, Boston, with a population of slightly more than 16,000, was larger than Philadelphia (13,000) and New York (11,000). By the time of the American Revolution, Boston was the smallest of the three, still with 16,000 inhabitants. Sub-

266   Of the 225,000 people who work within the area of downtown Boston, first colonized in 1630, 65 percent come by public transportation.

267   The Bonner map of 1722 shows a logical street pattern that was characteristic of many English towns.

268   Long Wharf, shown in this 1768 engraving, contained shops and warehouses that could load and unload at the dock.

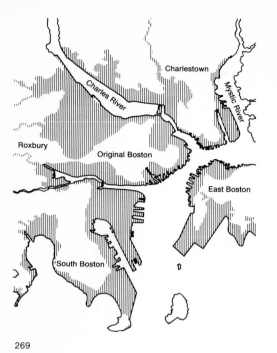

269

stantial increases in the population did not occur until the 19th century. At that time, the remaining flat lands were quickly populated. The hills, never seen as a great asset until then, suddenly became very valuable and were used for much of the early landfill on the marshy shores that surrounded the peninsula. Today only the greatly reduced Beacon Hill remains of the original three, while 60 percent of downtown Boston rests on landfill (269).

At the southern base of Beacon Hill and on what in 1634 was the western edge of Boston, the town purchased 45 acres (18 ha) of flat land for the still intact Boston Common. By 1722 the common was a "versatile community resource useful for pasturing cattle, training military companies, and hanging unwelcome Quakers,"[1] who had presumably vacationed too far north of Philadelphia. Because of an 1803 law the townhouses of Beacon Hill, Back Bay, and the South End—three distinct areas adjacent to the center—were built mostly of brick (with some of stone or other noncombustible materials) to help protect against the numerous and persistent fires, which sometimes destroyed hundreds of buildings.

Boston's zoning combines a low FAR with urban design controls which offer clear advantages to developers who choose the option of submitting to design review by the Boston Redevelopment Authority powers.

Rather than allowing highrise buildings with setback regulations, as other cities were doing at the time, Boston's first zoning ordinance, passed in 1924, was more an attempt to prevent highrises altogether. Very tall buildings were viewed as an unnecessary and burdensome intrusion upon the low scale of the city. To ban highrises in Boston, the city established a maximum height of 155 ft (47 m) for downtown buildings. This measure followed a clear precedent of height controls in Boston dating from at least as early as 1896. The 1924 code was an indirect (but inflexible) way of establishing FAR controls, which in this case worked out to allow a building to have an approximate FAR of 15.

After 11 years of discussion, study, and preparation, a new zoning resolution was adopted in 1964. It did away with height re-

strictions in favor of direct FAR controls. A building in the center could now reach an FAR of 10—one-third less than the 1924 ordinance. If the proposed building located across from a public open space, it could build to an FAR of 12; and if it included off-street parking, it could go to FAR 14. But the intent of the law was clearly to reduce the allowable square footage of a building from what had pertained under the 1924 provisions. An analysis of the history of the 1924 law showed that most buildings erected under it were only half as large as the zoning allowed; and as far as the lawmakers were concerned, that was just fine.

Most of the assumptions of the 1964 zoning change were immediately proven wrong. The late sixties were a time of building boom in Boston. From 1965 to 1970, the average annual increase in office space was almost 3 times as much as that between 1960 and 1965, and more than 11 times as much as that between 1950 and 1960. The pressure for buildings exceeding the base FAR of 10 was so great that developers regularly applied to the Board of Appeals for variances.

The zoning would have allowed the developer of the Keystone Building, for example, with the two bonuses listed above, to build 400,000 sq ft (38,000 sq m) on a site of 28,676 sq ft (2,662 sq m) [FAR 14]. Before the Board of Appeals, the developer argued that because of increased foundation costs due to poor soil conditions and because of land assemblage costs that were higher than originally foreseen, he would need to build a larger building which would have more rentable floor space to avoid a financial hardship. The Board of Appeals granted the developer an increase of 364,000 sq ft (34,500 sq m) above the allowable 400,000 sq ft for a total FAR of 26. The virtual doubling of the zoning's allowable bulk limits was not tied to any particular site improvements or public amenities. In fact, the opposite was true: setback requirements were relaxed and the number of required off-street loading bays was cut in half. The Board of Appeals responded not to the merits of the developer's arguments but rather to the size of neighboring buildings, not questioning the fact that the development of buildings that size was in direct conflict with the goals of the zoning code.

269 When first founded, Boston was virtually an island, to which over the years, 5 sq miles (13 sq km) of landfill were added.

The city's planning agency—the Boston Redevelopment Authority (BRA)—took a more creative approach than the Board of Appeals. The BRA sought to allow the developer to meet his proclaimed needs; but it also encouraged the developer, through incentives, to work with the BRA so that the proposed building would fit into a well-thought-out plan for a larger area. The BRA relied on the powers of urban renewal, planned development, and a special tax provision called 121A.

In urban renewal areas, the BRA could offer a developer a prime site cleared of tenants and buildings at reduced land costs. In exchange, the BRA would have design review powers over the developer's project to ensure that the building met the precise urban design guidelines of the BRA plan.

In Boston, a Planned Development Area is a site [the minimum size is 1 acre (.4 ha)] which the developer owns and on which he conforms to BRA urban design requirements. Once he produces a design acceptable to the BRA, the developer can, under the planned development procedures, apply to the Board of Appeals for a variance from all code restrictions, including FAR limitations; the BRA will support him before the board. In such cases, the Board of Appeals almost always grants the requested variance.

Under the provisions of section 121A, the city determines a building's tax payment as a percentage of the building's gross income over a fixed number of years (40 years in the case of One Beacon Street). Computing the tax in this way is advantageous to the developer because the tax rate itself is fixed and is tied directly to the building's occupancy, not the building's assessed valuation. To the city's advantage, developers are encouraged to build in areas the city wants to upgrade—areas where developers had previously been reluctant to build. Moreover, the BRA has design review powers over buildings using this tax formula.

With the cutback in urban renewal funds, the restrictive zoning code in Boston creates a situation where developers regularly apply to build under the provisions of planned development or section 121A, giving the BRA almost automatic design review—something most cities exercise in very few instances.

Urban renewal got off to as disastrous a start in Boston as anywhere. But under the leadership of Edward J. Logue and with both planning and implementation centered in a single agency, the Boston Redevelopment Authority became an extraordinary instrument for urban revitalization through urban design.

Many of the projects that have changed the face of Boston since 1958 have been initiated through urban renewal. The BRA actually grew out of the Boston Housing Authority and was responsible at first solely for urban renewal projects. Boston's West End, one of its first efforts, has become a sort of code name for many of the dismal human and urbanistic failings of urban renewal. The West End was primarily a low-income Italian working class neighborhood, not dissimilar in character to the neighboring North End. If not a middle-class version of city life, it was a vibrant area full of family and friends and convenient to jobs and shopping. As in so many cases around the country, probably because of what Bacon calls "the fallacy of the average," the area was arbitrarily labelled a "slum," and except for a few churches and *one* historic house, 47 acres (18.8 ha) were cleared. Ostensibly, the goal was to improve the lot of the poor souls resident in the "slum" by removing them from the "blight" in which they lived. Not incidentally, construction of new middle- and upper-income units was supposed to improve the city's tax base.

Herbert Gans in *The Urban Villagers* has taken exception to both of these premises and has vividly recorded the evil consequences of this policy for the West End. Forced to give up their community, to move far from family, friends, and work, the displaced residents were often forced to overcrowd in what housing was available to them on their small incomes—housing often inferior to what they had previously lived in. This is the stuff of which real slums are made. And the net effect: subsidy of the middle class in modern highrise buildings with views of the views (270). It is true that with the building costs of the sixties and seventies, housing must be subsidized for middle-income people as well as low-in-

270

271

186

270 The West End was one of Boston's earliest attempts at urban renewal. It provided subsidized middle-income housing at the expense of the poor, and its design bore little resemblance to the brilliant housing types traditional in neighboring Beacon Hill or Back Bay.

271 This West End shopping center seems to have "wandered in from the suburbs of another city."

come people, but surely the middle class should not be housed at the direct expense of lower-income groups.

The project also included a drive-in shopping center, motel, and movie house complex, which Walter Muir Whitehill accurately describes in *Boston: A Topographical History* as having "the air of having wandered in from the suburbs of another city"[2] (271).

When John F. Collins was elected Mayor in 1959, the urban renewal program, then in its infancy and with vast amounts of funds still available, was off to a disastrous start, having already alienated a large faction of the city's populace. Wishing to avoid future mistakes, Mayor Collins in 1960 appointed Edward J. Logue, first as a consultant and soon after as development administrator of the BRA. The respected Right Reverend Monsignor Francis J. Lally became the BRA's chairman. Both men helped restore a missing sense of integrity to the immensely powerful agency. The BRA in fact soon became even more powerful, as the City Planning Board was merged into it. Plans were announced almost immediately after Logue's appointment for projects encompassing fully 25 percent of the land area of Boston. To carry them out Logue put together a talented staff, which included architect and planner David Crane as planning administrator.

Government Center exemplifies imaginative use of urban renewal and the Logue-Crane theories of "Capital Design" and "Capital Web," supported by superior architecture at the level of urban design.

Of all the projects proposed, the most ambitious was the redevelopment of 60 acres (24 ha) of prime land known as "Scollay Square." Situated among the financial district of downtown Boston, Beacon Hill, the famous Massachusetts State House designed by Bulfinch, and several other important landmarks, Scollay Square was always an important, easily accessible area. In the middle of the 19th century the city's best hotels, restaurants, and entertainment facilities clustered here.

The close proximity of Scollay Square to the naval shipyards in Charlestown and a succession of wars brought thousands of sailors and a gradual change in the nature of

the area. When Logue arrived on the scene, Scollay Square, after half a century of neglect, was a collection of dilapidated buildings housing a good cross-section of the world's honky-tonk.

Plans for the redevelopment of Scollay Square as a government center dated back as far as 1917. Logue's proposal appended itself to this genealogy at an especially propitious time, for in the preceding few years federal, commonwealth, and city agencies had all stated the need for new office buildings, and some major appropriations had been set aside. A study released in 1956 by a special mayoral board had reaffirmed that Scollay Square was the best location for such a group of buildings.

Logue and Crane introduced to Boston the concept of "Capital Design" and the theory of "Capital Web." In Capital Design the city makes sure that its capital investment results in public buildings and other public works that are intelligently designed and sited. This public investment is supposed to have a lasting beneficial impact on the surrounding area, encouraging private investment for renovation and new construction. Capital Web is an extension of Capital Design. Under Capital Web public buildings and community facilities are interconnected by well-maintained public pedestrian ways and public open spaces and a safe network of important local streets. In theory, this structure of the public domain improves the use of community facilities, sparks new construction in a more coherent manner, and in general increases property values.

Both of these tools were at work in the Government Center project when Logue hired I. M. Pei not only to design the site plan for the Goverment Center, but also to establish specific urban design controls for each parcel therein. The Pei plan modified an earlier master plan by John Myer of Arrowstreet in association with Adams, Howard and Greeley; Anderson, Beckwith and Haible; Sasaki, Walker and Associates; Kevin Lynch; and Paul Spreiregen. The controls Pei designed included height and bulk limits, required setbacks, and specification of the relationships of buildings. There were 25 parcels in all, 20 for private development and 5 for government buildings. Pei's plan reduced the site's maze of 22 streets to just

272

273

272 BRA director Edward Logue insisted that distinguished architects be hired to build within the I. M. Pei master plan for the Government Center.

273 A generous pedestrian shopping arcade extends the 875-ft (260-m) length of the One-Two-Three Center Plaza Building across from City Hall.

6, allowing the creation of large pedestrian areas. The layout of proposed buildings reinforced historic streets and important views. The location of the City Hall and the rough dimensions of the plaza it was to sit on were outlined in the plan. Finally, the best of the historic buildings were to be preserved.

Logue insisted that buildings in the government center be designed by architects of the highest abilities. "Beauty once flourished in Boston," said Logue. "It must again."[3] The focal point of the Government Center was to be the City Hall (272). The commission to design this unique building went to architects Kallmann, McKinnell, and Knowles—selected in 1961 from 250 participants in a national design competition. The City Hall and its plazas are surrounded to the north by the John F. Kennedy Federal Office Building (The Architects Collaborative and Samuel Glaser), the Government Center Parking Garage (Kallmann and McKinnell), and just beyond, the State Service Center (Paul Rudolph, design coordinator; Desmond and Lord; Sheply, Bulfinch, Richardson and Abbott; and M. A. Dyer and Pedersen and Tilney); and to the west by One-Two-Three Center Plaza—a curved 8-story, 875-ft (270-m) long office building with a shopping arcade at its base (273) (Welton Becket and Associates)—and Pemberton Plaza behind it (Kallmann and McKinnell); to the south by the renovated Sears Block (F. A. Stahl), the One Washington Mall office building (Edwardo Catalano), and the 40-story New England Merchants Bank office building (Edward Larrabee Barnes).

To the east, there was to have been a bridge connection over Congress Street to the renovated Faneuil Hall and plaza, Quincy Markets and more plazas (Benjamin Thompson and Associates), and the 37-story Sixty State Street office building (SOM). The bridge was nixed by Mayor Kevin White, who said he didn't like the SOM design. Some say that what he mainly doesn't like is the politics of the developers of Sixty State Street, Cabot, Cabot, and Forbes, who supported White's opponent in the last election. In the midst of all this, the public is denied an important pedestrian connection over the heavy traffic on Congress Street.

City Hall Plaza is one of the few outdoor public spaces in the United States that rivals in elegance, refinement, and usage the great plazas of Europe (274). An inviting space with ample seating, trees, and fountains, it takes its life in part from the retail activities at the base of the Center Plaza Building and from the Sears Block with its outdoor cafe. The lower floors of City Hall itself house those agencies of city government that directly serve the public. No doubt the plaza would have encouraged even more pedestrian activity had the base of the lower portion of the JFK Federal Building been devoted to retail shops, restaurants, and cafes. But until very recently, this approach of mixing in a few other uses—even in a modest way—seemed beyond the imagination of the federal government. This partial lack, however, is compensated for by the numerous food kiosks the city allows on the plaza at noontime.

There is no question that the zoning techniques used in New York and San Francisco can create competent, responsible architecture. But zoning cannot guarantee brilliant architecture and great urban spaces. With the government center complex virtually complete after 20 years of planning, design, and construction, it can be seen that imaginative use of urban renewal has been able to achieve some outstanding buildings and significant urban spaces across a very large area. And much to Logue's credit, although Boston ranks sixteenth in size of U.S. cities, it was third in receiving federal urban renewal funds.

With some notable exceptions and despite the urban design controls, many of the tall buildings outside Government Center seem out of scale with Boston's fine network of small streets and typically low buildings.

On the site immediately south of the One-Two-Three Center Plaza Building and Pemberton Plaza is a 38-story office building, One Beacon Street, which was designed by SOM's New York office and built under section 121A. By following urban design guidelines established by the BRA, the building gained an additional 100,000 sq ft (9,500 sq m) of floor space (which essentially increased the building by 4 stories).

274

275

274 City Hall Plaza is one of the most important public spaces built in the United States.

275 Despite BRA urban design requirements, it may be impossible for huge buildings like One Beacon Street—which was required to set back in order to provide the view of King's Chapel—to relate to the delicate scale of old Boston.

One of the main concerns of the BRA was that the color of the building be in harmony with the character and red brick color of the residential section of neighboring Beacon Hill. For this reason, the BRA vetoed SOM's first proposal for a building in Corten steel.[4] Other concerns of the BRA were that the building be sited so it would leave a view of King's Chapel at the end of Beacon Street; that the plaza created by setting the building back, to provide the view, be paved in brick (275); that there be a movie theater to replace the one torn down for the redevelopment; that the building have a restaurant along Beacon Street; and that there be a second-level lobby that would then connect directly to Pemberton Plaza.

Despite these urban design stipulations, One Beacon Street and many other tall buildings outside the Government Center seem way out of scale located in Boston's fine network of small streets and alleyways and typically low buildings.

An exception is Barnes's New England Merchants Bank, which was well sited in the Pei plan: the building leaves a view of the Old State House down a pedestrian street designed by Kallmann and McKinnell (276), and it is well designed into the sloping site by Barnes. Another exception is the carefully studied design solution for the Shawmut Bank by The Architects Collaborative. The tower portion of the building grows out of a base that covers the entire site, reacting sensitively to the divergent street pattern and surrounding buildings (277).

More typical effects of the imposition of these massive buildings can be seen in the 37-story First National Bank Building and the 41-story Boston Company (278, 279). But the real tragedy of insensitive design is the 52-story Prudential Building and its attendant collection of scaleless apartment buildings, all built on the air rights of the Massachusetts Turnpike (280). The Prudential Center is 1½ miles (2.4 km) west of the downtown; but it is at the very edge of the Back Bay area, with its tree-lined shopping streets, its fine red brick buildings, and its height limitation of 70 ft (22 m). The 25-acre (10-ha) Prudential complex is surrounded by a 2-story stone wall, with stairs and escalators every so often leading to a lifeless plaza and stores. It is the very anti-

thesis of all the urban design lessons to be learned from the Back Bay.

It may be impossible for taller new construction to relate to the scale and character at the very center of Boston's downtown area in the sensitive way Kallmann and McKinnell have managed in their design for the Boston Five Cents Savings Bank and its very usable plaza created out of a traffic island (281). With the exceptions noted above, the huge highrises are too massive for the smaller sites and seem best when located on the larger blocks farther away from the oldest section of the downtown.

Now that urban renewal funds have evaporated, Boston has been investigating the uses of incentive zoning, and a "Tremont Street Special District" would be the outgrowth of a report by Bill Fain proposing a new dimension for incentive zoning: tax incentives for the restoration of older buildings.

Because urban renewal funds have evaporated, Boston has investigated the use of incentive zoning as a way to maintain some leverage for the creation and control of public amenities built by the private sector in conjunction with large downtown buildings.

The Tremont Street Special District, though yet to be adopted as city policy, is an outgrowth of a report by David R. Barrett to the BRA on incentive zoning for Boston. Bill Fain, author and architect of the Tremont Street District, drew also on his experience as one of the urban designers on New York's Fifth Avenue Special District and his analysis of urban design policies in San Francisco. Since many of the buildings in the Tremont District are worth preserving, the Fain approach would add a new dimension to the use of incentive zoning—tax incentives for the restoration of older buildings. This is the opposite of the more conventional approach of encouraging larger buildings by increasing the floor areas of new construction through bonuses for the provision of certain amenities. The Tremont District places emphasis on shopping streets, protection of historic buildings, views of historic buildings, and pedestrian amenities (282). It also recommends restricted hours for deliveries, prohi-

276

277

278

279

282

276   The New England Merchant's Bank fits well into the Pei plan (left of City Hall in 272), and the pedestrian street in front of the bank preserves a view of the old State House.

277   The Shawmut Bank, located slightly away from the oldest part of the center, has been carefully designed to relate to the scale of the surrounding buildings.

278-279   The First National Bank Building (278)—known in Boston as the "pregnant building"—and the Boston Company (279) are awkward impositions on the oldest part of the downtown area.

280   The Prudential Center complex, though an economic boost to the city and especially the area surrounding it, has completely ignored the urban design aspects of the Back Bay.

281   Boston Five Cents Savings Bank is a model of urban design sensitivity in the tight downtown area. It may be that buildings in that immediate part of the historic core cannot, or rather should not, be allowed to be much taller than the surrounding buildings.

282   The Tremont Street Special District is an attempt to provide an urban design framework for a specific area. Emphasis is on protecting significant views and preserving historic buildings through tax incentives.

280

281

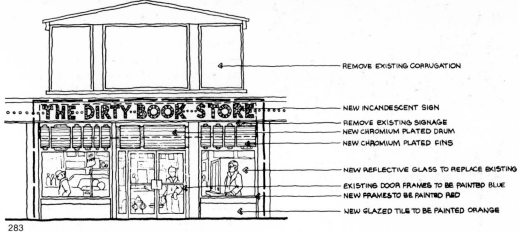

REMOVE EXISTING CORRUGATION

NEW INCANDESCENT SIGN
REMOVE EXISTING SIGNAGE
NEW CHROMIUM PLATED DRUM
NEW CHROMIUM PLATED FINS
NEW REFLECTIVE GLASS TO REPLACE EXISTING
EXISTING DOOR FRAMES TO BE PAINTED BLUE
NEW FRAMES TO BE PAINTED RED
NEW GLAZED TILE TO BE PAINTED ORANGE

283

284

285

283 The BRA offers a free design service for renovation of shop fronts in the city's pornography district.

284-285 Urban renewal funds have helped restore the Quincy Markets to a vibrant commercial center, with great attention to detail (285). There are specialty shops, restaurants, and cafes throughout.

bition of all off-street parking, and a series of street closings within the area.

The concern with urban amenity extends even to the "Combat Zone"; Boston (of all places) has established a "Special Adult Entertainment District" complete with urban design controls and incentives and even a historic preservation effort.

When the old Scollay Square was torn down, so were a variety of shops and cinemas that would inevitably crop up somewhere else—those purveying "adult entertainment." Irony of ironies, the city that made "Banned in Boston" a household phrase has outwitted even liberal old New York by setting aside a special district at the edge of downtown for such use. The appearance of the buildings is strictly regulated to prevent sleazy facades. (By contrast, New York's past policy of harassment made proprietors uncertain of the future and consequently unwilling to invest in assets they couldn't carry away under their raincoats.)

Specifically, Boston's Special Adult Entertainment District law precludes the licensing of a shop which excludes minors in any part of the city other than its clearly delineated 2-block "Combat Zone." The zoning permits flashing lights—forbidden elsewhere in the city. To encourage facade renovation, the BRA offers building owners in the Combat Zone free consultation and even specific designs for storefront rehabilitation and new signs, with working drawings and cost estimates all at no charge (238). In addition, the city has proposed a system of theatrical-type lighting to outline the distinctive architectural characteristics of each building—such as arches. The city has built an attractive minipark in the heart of the Combat Zone, with brick paving, benches, trees, and new lighting; and it is working with local preservation groups to find ways to renovate existing buildings within the district—many of which are late 19th-century commercial structures of significant historic value. In all, it is an enlightened approach towards something that has been a part of every city since Adam and Eve started the first new town.

Landmarks preservation in Boston has generally been an ad hoc affair, but in 1976 a Landmarks Commission was established.

After six years of politicking, Boston finally established a Landmarks Commission in December 1976. Preservationists hope they will now be able to save some of the city's important late 19th- and early 20th-century architecture, which had not previously stood out as historically important in a city as old as Boston.

Prior to establishment of the Landmarks Commission, preservation in Boston was generally on an ad hoc basis. In the center of the city, the Freedom Trail Foundation watched over major points of interest, establishing a walking tour that included the old North Church (1723); Old South Meeting House (1729); Kings Chapel (1749); the Old City Hall (1879); the Old State House (1711); Faneuil Hall (1789); and Paul Revere's House (1681). It is Boston's good fortune that four of these structures are churches and the rest equally sacrosanct, or the walking tour might have included precious little, save for the winding street pattern, to remind future generations of Boston's history.

The Landmarks Commission is not going to have an easy time preserving the city's 19th-century heritage downtown where development pressures are intense. In fact, it was the influence of the developers that significantly altered the final landmarks ordinance to exclude the center from one of the ordinance's toughest features—historic designation of a whole district. Designation in the center must be on a piecemeal, building-by-building basis.

A major preservation achievement, the restoration of Faneuil Hall and Quincy Market, has been accomplished as part of the city's waterfront urban renewal project.

On the brighter side of the preservation problem, the restoration of Faneuil Hall and Quincy Market in the heart of the downtown has now been completed. The three 500-ft (150-m) long market buildings behind Faneuil Hall were built in 1826 to the Greek Revival design of architect Alexander Parris (284). They were originally called the Faneuil Hall Markets but were later renamed Quincy Markets after Mayor Josiah Quincy, who had them built. These structures once housed the city's wholesale markets; the meat and vegetable dealers have since moved to new facilities which have better

286

287

286 The elevated highway cut off the North End from the downtown with a maze of ramps, parking lots, and chain-link fences.

287 In an effort to reverse the negative impact of the highway and regain pedestrian access to the harbor, three ramps have been eliminated from the highway and a straight pedestrian connection (foreground) has been made between the Quincy Markets and the 4-acre (1.6-ha) waterfront park, which was formed by realigning Atlantic Avenue.

access to the region's transportation network.

The BRA and the City of Boston obtained the structures as part of the waterfront urban renewal district. However, the anticipated price tag for the renovation—$20 million—cast doubt on the whole project; that is, until the prestigious James Rouse Company, making a commitment to the future of downtown Boston similar to the one it had made to downtown Philadelphia, agreed to become the developer, with Benjamin Thompson and Associates as architects. Then with a $2.7 million federal preservation grant from HUD for exterior renovation, the project moved steadily to completion. North and South Streets, which were service streets for the markets, have been closed to traffic and now form a pedestrian precinct. There is a combination of brick, cobblestone, and granite paving with trees, flowers, benches, and outdoor cafes (285). The markets contain about 100 restaurants, boutiques, and specialty stores at ground level, with offices located above. Although it is an extremely appealing renovation, some critics charge that it has created a sophistication of ambiance that betrays what had been the market's more humble clientele.

Boston has been as afflicted as any city by elevated highway construction, but it has had perhaps the most remarkable rebound from this kind of problem; three ramps of its monster have actually already been removed from the center; the entire elevated highway through downtown may be taken down and replaced by a submerged highway; and aided by an Urban Mass Transportation Administration grant, the city may create a 10-block auto-free zone in its retail core which will include a $220 million mixed-use development project.

The fragile scale of downtown Boston has been as brutally assaulted as San Francisco's by elevated highway construction. And Boston residents have become as perturbed as San Franciscans about the intrusion of this elevated, blighting monster, which serves so few of the tens of thousands of center city residents. In the process of bringing out-of-towners and their automobiles into town—dead center—the highways spill ramp upon ramp of motorists into historic Boston and at the same time

cut the North End off from the center (286). Those wishing to make what had been a simple walking trip to or from the North End now have to walk a fair distance to find one of the few ways to get past the barrier. Next, they have to walk several steps down to get under the ill-conceived ramps and then by a circuitous route through parked cars and chain link fences before getting a glimpse of daylight. Renewed interest in the center, the North End, and the waterfront have focused directly on the problem of the highway.

To eliminate some of the unnecessary congestion produced in the center, three ramps of the highway were removed. This feat, coupled with a realignment of Atlantic Avenue along the waterfront, has allowed creation of a 4-acre (1.6-ha) park (287), which has a straight pedestrian connection under the highway to Quincy Market, Faneuil Hall, City Hall Plaza, through the Center Plaza Building up to Pemberton Square and the State House, and into the fine streets of Beacon Hill and the Boston Common beyond. This pedestrian route is called "walk to the sea" and suggests how well the Capital Web theory can work in reality.

More impressive, though, is the fact that the entire elevated highway may be taken down in favor of a submerged highway, allowing emphasis on the pedestrian in downtown Boston. Close to 30 percent of the billion-dollar funding needed for this project has been approved at the federal level, and implementation only awaits an environmental impact statement plus review and comment by community groups. The more difficult and costly center portion of the total project has not been approved yet—as what is predicted to be 12 years of construction begins to redress the wrongs of the wasteful and destructive highway program in this historic city.

Community reaction to the continuation of the highway program led Governor Sargent in 1970 to impose a moratorium on all highway construction along Route 128, the circumferential highway that bypasses Boston, pending the findings of a comprehensive transportation study. These findings prompted the Governor's 1972 decision to stop all highway construction within Route 128 and place emphasis on public transit improvements.

288

289

290

291

288 Washington Street Mall is the first attempt to gradually reduce vehicular access in the downtown area.

289-290 Boston's remodeled subway stations: before (289) and after (290) the renovation of Arlington Station.

291 The graphic system developed for Boston's subway has become a model for subways across the country because of its quality and legibility.

Boston was later awarded a demonstration grant from the Urban Mass Transportation Administration (UMTA) to help create an auto-free zone in the heart of the retail core downtown, covering an area of approximately 10 blocks, or about 15 percent of the downtown. The proposed pedestrian precinct will include a $220 million development project consisting of a new department store for Jordon Marsh, other retail facilities, a hotel and office space, and a 1,500-space parking garage to replace the number of spaces removed (federal law allows replacement only of removed spaces).

Through the BRA, the city has made a commitment to build a variety of public improvements in the area. To accomplish these projects, voters approved an $11.2 million bond issue. The first city undertaking paid for by the bond issue is the Washington Street Mall located in the heart of the downtown shopping district. Senior BRA architect John Sloan drafted guidelines, and the architectural office of Arrowstreet produced the final design. The first phase of the project narrows the three lanes of traffic along a 2 block stretch of Washington Street down to two lanes, thereby enabling both sidewalks to be 20 ft (6 m) wide. A plexiglass canopy has been placed over sidewalks not already protected (288). It is a modest proposal based on a compromise—it still allows two lanes of automobile traffic in deference to the wishes of the merchants, and it has one lay-by lane for deliveries. If the first phase is successful—that is, if no unmanageable traffic problems ensue—then the roadway will further be reduced to only one traffic lane.

The scale of the center of Boston is perhaps the most analogous of all U.S. center cities to that of many European cities. It is ideally suited to a vast program of pedestrianization similar to those instituted in more than 100 European centers. Such a program could place Boston in an enviable position for a U.S. city. But in many ways, Washington Street illustrates the problems such an endeavor would confront. Plans to make Washington Street a pedestrian mall have been afoot for more than 14 years. The plan still permits automobiles; and in fact, by allowing a 1,500-space garage, the plan can be said to encourage the automobile. Few retailers are willing to gamble that public transportation can comfortably and safely bring shoppers downtown.

It is believed that Boston's mass transit system could handle substantially increased ridership if there were a forced shift away from the automobile. The system could accomplish this goal by running longer trains, by having new trains with more doors (Boston has been purchasing new subway and trolley cars), by running trains more frequently, and by encouraging the expansion of staggered working hours. These are but a few of the technical adjustments that could be made to accommodate ridership.

And Boston's subway system has never looked better (289, 290). The stations have almost all been remodeled in accordance with standards established by the Cambridge Seven architects under contract from the MBTA (with two-thirds of the funding coming from the federal government). The graphic system is one of the most comprehensive and sophisticated ever produced for a U.S. transit system (291). The four main lines have been color coded, and trains, stations, and signs are painted in accordance with the particular color for that particular route.

One problem in Boston (it is a characteristic problem of most cities) can be seen in a lack of continuity of commitment by city government. As in the case of the Washington Street project, there have been numerous project directors over the years. Each one pushes the proposal so far. And even if it arrives at a point where it is thought to be public policy, once the director of any particular project moves on to something else—another job, another city—the more permanent civil servants in the bureaucracy may focus on a completely different set of priorities—often deliberately to avoid the more controversial projects like street closings.

Without the kind of commitment that Edmund Bacon made to Philadelphia, these more difficult projects will too often remain unbuilt.

Atlanta

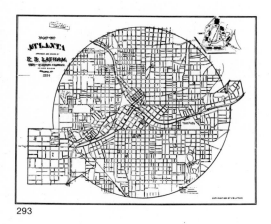

293

Atlanta's growth as a major center can be attributed to the architect/developer John Portman's commitment to the downtown and his unique design and development of hotels and office buildings which include major interior and exterior spaces of a scale and quality heretofore unheard of in speculative development. The success of Portman's buildings has been so great that, to compete for business in downtown Atlanta, four large developers have all felt obligated to follow Portman's design concepts in their projects to attract users; and hotel design all over the country has been strongly influenced.

Population and geography
With only a few major interruptions—like when Sherman burned Atlanta to the ground towards the close of the Civil War and the filming of "Gone With the Wind"—Atlanta has grown to a population of 457,000 in an area of 136 sq miles (350 sq km). Exclusive of Atlanta, its seven-county almost 2,000-sq mile (5,000-sq-km) region in northwest Georgia has a population of 1,200,000. In the downtown section of Atlanta (292) an estimated 100,000 people work; 30 percent come to work by public transportation—that is, by bus, until Atlanta's new rapid transit system is completed. The remaining 70 percent come to work by automobile.

Historical development
The pressure to open up northwestern Georgia, which eventually led to the creation of Atlanta as the center of a vast unexplored region and later the state capital, coincided with a series of conditions and events in the first half of the 19th century.

Settled in the early 18th century a short distance inland from the Atlantic Ocean, Savannah was Georgia's principal city, another in a string of early U.S. cities on the important eastern seaboard. Large landholdings by a few wealthy landlords, who depended on slave labor, frustrated the desires of many would-be small farmers. But where could they go? All the potential farmland of northwestern Georgia was an Indian reservation under the auspices of the U.S. government, where the Creeks and the Cherokees lived, separated by the Chattahoochee River.

Pressures mounted within Georgia to relocate the Indians—preferably just across the state's western border. Other Southern states were sympathetic to Georgia's claim that the U.S. government in guaranteeing the sovereignty of Indian reservations was superseding the right of states to govern their own internal affairs. The collective strength of the Southern states was sufficient for Congress to pass a law in 1827 providing for the removal of all Indians not just across Georgia's western border, but 700 miles (1,100 km) across the border to the all-new Indian territory. It took 10 years for Georgia to enforce the eviction notice, which by then affected the remaining 15,000 Cherokees. While the Indians were reluctantly packing, the state began surveying the Indian holdings. Thousands gathered at the edge of the Cherokee Nation waiting for the original inhabitants to begin their long trek across the United States. A rough winter coupled with several epidemics made it a journey, known as "The Trail of Tears," which one-quarter of the Indians would not finish.

292   Of the 100,000 people who work in downtown Atlanta, 65 percent come by automobile.

293   Atlanta grew without a predetermined plan. Instead, lots were parceled out in gridlike patterns between either the radiating network of trails or railroad lines. Characteristic of early towns in Georgia, Atlanta originally comprised a circular area with a 1-mile (1.6-km) radius.

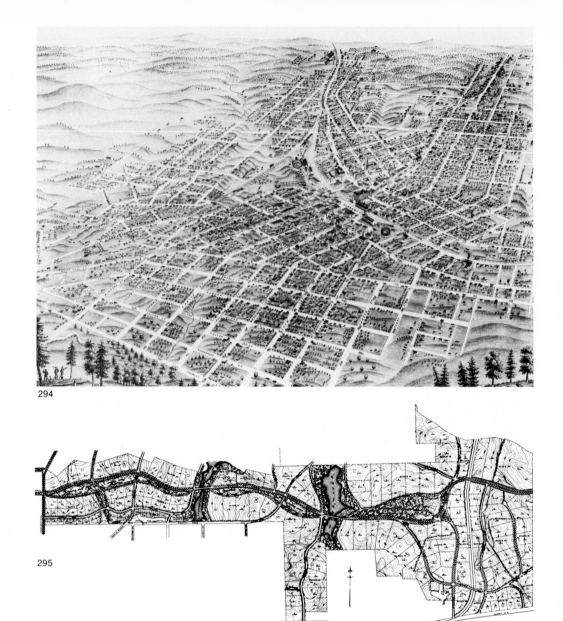

294

295

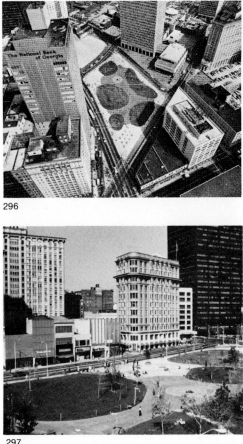

296

297

With the Indians departed, the new occupants began to systematically mine the region's gold—a major source of interest. Cotton too became an important crop and sparked railroad construction. By 1836 a survey established a point between a series of ridges 7 miles (11 m) southeast of the Chattahoochee River as the ideal termination of two railroads within Georgia then under construction: one from Augusta, the other from Macon. Several other railroads would eventually radiate from that point, which would become the distribution center of the southeastern United States. The dot on the map was appropriately named Terminus. The state further agreed to construct a railroad that would connect Terminus north to the Tennessee River where it would meet a railroad then under construction from Cincinnati.

When Terminus outgrew an early prophesy that it would only be "a good location for one tavern, a blacksmith shop, a grocery store, and nothing else"[1]—that is, when Terminus was no longer merely a terminal but actually a town—its name was changed to Marthasville in honor of the daughter of one of the state's favorite sons. A good idea at first, but a little folksy once the real significance of the town was apparent. By 1845 Marthasville was renamed Atlanta—supposedly a feminine version of Atlantic—that would continue to symbolize the terminus of the Western and Atlantic Railroad.

With the Indians removed, the railroads in place, and its new name intact, Atlanta began to grow—not to any predetermined plan, for early inhabitants steadfastly refused to allow the city administrators to survey the land in any ordered way, fearing the cost of this procedure would increase taxes. Instead they continued to build on sites gerrymandered along old Indian trails and cowpaths. The major trails and some of the cowpaths met at a spring adjacent to an area called "Five Points" that even today is considered the center of downtown Atlanta (293, 294).

In fact, growth during Atlanta's 140-year history has never conformed to an overall plan. The city does, however, have several residential sections, which in themselves capture the spirit of the popular late 19th-century planning movement in the north,

which sought to preserve natural features of the landscape.

In the early 1890s Daniel Burnham was designing the Equitable Building in Atlanta, and upon his recommendation the developer engaged Frederick Law Olmsted to design a residential section called "Inland Park." This was the beginning of many projects Olmsted's office designed in Atlanta—most notably Druid Hills, a 1,400-acre (560-ha) suburb with parkways throughout (295).

Lamentably, none of Olmsted's efforts pierced the downtown area the way Central Park does in New York. And until very recently, when an anonymous donor contributed $13 million for central city parks, Atlanta was without significant open space downtown. Most of the gift went to clear a grouping of older buildings adjacent to Five Points. The resultant Central City Park designed by the city's own parks department staff—very far from the spirit of Olmsted's work—was deliberately designed with no benches to avoid loitering. People make do as best they can sitting on berms of grass, steps, and retaining walls. What qualities the park may have are weakened by the nature of the surrounding buildings—especially the Trust Company of Georgia, which sits on its own plaza and does little to relate to the park across the street (296, 297).

It is mainly private initiative in Atlanta rather than public responsibility that creates plans for downtown Atlanta, and this may very well be the preference of the business community. Through the Central Atlanta Progress (CAP), the planning arm of the business community, designs presented are seemingly altruistic, but obviously are what the business community perceives to be in its own interests. In the guide book to Atlanta, put out by the Atlanta chapter of the American Institute of Architects, H. Randal Roark says that "Atlanta is a private city and history has shown that the public hasn't spent the money on itself if it hasn't had to."[2] Both the Central City Park and the Georgia Trust Company building would tend to support this view, as would the unbuilt 1909 Bleckley plan to deck over the railroad tracks downtown.

It was apparent at the turn of the century that the increasing railroad traffic could not

294   Burned down during the Civil War, Atlanta by 1871 was once again a thriving town.

295   Although Olmsted designed several subdivisions in parklike settings in the Atlanta area, the city did not benefit from a large urban park like those Olmsted was so famous for designing in San Francisco, Chicago, and New York.

296-297   With a private donation, the city has built Central City Park, though surrounding buildings—like the Trust Company of Georgia (shown at the top of 296)—make it a poorly defined space. The park itself was deliberately designed with few places to sit, but people make do as best they can.

298

299

300

301

298 The unbuilt 1909 Bleckley plan offered a comprehensive approach to decking over the railroad tracks.

299 Ultimately, only a system of the most basic viaducts was built above the railroads.

300 The Equitable Building is typical of recent construction that relates more to a simplified version of modern structures than to the historic shape of the actual site.

301 No doubt older buildings, like the Georgia Savings Bank (1897), were built to lot lines more for reasons of economics than aesthetics. Historically, though, this is a basic principle for more clearly defined public streets and spaces.

coexist with all the other surface traffic. Architect Haralson Bleckley, having studied in Paris, produced a scheme in the City Beautiful/Beaux-Arts tradition, which showed how the city could establish a new level above the railroad tracks, much as the New York Central Railroad did over the New York City tracks when it decked over them to create Park Avenue. Bleckley's proposed concrete platform would also have provided tree-lined walkways, boulevards, and fountains (298). In 1928 when it finally came time to actually do something, the body of Bleckley's plan was ignored for its skeleton: a system of viaducts creating the new street level (299). New buildings went where the open space was to be in the plan, and older buildings closed their lower levels and opened second-level shops. In 1968 a 4-block section of the lower level was reopened. Called Underground Atlanta, it quicky became a tourist attraction providing needed nightlife activity for the downtown.

Newer buildings in the oldest parts of the downtown, like the Trust Company of Georgia and SOM's Equitable Building, defy the contorted street network and are often built as rectangular towers despite the shape of the sites (300). So the many elegant buildings of the past, like Bradford Gilbert's 1897 Georgia Savings Bank, may unfortunately be urban design solutions of the past as well (301).

Atlanta's zoning has focused mainly on separation of "incompatible" uses and does little to limit very large developments, reflecting an official intent to let market demand exert its influence.

Atlanta and Houston are but two of several Southern cities in the midst of a Southern renaissance experiencing dramatic increases in economic productivity. Unlike Houston, though, Atlanta does use zoning as a tool to regulate development. The adoption of zoning in Atlanta in 1922 was primarily to separate or zone incompatible uses from one another. Separating incompatible uses in Atlanta at that time, and in fact until very recently, meant separating blacks from whites. Residential districts fell into three categories: "white, colored, and undetermined." Large swatches of land were zoned as commercial districts. There

was no need for so much commercial area, but it served as an effective buffer between the different residential "uses." Railroad tracks also provided ideal barriers. Where railroad tracks did not exist, streets were dead-ended, and the few streets that did connect black and white areas changed names as they changed districts.

Those parts of the zoning that managed to deal with buildings did not restrict a developer from building as much as he wanted of a permitted use on a particular downtown site. The 1954 zoning change did limit the total square footage of a downtown building to 25 times the land area of the site (FAR 25). This, as has been seen in many other cities, was hardly any control at all. Height and setback requirements were introduced but repealed a few years later. The main purpose of the 1954 zoning ordinance was to produce a uniform zoning code over the 82 sq miles (210 sq km) annexed in 1952.

Presently, the city is about to propose a new ordinance that would slightly reduce the FAR from 25 to 20 at the center of the downtown, where two major subway lines will cross, and down to FAR 16 in a surrounding zone also serviced by subway stops. Even with these reductions, the zoning is close to what New York City allows and will do little to limit extremely large developments. City officials admit to being leery of regulating too strictly beyond the very general bulk limitations and take a position of allowing the market demand to influence development, including ground-floor uses.[3]

On a few streets, however, the zoning will insist that developers either set back proposed buildings or provide an arcade at the base of the building to increase pedestrian space. Other than that, the plan allows developers to connect to adjacent buildings at various levels, by various means, such as the bridge connections common in Minneapolis. But the city neither insists on nor encourages a developer to make these connections.

The resurgence of downtown Atlanta, especially as a convention city rivaling the attractions of New York and Chicago, is rightly attributable to architect John Portman. But that might be the smallest part of his contribution to urban design, for

he has not only redefined what modern architecture can be but also reworked what might be the architect's involvement in this new definition.

By parlaying his fees into part of an equity investment in the projects he was designing, John Portman has created a large architecture office plus the real estate development firm of Portman Properties. Portman's serving as the architect for much of the real estate side of the ledger led the American Institute of Architects' ethics committee to investigate possible conflicts of interest. Traditionally it had been believed that if the architect served as developer he would know better than most where to cut corners to minimize costs—which might mean minimal quality—in order to maximize profits. In this way, as the conventional wisdom had it, the architect would endanger his or her advocacy role for quality and the larger concerns for the community that transcend the usually narrow scope of developers.

In working for developers, architects are often put in an adversary position and therefore must be especially good at selling, which may explain why the profession puts so much emphasis on presentation techniques. Once the developer sees through the camouflage and understands what the architect is doing or what it is costing the developer (in smaller profits), the developer is likely to take out his trusty pink eraser, causing many a stern-faced architect to weep.

John Portman is a good salesman, but he knew that wasn't enough. After 10 years of his intense building activity in several American cities, the rest of the profession could only look with envy at the work of this man. For it is work on a scale, of a quality, and with the types of spaces most architects can only fantasize the opportunity to build as they putter across France in their Volkswagens taking pictures of Gothic cathedrals. (It was the belief that such spaces were no longer possible because of modern financing limitations and the dearth of royal patrons that caused several internationally renowned architects to independently come to a design philosophy that makes the building a cohesive whole by designing its circulation systems in innovative ways.)

Accordingly, there has been no censure of Portman's practice, but rather an admonition to the rest of the profession that it might be not only in the interests of the profession, but of society at large, for architects to emulate the Portman approach. Besides as only the naive in the profession learned in the scandals involving government contracts for work in Maryland, the very nature of an architect's subservient relationship with developers can place architects in a vulnerable exploitative situation.

Portman has reversed the rules and probably has dozens of developers across the country cursing him for it. In Atlanta alone, Portman's impact on all hotel and office projects has been profound. There are four major developments in or near the downtown. All are probably much larger in scale and vastly more expensive than a developer in any other city, let alone Atlanta, would previously ever have contemplated. But in Atlanta, Portman's multiuse Peachtree Center, and especially its huge flamboyant public spaces, has set the tone with which other developers must compete. And to compete, the base line of the four major developments—Omni International, Atlanta Center, Peachtree Summit, and Colony Square—is the concept of multiuse buildings with large enclosed public spaces. The clear aim of these other developments is to out-Portman Portman. Only in this way could they hope to capture a share of the hotel and office market as Portman's Peachtree Center itself continues to expand. If the economy is not quite right, the developer may get hurt worse than before; but the public has gained some remarkable, well-thought-out urban spaces that were designed to lure them there. (It is also a far cry from the schlock developers have been allowed to build in most American cities.)

It is easy to nit-pick about certain Portman design details or even to disagree more substantively over some urban design aspects of his projects. However, Portman must first be put into a larger perspective that duly recognizes the ingenious way he has approached his work. As an architect-developer he has given many architects the upper hand in large-scale development—the upper hand in the sense of finally being able to incorporate urban spaces—to design for human enjoyment—without fear of having the developer slap the architect's hand or, worse yet, have the job given to another less ambitious architect.

Whether all architects who exercise their new powers will be as sensitive in using them as Portman has been in most of his work remains to be seen. But in Atlanta, developers are going to prestigious design-oriented firms to undertake their large-scale plans.

As important as this change of roles for architects may be, the central theme is financing. And this is where Portman has performed his greatest service to the profession. He has proven what many in the profession have long suspected: the quality of architecture is tied directly to a developer's attitude about financing. (Of course, it would be a mistake here to minimize the role of a conservative banker.) Most developers have little of their own money in a development—none, in fact, in the case of an extremely competent developer. (As Harvard real estate economist Mort Zuckerman puts it, "A developer is a person who would marry Elizabeth Taylor for her money.") The central issue is how much can be borrowed, at what rates, and for how long. If the project is to cost $100 million, why not $105 million? With good credit comes higher, longer-term borrowing at lower interest rates. So Portman has not only shown architects how to do it, but he has set a standard that many developers must follow if their creations are to be financially successful and that bankers must back if they too wish to continue to have a piece of the action. It is not too difficult to imagine the ripple effect of this approach on housing and other building types.

Peachtree Center, Portman's main work in Atlanta, is just a few blocks north of the older downtown area. It has much of the same elegance and sense of urbanity as upper Michigan Avenue in Chicago. It is one of the few large-scale developments in the United States that comes even close to the quality of Rockefeller Center, after which it is obviously patterned.

Today Peachtree Center is a collection of five major office buildings ranging in size from 25 to 31 stories; two hotels—one of which, the 70-story Peachtree Center Plaza,

is billed as the tallest in the world—each with the interior atrium space that has become Portman's trademark; a 22-story, 2 million-sq-ft (190,000-sq-m) Merchandise Mart; a bus terminal with a 1,000-car parking garage and another 500-car parking garage; a 6-story 135,000-sq-ft (12,700-sq-m) glass-enclosed shopping galleria; and a 475-seat dinner theater (302). Plans call for additional retail space that will connect to the future Peachtree Center rapid transit stop and a major legitimate theater atop the bus terminal garage. If Portman gets his way (there is little reason to assume he won't), several hundred units of housing will also be built. To date, the project spans a 5-square-block area. All buildings are connected either by underground or ground-level shopping concourses or overhead bridges (303, 304, 305).

The architecture is a curious, sometimes kitsch, usually successful blend of the styles of Le Corbusier, Mies van der Rohe, and Frank Lloyd Wright. But in the end it is Portman.

Portman's promotion of, and financial interest in, the highly successful Merchandise Mart is what got Peachtree Center off the ground. It was a gamble on a facility that to work had to attract and service the commercial needs of 11 southeastern states. And it was a commitment to the viability of downtown Atlanta made in the midst of the move to the suburbs. Says Portman, "We must not erode the tax base of the city. The suburbs can't keep us alive."[4]

The gamble worked, attracting in 1961, its first year of operation, 50,000 buyers—and by 1975 well over 200,000 buyers. Although the Merchandise Mart was deliberately built in an area that already had hotels, it was clear to Portman that more hotels were needed. So up went the Hyatt Regency. Despite Conrad Hilton's observation of the hotel under construction, "That concrete monster will never fly,"[5] it flew. And it fostered a minor revolution in the hotel industry. With it all came heavy doses of Portman's philosophy: the hotel is a microcosm of the city. The atrium space is the "city square," complete with fountains, flowers, sculpture, and cafes. The square is surrounded by the dwelling units (hotel rooms), community rooms (meeting

302

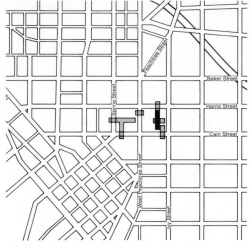

303

Scale: ⅛ in. represents 200 ft

☐ Bridge
■ Underground tunnel

304

305

302   The resurgence of downtown Atlanta owes much to John Portman's Peachtree Center development.

303-304   Buildings in Peachtree Center are connected by overhead bridges or underground and ground-level shopping concourses.

305   Much of the sense of urbanity often associated with Rockefeller Center has been captured here.

306

307

rooms), and there are shops and restaurants throughout. Maybe. But the overall combination of all the buildings—hotels *and* offices *and* housing *and* industry *and* so on —with their interior *and* exterior spaces, interior *and* exterior shops, cafes, restaurants, and bridges, would seem to come closer to a paradigm of a city. Currently, over 15,000 people work in Portman's city, not counting hotel guests and visitors.

In the case of the Hyatt Regency atrium, the city square is a 21-story high space, 120 by 120 ft (36 by 36 m) (306). Across West Peachtree Street and a block or so south is the 70-story Peachtree Center Plaza Hotel and its glass-enclosed 5-story space that wraps about the base of the circular tower that houses the hotel rooms (307, 308, 309). It is an undeniably dramatic and exciting space with generous seating at the different overhanging levels. Seating areas at the lowest level literally seem to float in a pool of water.

Detractors have characterized much of the Portman style as Disneylandish. Meant to be a derogatory remark, it reflects a failure to understand Portman's accomplishments. Still, Portman himself does not object to the term, since both Disneyland and his own creations seem to provide a framework in which people *do* enjoy themselves. Both of Portman's Atlanta hotels come close to fulfilling Maki's idea about city rooms. Portman's words and especially his deeds show his spaces to be public rooms which are not intimidating, though they could be more easily accessible.

For the most part Portman's buildings fill their entire sites—usually whole blocks. This is because the stress is on the internal spaces. And no wonder. Portman's favorite building is New York City's Guggenheim Museum. His favorite place for ambiance is Copenhagen's Tivoli gardens. And for street life it's the sidewalk cafes of Paris. It is this last point on which some nit-picking might be in order and where there may be a contradiction between what Portman claims he aspires to create and what an observer borrowing Jane Jacobs' eyes for a few moments might see and therefore dispute. As noted, Portman buildings usually come right up to the existing sidewalks, which they almost all do along West

Peachtree Street. They are all oriented to bring the potential user inside, for there are very few ground-level shops—although it would seem there could be many. Perhaps this is intentional so as not to compete with the large amount of interior shopping that must be rented. But a New Yorker or a Chicagoan, while relishing the exciting interior spaces, might be a little disappointed at the exterior street level.

Look closely at the two hotels, for example. The entire frontage of the Hyatt Regency is devoted to a driveway for drop-offs and pick-ups, thus there are two breaks in the sidewalk for private automobiles and taxis, which serve mainly out-of-towners (310). The 5-story base building that fills the entire site for the Peachtree Center Plaza is all concrete. Therefore the animation of a building wall with windows is lost. The section through the building indicates plenty of opportunities for windows, which would no doubt make the interior spaces more pleasant (311, 312). The concrete wall, then, is a deliberate gesture meant to lure the unsuspecting into the total surprise inside. Except for the intentionally small entrance to the Peachtree Center Plaza Hotel along West Peachtree Street, the rest of the frontage is devoted to a long, low, concrete bench, which is pleasant enough and is protected by a canopy above. Behind the benches are display windows for shops inside the building. But these are not Paris sidewalks! This is precisely the way Portman went awry of urban designers in New York. In his proposed hotel for Times Square, there is a glass-enclosed cafe on Broadway, but the rest of the building was to be raised on columns. The result would be a loss of ground-floor retail space, and therefore none of the accustomed street activity which is so much a part of New York City life.

Immediately south of Peachtree Center is Davidson's, a major department store in the midst of a shopping street. The Peachtree Center Plaza does have an interior connection to Davidson's. Portman might argue, though, with some justification that the disintegration of downtown Atlanta over the past few years has left little urban pattern to emulate or build upon.

Most cities enthusiastically welcome Portman's grand vision for the city's future,

306   The Hyatt Regency was the first contemporary hotel to feature the now well-known Portman trademark: a large glass-covered atrium space.

307   The latest addition to Peachtree Center is the Peachtree Plaza Hotel.

308

309

310

311

308-309   The interior of the Peachtree Plaza Hotel offers a series of overlapping balconies and seating areas "floating" on water.

310   In general, the sidewalks in and about Peachtree Center are designed more for the service functions of a building than for pedestrian-generating activities.

311-312   Lower floors of the Peachtree Plaza Hotel are encased in concrete—clearly intended to lure the pedestrian into the exciting interior space. Still, that is at the direct expense of providing a more animated facade and therefore a more active and interesting streetscape.

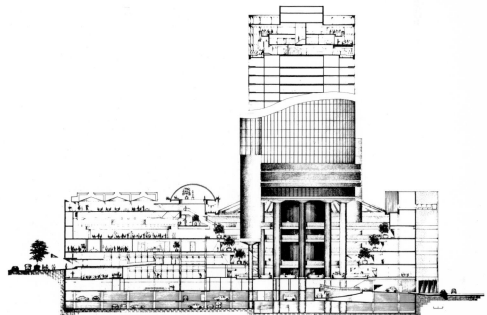
312

313

314

313 Omni International is built above railroad tracks at the edge of the center. The area of the major space is outlined by the skylights. Its relationship to Peachtree Center can be seen in 302—it is to the right and behind the cylindrical Peachtree Plaza Hotel.

314 Evidently, to compete with Peachtree Center, developers in Atlanta have found it necessary to build mixed-use complexes with emphasis on big interior spaces. The Omni International has created just such a space, active in itself and surrounded by shops, restaurants, a hotel, offices, and a major amusement center.

315 Peachtree Summit has the appearance of a sleek piece of urban sculpture, but urbanistically it has been designed to fit its site and to connect to the future subway. The subway will actually be built on this section of West Peachtree Street, creating a new street level above the subway.

316 Peachtree Summit has provided a multilevel lobby space. Another such space, with shopping, will be built across the highway to be north, thereby connecting to a second office tower.

316

315

for the vision is tied to an immense economic shot in the arm, and the finished building or complex is a tourist attraction for years to come. Whether it is always in the city's best urban design interests that buildings be constructed precisely as Portman has designed them is the subject of intense debate. Of the cities surveyed here, New York and San Francisco have the most restrictive urban design policies, which are directly tied to their own vision of their future. In both these cities Portman has had to moderate his vision to fit what experienced urban designers felt were more appropriate urban solutions given a different understanding of the nature of those cities. Nitpicking? Perhaps. But still critical aspects of such large-scale urban work.

Five blocks west of Peachtree Center is Omni International, an expansive complex of buildings on a 34-acre (13.6-ha) air-rights site above railroad tracks.

The complex has a 2,000-car parking garage and the 18,000-seat Omni Sports Coliseum. Spurred on by the acceptability of building on the edge of downtown, the developers—International City Corporation—retained the architects who designed the coliseum (Thompson, Ventulett and Stainback) when they approached the next and most ambitious part of the project, the Omni International.

What the architects like to call a 14-story multiuse megastructure, the Omni International is a grouping of four major buildings around a huge enclosed space (313, 314). The buildings consist of two office structures, with a total of 480,000 sq ft (45,500 sq m); a 472-room hotel; and the 8-story fantasy "World of Sid and Marty Krofft," where adults are as amused and entertained as children. The buildings are connected by glass walls between them and interconnected at the base by several levels of shops occupying 200,000 sq ft (19,000 sq m) of space and overlooking an olympic-size ice skating rink. Besides the shops, which read like a who's who of Via Condotti, there are also 6 movie theaters and 10 restaurants. And there are glass-enclosed elevators à la Portman, an 8-story escalator to the upper level of Sid and Marty's World, balconies off hotel rooms and corridors, and lighting sculptures day and night.

While on the exterior the buildings have some shop windows, the complex is very much like Portman's architecture—an internally oriented scheme. The very nature of the surrounding buildings—the coliseum and the newly completed Georgia World Congress Center for state conventions and trade fairs—may dictate this approach, although the architects may have been more influenced by the nature of that area of the city which, along with the railroad tracks, is rather rundown and dilapidated.

Three blocks north of Peachtree Center, which places it eight blocks north of Five Points and puts it at the edge of the interstate freeway, is Peachtree Summit, another ambitious office project in the special tradition that Atlanta may become famous for.

Market conditions will probably reduce an earlier master plan calling for three office towers to two. The first tower, designed by architects Toombs, Amisano and Wells, is now complete and virtually fills its triangular site along West Peachtree Street at the southern edge of the freeway. Although at first glance it appears to be yet another building designed as a piece of sleek sculpture (315), its overall urban design aspects make it a significant, thoughtful urban complex.

With a 3-story glass-enclosed garden at its base (316), the building is designed to connect directly with the future rapid transit stop. Because of a combination of conditions in that area—including the topography, which is higher downtown and falls away towards Peachtree Summit, and the presence of the submerged freeway—this particular section of the rapid transit line will actually be constructed directly on West Peachtree Street. And in the tradition of Atlanta, a new street will be built above. Peachtree Summit is designed accordingly, and will also serve as an interchange between the transit station and a smaller people-mover the transit authority will construct from the eastern edge of Peachtree Summit to the existing Civic Center several blocks further east. The pedestrian connection between these two transit facilities will be through another three-level glass-enclosed shopping area built above the air rights of the freeway; the shopping area will

317

318

317 MARTA is Atlanta's attempt to reduce dependence on the automobile. Partial service will begin in 1981.

318 Munich's *Kaufingerstrasse* may be a valid model for the type of urban street MARTA could help make possible in downtown Atlanta.

also serve as a link between the existing office tower and the future tower on the northern side of the freeway.

A new metropolitan rapid transit system offers the prospect of significant stimulus to downtown revitalization, the first major commitment of public funds to stem the deterioration of Atlanta's older core.

Like Peachtree Summit, Peachtree Center and Omni International are both built adjacent to future rapid transit stops. And although all these projects have provided large amounts of parking, it is the success of the rapid transit that may determine the future viability of these and other large real estate ventures.

MARTA (Metropolitan Atlanta Rapid Transit Authority) came into being when voters in the two-county area in which Atlanta is located approved a referendum in 1971 for a metropolitan-wide bus and rapid transit proposal. Two other surrounding counties—far more rural in nature—turned the proposal down. In short, the voters approved a 1 percent sales tax increase, half of which enabled MARTA to purchase the privately owned and operated bus company, buy new buses, build park-and-ride facilities, reorganize bus routes, and lower the 40-cent fare (plus 5 cents for a transfer) to 15 cents, with a free transfer between buses and/or subways, among other things. In fact, the referendum established by law the 15-cent bus fare, regardless of the length of the ride until 1979. For each of the three years after 1979, the fare will increase 5 cents until it reaches 30 cents, since, as also required by the same law, the fare by that time must cover at least half of the system's operating costs. Since the 1972 fare reduction, bus ridership for work trips has increased by 25 percent and for nonwork trips by 38 percent.

The other half of the revenues produced by the 1 percent sales tax increase goes towards the city's share of the construction costs of the rapid transit system. The 54 miles (86 km) of track is in essentially two major rail lines, portions of which are either below grade, at grade, or elevated. The two lines cross in the downtown at Five Points. The first phase of about 14 miles (22 km) should be in service by 1981 and the re-

maining 40 miles (64 km) by about 1985. Buses will be rerouted to service the transit stops (317).

MARTA plans to close several streets in the vicinity of the Five Points station to accommodate the heavy pedestrian traffic. Following MARTA's lead, the city's planning office has proposed closing the rest of West Peachtree Street north as far as the end of Peachtree Center to create a pedestrian mall without buses or cars but accessible for emergency vehicles and certain deliveries. Both Davidson's management and Portman oppose the proposed mall, contending that automobile accessibility is essential to the vitality of the street. The city claims merchants in the older downtown section favor the mall. A compromise solution may be in order which at least allows buses and service, for the street does seem very wide to be only for pedestrian use. But there are fine examples in Europe, especially Munich's Kaufingerstrasse/Neuhauserstrasse, where the street, as an exclusive pedestrian environment between two rapid transit stops—as would be the case in Atlanta—works extremely well (318).

What does seem to be most important here is the commitment of public funds to stem a deteriorating core. The large-scale new development projects are necessarily where assemblage of larger contiguous land parcels at lower prices is feasible—outside the older center. So development dollars have shifted attention away from the core, leaving it stagnant. MARTA, the work of Central Atlanta Progress and the city's street improvement program may reverse this trend and spark redevelopment and renovation of smaller parcels within the older downtown.

Minneapolis

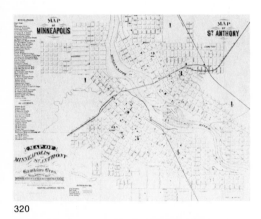

320

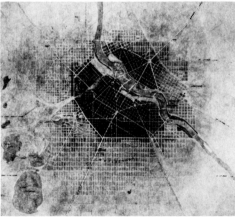

321

319   This view of Minneapolis illustrates the all too familiar condition of American downtown areas—a handsome region abruptly terminating in parking lots. Of the 82,500 people who work in downtown Minneapolis, 50 percent drive there and the other half come by bus.

320   As the city grew, the 1855 grid plan was constantly adjusted to accommodate the bends of the Mississippi River.

321   Edward Bennett's 1917 plan for Minneapolis featured the best of Vienna and Paris, but was shelved for want of a king to carry it out.

Minneapolis is one of the most successful examples in the U.S. of the cooperative efforts of private and public agencies working together to provide an urban design structure that has dramatically transformed the quality of life in the downtown. The two major developments are the skyway system, which connects almost all the major buildings at an upper level by bridges, and the Nicollet Mall, which has become a national model for the quality of urban streets American downtowns should try to achieve.

Population and geography
Minneapolis and St. Paul (the Twin Cities) form the nucleus of a 600-sq-mile (1,550-sq-km) metropolitan area housing 1.8 million people. The physical structure of Minneapolis, even with a population of only about 400,000 people in an area of 59 sq miles (153 sq km), is still similar to most larger American cities; but perhaps because of its small scale, its incongruities are more apparent. From the air, a virtual forest of trees ends abruptly at a sea of cars surrounding the compact downtown area (319).

Downtown Minneapolis is an 8-block-square area. Each block of its formal grid is 330 ft (100 m) to a side, with 80 ft (24 m) of street and sidewalk between blocks. Within this core approximately 82,500 people work, half of them commuting by bus and the other half by automobile.

Historical development
Like Mark Twain, Minneapolis grew up around the Mississippi River. A regional center for lumbering and milling, the rapidly expanding and prospering city in 1855 established a grid plan to regulate its growth (320). The grid proved flexible, easily adjusting itself to the bends of the river.

In 1917, Minneapolis commissioned Edward H. Bennett to design a new master plan. Bennett, envisioning Minneapolis as a composite of Vienna and Paris, produced yet another in his series of City Beautiful plans (321). Alas, this City Beautiful was not to be, or surely the world would know more about Minneapolis than it does.

More recently, plans reflecting the modern perspective about city centers—with people-movers, active riverfronts, and a whole host of other urban treats—were generated under a variety of programs sponsored by the National Endowment for the Arts. The plans, however, go begging for other federal agencies to help finance their implementation.

The city's Metro Center '85 master plan, produced under the direction of Weiming Lu, may be appealing (like most master plans); but it does not necessarily represent public policy. As a compilation of city history, resources, and the activities of public and private agencies, it is a useful document and has served as a guide to the formulation of some policies, enabling the city to organize the divergent planning activities of different city agencies. As a start the city has passed a Development District Bill, which has procedures and powers similar to urban renewal, and a historic preservation bill. Still pending is a bill empowering the Department of Development and Planning to create design districts, as in New York, with review powers for buildings in special locations, as in San Francisco.

322

323

322 Nicollet Mall was designed to allow the Northwestern National Life Insurance Building to serve as a terminus. In its quest for grandeur, the building eluded its urbanistic responsibilities.

323 The mall serves as a viable model for what many U.S. downtowns could be like. The exclusive bus lane represents the importance of buses that radiate from the mall to every part of the city.

The FAR per building in Minneapolis—with all possible premiums—could reach 35, twice that of New York.

In downtown Minneapolis, the basic FAR is 14. In addition, there are bonuses for through-block walkways, exterior and interior arcades, plazas, connections to parking garages, off-street passenger loading, and off-street freight loading. In some cities, many of the same items that are rewarded in Minneapolis are required as essential features of a building without bonuses. Although the average building does not appear to exceed the basic FAR of 14, this zoning does allow some extraordinarily large buildings to occur and reduces the city's leverage in achieving a coherent urban design policy within which each new building would fit.

The 8-block Nicollet Mall—approximately ⅔ mile (1.1 km) long—occupies the heart of Minneapolis's shopping district. And although perhaps the least of the mall's objectives, it is the first example of what much of downtown Minneapolis and, for that matter, the downtowns of many similar American cities could be like.

For the first time in Minneapolis's recent history, the city's undulating and densely green landscape penetrates the center, and a balance is struck between the automobile and the bus, with buses having an exclusive right-of-way on the mall in a final recognition of their vital role in the city's transportation system, limited as it is.

The Nicollet Mall was the brainchild of the business community which in 1955, organized itself into an effective lobby called the "Downtown Council." Shortly thereafter, the Downtown Council was instrumental in revitalizing the city's planning office. Larry Irvin was appointed planning director, and as the Downtown Council's own plans for Nicollet Mall progressed, with Barton-Aschman Associates as its transportation consultants, much of the planning criteria established by Irvin's group was adopted.

It was 1957 when the discussions about improving Nicollet Avenue began as an attempt to revitalize the downtown—the objective being to retain its regional importance and help stem retail declines. General

Mills had recently moved to the suburbs, where several shopping centers were under construction. By 1963, the Minneapolis City Council had approved the final plans, and in 1967 the mall finally opened.

Of the mall's approximate $4 million cost, only 25 percent came from the federal government: $512,000 from an urban mass transportation demonstration grant and $483,000 as an urban beautification grant. The remaining costs were financed by a bond issue to be redeemed by a complicated assessment levied on the properties benefiting from the mall, including those with direct frontage and extending to others up to 350 ft (110 m) from the mall. The assessment formula is based partly on frontage, partly on square footage, and partly on proximity to the north-south axis of the mall.

The removal of the automobile won support when a traffic survey showed 80 percent of Nicollet Avenue's traffic had other destinations. Furthermore, every neighborhood in Minneapolis is connected to the center area by bus; and with the exception of one line, every bus would cross the proposed mall, would operate directly on it, or would run 1 block parallel to it.

The mall's curvilinear alignment was proposed by Barton-Aschman, and was originally to extend the mall's full 8 blocks. However, the design was adjusted to provide a terminal view of Yamasaki's not-quite-transparent-enough office building for the Northwestern National Life Insurance Company (322).

At the insistence of prominent merchants, it was agreed that the mall would be an urbane street of quality construction and design. Lawrence Halprin and Associates was hired as the landscape architect. Each block was to be distinguished by its own individual character, with continuity provided by lighting, graphics, street furniture, and paving.

As built the mall has heated bus shelters; six fountains, some of which are heated to expand operation by several months a year; flagpoles; benches; and sculpture (323). Flowers are planted seasonally. Nine-tenths of the mall's maintenance costs are borne by the merchants as part of another special

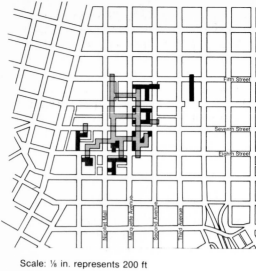

Scale: ⅛ in. represents 200 ft

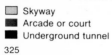 Skyway
Arcade or court
Underground tunnel

325

324

326

327

328

324 The skyway system is ideally suited to the city's harsh winter climate.

325 Presently 14 bridges connect over 30 buildings located on 16 blocks. Urban designers would like to see the second-level system connect the entire 64-block center with 77 bridges.

326 The city has established design standards for the bridges which, during winter, serve an average of 18,000 people a day.

327-328 The skyway system is interconnected by stairs, escalators, and elevators to the ground or arcade levels, which also have shops. The skyway system itself passes through department stores (327), other shopping facilities, and a series of interesting multilevel banking floors (328).

assessment. The success of the mall—retail sales along the mall have increased by a minimum of 15 percent—has led the city to experiment with exclusive bus lanes on other downtown streets, which flow in the opposite direction of the otherwise one-way traffic.

If it is true that Minneapolis has only two seasons—winter and the second week in July—then the city's skyway program, which connects buildings at the second level with glass-enclosed pedestrian bridges at midblock, is a significant aid to year-around pedestrian movement.

The skyway program has thus far been financed completely by private development. Since 1962 14 skyways have been built and several more are planned (324). The system presently connects over 30 buildings located on 16 city blocks. On any given day, about 7,000 people pass through each skyway and in the winter about 18,000 (325). When the system has been completed and connected to the peripheral parking garages, an estimated 40,000 people a day will travel through a typical skyway (326).

Following the lead of several developers, the Minneapolis Department of City Planning has done studies to guide the location of future skyways which, if built according to plan, could connect the 64 center city blocks with 77 bridges.

The skyway system is interconnected by stairs and escalators leading to interior arcades. Often, second-story office space has been converted to retail frontage. These second-story pedestrian routes also pass through department stores (327), several grand old multistoried banking lobbies (328), and parking garages, which have been designed to have retail space on both first and second levels. Newer construction and renovation add to the system, providing several enclosed spaces that are heavily used and often have lunchtime events.

In Minneapolis, private property extends to the center line of all abutting streets. The city has easement rights, upon which are built the streets and sidewalks. Because of these easement rights, the city must grant the right of encroachment to anyone wishing to construct a skyway. The right of encroachment is subject to design review by the city based on the following standards: ards:

–A clear walking path at least 12 ft (3.6 m) wide [20 ft (6 m) wide for all routes connecting to major peripheral parking ramps]

–A minimum vertical headroom of 8 ft (2.4 m)

–Heat, air-conditioning, and adequate lighting

–The inclusion of multilevel courts and ground-level interior arcades to link the street and second-level systems

–A maximum openness and use of glass

–A carefully located system of open spaces within arcades

–A well-designed sign system and clearly marked skyway entries from the street level

–Diverse activities along the routes, which should not compete strongly with similar functions on the street level

Before the second level was developed, there was little retail space available; and low pedestrian volumes meant that retail trades did not want to locate on streets adjacent to the mall, which were rented for institutional uses that helped create lifeless streets—bringing the situation full circle. Opening up the second level, especially in areas away from the major shopping street, gave retail activities unable to pay prime rentals an important opportunity for expansion. By now, however, rentals for second-level space are approximately the same as rates on the ground level, but with no apparent depreciation of ground-floor values.

At the very heart of the skyway system stands the IDS building designed by architects Philip Johnson and John Burgee. It is a superb embodiment of several urban design principles.

Developed on 1 square city block of approximately 2½ acres (1 ha), the project includes a 57-story office tower, a 19-story hotel, an 8-story office building, and a 2-

329

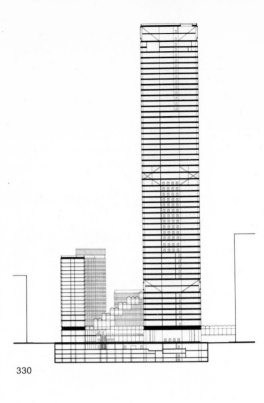

330

329-330   The Crystal Court was created by wrapping a four-building complex around a space, which was then glass-enclosed.

story building for Woolworth's (329, 330). All these buildings wrap around what is surely one of the most remarkable urban spaces ever built in the United States—the 10-story, glass-enclosed, 20,000 sq ft (1,900 sq m) "Crystal Court." This elegant space serves as a "town square" for the entire center (331, 332).

Rarely do American cities provide such enclosed public, though privately owned, urban space, although the great cities of Europe abound with them. Kevin Roche's Ford Foundation building in New York, one enormous effort in this direction, is unfortunately not the center of an interconnected urban network, as the IDS building is, and therefore has much less pedestrian traffic (333). Moreover, even if it were in such a location, the Ford space was designed for passive enjoyment—meant to be viewed—and not for cafes and small shops: its no-sitting policy is strictly enforced. The grandiose hotel lobbies of John Portman, as has been seen, come much closer to the mark. But even Portman's spaces are relatively inaccessible to the average pedestrian; and despite his efforts to make the hotel lobbies public rooms, there is often the sense that they are, in fact, spaces created for the hotel patron. What is remarkable in Johnson and Burgee's Crystal Court is its sense of being a public space; one might almost think it was built by the city.

The main space of the IDS Building seems literally to bleed out into the Nicollet Mall through a 40-foot (12-m) wide glass entrance. This space connects by escalators to the skyway's second level, from which four skyways radiate (334). There are restaurants on four levels and retail shops on three levels, with an emphasis on maintaining shopping frontage on all the streets, especially the mall.

Like so many buildings in other American cities, the IDS Building points to the contradictions in the bonus provisions of different zoning resolutions. Often no relationship exists between what zoning permits (indeed encourages) and what is actually built.

The city rewarded the IDS development with four bonus points of FAR for two internal walkways (at two points of FAR each) and an additional two points of FAR for off-street loading facilities. Starting from a base of 14, the IDS Building could have aimed for an FAR of 20, although in fact it *only* reached 17. No bonus was awarded for the spectacular interior space, nor for the essential skyway connections. Apparently, the economic incentive is considered so strong that skyways need not be bonused; economic incentive notwithstanding, they probably should be mandatory. Of course, it would be folly to put a development in that or any location and not take advantage of the opportunity to connect it to an established shopping system; however, the abundance of disruptive urban buildings suggests that there are no absolute guarantees of wisdom in urban development.

Minneapolis was only lucky that the architect and developer did everything they should have and much more. But the case of the IDS Building demonstrates that zoning in general must be used even more tightly as a tool in controlling new development to make it urbanistically sound. Without inhibiting excellent architecture, zoning should at the same time specifically encourage development of the most useful urban design elements. Minneapolis should consider restructuring its bonus system accordingly (as indeed should many other cities): the next time Minneapolis may be unlucky and get a Sears Tower of its very own.

In a noble effort to create public spaces for all seasons and all types—both exterior and interior, paved and landscaped—John Carl Warnecke's Hennepin County Government Center has not entirely succeeded.

By straddling a public street that divides the 2-square-block site, the Hennepin County Government Center was given a questionable prominence, and it creates a very unpleasant block to walk across (335, 336). The building is connected to the City Hall by an underground passage and provides, to the architect's credit, for the continuation of the skyway system, which will connect to future developments on adjacent sites via diagonal bridges.

But neither the paved plaza on one side of the building nor the landscaped plaza on the other are of the stuff that make up great

333

331

334

SECOND FLOOR PLAN

332

337

338

335

331-332   The 20,000-sq-ft (1,900-sq-m) Crystal Court is surrounded by three levels of retail space—one below ground, one at ground level, and one at the skyway level. The space has become the town square for Minneapolis, a place to linger while waiting for a friend. And in its own way it is as interesting and exciting as an Italian piazza.

333   Although the glass-enclosed central space of the Ford Foundation Building in New York equals in effort the IDS Crystal Court, it has been designed as a passive space: more to be viewed by those working in the building, for sitting is prohibited there, let alone eating a sandwich.

334   Although it was not an urban design requirement, the IDS Building made a bridge connection to each of the four surrounding blocks.

335-336   An apparently confused urban design solution, nonetheless, the Hennepin County Courthouse has been designed so that its second level can be connected to future development on adjacent blocks. Built across a street, the courthouse creates a street under the building that is not only dark, but unpleasant to walk along (336).

337-338   Neither the paved plaza (337) nor the landscaped plaza (338) provided by this solution seem particularly worth the effort and expense of spanning the building across a downtown street.

336

339

340

341

342

urban spaces. It is impossible not to ask if the project would not have been better had the tower been contained to one block, allowing for a single major exterior space on the other block (337, 338). Yet the 24-story skylighted atrium space is extremely impressive. Although it could have been more actively programmed, this may still happen if and when future bridge connections are made to it (339).

It is interesting to imagine what Warnecke's Pahlavi Foundation on Fifth Avenue in New York[1](47) might have been like if the legally binding urban design controls had been absent. Requirements *were* present, and it is an excellent urban building, more responsive to its urban environment than the Hennepin County Government Center.

The Loring Park Development District is the first to be established under a city ordinance intended to encourage a strictly local approach to neighborhood rehabilitation.

The city of Minneapolis's Development District legislative ordinance enables the city to sell general obligation bonds—the funds from which can be used to buy up land—use condemnation powers, when and if necessary; relocate present occupants; demolish existing structures; and administer the program. It is with these powers that the Loring Park Development District was established in 1972. The new district will replace 1,040 deteriorated dwelling units with 2,700 new dwelling units, increasing tax revenues fivefold.

Paul Friedberg and Associates were invited to develop an urban design framework for the Loring Park project. Working with Barton-Aschman Associates, Friedberg has also designed a 4-block extension to Nicollet Mall which connects to Loring Park by the Loring Greenway, an auto-free pedestrian area with shopping and recreational activities that serves as a spine throughout the new development (340). Several streets have been dead-ended and another depressed to create the Greenway that Friedberg says parallels a feature of the long-ago Bennett plan, which sought to tie Loring Park to the center of the city by a boulevard.

The urban design guidelines for the Loring Park Development District establish the lo-

cation and design of the Loring Greenway; location and size of private development parcels; maximum number of dwelling units in each parcel; maximum square footage of open space; and building heights and locations for reasons of security and sunlight (341).

Examining one of the developed parcels shows the relationship between the urban design guidelines and the built architecture. The maximum FAR was set at 3.5, with not more than 337 dwelling units. Among the other requirements the project had to meet was that the view of a church at the end of the Greenway remain unobstructed. At the same time, the building on that side of the project had to relate in scale to the height of the church. There had to be one story of continuous shopping along the Greenway. Provision was also made for an interparcel weather-protected pedestrian way that could in the future connect to the skyway system. The design scheme for this parcel, by architects James Stageberg and Tom Hodne, is a sensitive solution that fits well into the urban design plan (342).

An architectural solution has made feasible the recycling of the first designated landmark in downtown Minneapolis in a neighborhood of older buildings separated from downtown by the city's entertainment strip, Hennepin Avenue. By providing the first elevated pedestrian connection from a new peripheral parking garage through the recycled building to the downtown center, the city hopes to attract more private investment to the old neighborhood.

Hennepin Avenue is the entertainment strip of Minneapolis and the street that divides the downtown area from many older buildings originally used for manufacturing and warehousing. The Butler Building—the first designated landmark downtown—is only one of several buildings of the type which housed industrial activities that have become obsolete in the downtown areas of American cities (343).

In the Butler Building, the size of the floors were so vast that their interior spaces were unrentable for contemporary office or apartment use. Architects Miller, Hanson and Westerbeck overcame this problem by cutting out several bays from the interior

339   The interior space may become more active with future skyway connections.

340-341   The Loring Park Development District is tied to the center by the 4-block extension of Nicollet Mall, which connects through the development district to Loring Park by the Loring Greenway. Urban design controls have been established for all parcels within the development district (341).

342   The design solution for parcel 1C within the development district incorporates all the urban design requirements.

343

343   To function for modern office use, the landmark Butler Building was renovated, in part, by cutting a huge light well out of the building's heavy timber construction. The building connects directly with a peripheral parking garage.

344   With the removal of structural bays from the interior, the very deep Butler Building, originally designed in 1906 as a warehouse, now functions as an office building in the front half. A similar conversion of the back half is planned to turn it into a hotel.

345   The numerous curb cuts that provide automobile access to parking lots are a major problem confronting all pedestrians.

346   Though not a public policy, an interesting urban design solution has often been used in Minneapolis that overcomes the problem of driveways to parking garages in midblock downtown streets. A steeply inclined ramp brings automobiles up to second-level parking, with the sidewalk wrapped under and around the ramp.

347   An even better solution than that shown in 346 is for underground parking, leaving the sidewalk free of all barriers. This example is in Toronto.

344

345

346

347

structural system to create a major central skylighted space (344).

By providing the first elevated pedestrian connection from a new peripheral parking garage located above the innerbelt highway system through the Butler Building and eventually across Hennepin Avenue to the center, the city seeks to make this other side of Hennepin Avenue an attractive area for private investment, which will follow established urban design guidelines and eventually connect to a glass-enclosed shopping arcade linking it to the Nicollet Mall.

Midblock access to midcity parking garages that doesn't interfere with pedestrian movement is provided by ramps, steeply inclined up to the second level with arcaded sidewalks beneath.

Along with the bus, the automobile is thus far an equally important component in Minneapolis's transportation system. However, with the automobile come accidents, noise and air pollution, and parking problems. To solve at least some of the parking problems, Minneapolis is engaged in a program of building peripheral parking garages, but there are still many garages in the center of downtown. Numerous driveways are a particular problem with center-city parking. The pedestrian, aside from contending with the ill effects of autos and from confronting them directly at intersections, must usually face cars once again at midblock as they enter and leave the garage (345). The space for the driveways cuts the continuity of shopping, thus making the sidewalk unpleasant for adults and dangerous for children, the handicapped, and the elderly.

Minneapolis seems to have found a good solution to this problem. The solution lies in giving over part of the sidewalk to a steeply inclined ramp leading up to the second level, although none of the several garages built this way are as aesthetically successful as they are technically workable. The sidewalk is wrapped through an arcaded space under the ramp (346). Most of these pedestrian routes, although not overly circuitous, are often dark and a bit oppressive; but many of them do contain shopping.

It may only be a question of design, but an even better solution would seem to be ramping down instead of up (347). If, for whatever reason, all the building's parking requirements could not be below ground level, then there could be ramps or elevators to upper parking levels within the development parcel.

At both ends of Nicollet Mall, large urban spaces have been created in conjunction with new developments—at one end, landscape architect Paul Friedberg's Peavy Park Plaza; at the other, Gunnar Birkerts' Federal Reserve Building.

In the Federal Reserve Building, excessive emphasis seems to have been placed on achieving a "statement" that relies on architectural acrobatics instead of a building that could have contributed something to Nicollet Mall or have provided a truly useful urban space (348).

Hung by means of a catenary structure, the building is raised off the ground 1 story. This seems awfully meager of the federal government, having allowed Kevin Roche to propose raising the Federal Reserve Building in New York off the ground 14 stories (104, 105). But even raising it off the ground *only* 1 story is enough to suggest: "people beware." The Minneapolis Federal Reserve Building—disguised in mirrored glass—is totally aloof and unrelated to its prominent location as the first building in a shopping mall. Perhaps it has taken its clue from Yamasaki's building across the street (322).

The benches on the plaza in front of the building are apparently designed for an anatomical creature of serpentine-like shape, a very distant relative to the human race (349). This may explain why the city's inhabitants seem to ignore the benches and the steeply sloped "innertube" plaza—from which it is impossible to enter the building—and in general are "staying away in droves" as one local magazine put it.

If a public place had to be created and had there been a keener recognition of the city's long, cold winters, perhaps a completely different type of space might have occurred. But even as an outdoor space, it should be compared with landscape archi-

349

348

350

348 The Federal Reserve Building is an architectural statement that on balance offers little either as part of the Nicollet Mall on which it is situated or as a usable public space.

349 Federal Reserve Plaza's ridiculous and unusable metal benches (freezing in the winter, blistering hot in the summer) are representative of the design solution in general. Despite the existence of so many excellent types of urban benches, the need of so many architects to design everything anew, often with little regard to the object's functional intent, is both absurd and disturbing.

350 Peavey Park, at the opposite end of Nicollet Mall, offers a striking contrast from which to judge the Federal Reserve Plaza.

tect Paul Friedberg's Peavey Park Plaza, built in conjunction with the newly opened Orchestra Hall and situated at the opposite end of the Nicollet Mall extension (350).

Architecture is not sculpture in the classical sense. Buildings are not objects on a plaza to be admired. First and foremost, buildings are to be used by people—both those who work within a particular building and those who work around it. A building must therefore function accordingly by becoming an integral part of the urban environment. This accomplished, a building can then be "distinguished" and provide space which is "exciting" to see and be a part of, but it must be a space that, like the building, is usable.

Architectural gymnastics are fine when they honestly perform divorced from the public realm, but when they are located in a setting with an established urban pattern, then it would seem only logical that a building defer to the environment in which it is built.

It is apparent that a city the size of Minneapolis with an able urban design staff can stay on top of new developments. But without a vision for the center that is codified into a legally binding framework, even Minneapolis can miss great opportunities. Still, the relationship in Minneapolis between the private and public sectors has produced some of the most interesting urban design ideas of any city in the United States, ideas that have dramatically improved the quality of the urban environment in Minneapolis and could do the same in many larger cities.

Epilogue

The steady disintegration of the central city in America has been a direct consequence of clearly established, if unwitting, national policy since World War II. Although in recent years signs of a resurgent strength are evident in the downtown areas of American cities, there are still enormous problems ahead. One major problem, not easily solved, lies in the demography of the older, larger American city. In most metropolitan areas, the suburbs are now richer and more powerful than the cities they surround. The power comes from the collective numbers of people in the suburban ring, now often greater than those in the center city, and effectively represented in Congress.

Much of the money for the good life in suburbia, however, is still earned in the downtown area of cities. Suburbs, many of which were subsidized to begin with through FHA (Federal Housing Administration) low-interest home loan guarantees and federally funded highways that get suburbanites to and from the downtown while greatly disrupting the urban landscape in the process, further exploit the wealth of the city through their exclusionary zoning practices, placing the burden of maintaining the poor solely on the city. In Shadrach Woods' opinion, "suburbs are neo-colonists."[1]

Central banks too share some of the responsibility for the present condition of American cities. While the banks provided much of the financing for the suburbs, they cut off help to older, poorer sections of the center city through red-lining and other discriminatory lending practices.

To compensate for some of the inequities in New York, Mayor Lindsay instituted an income tax on those who earned their money in the city and lived outside it, who previously, as nonresidents, had paid no city taxes to support the city services they freely took advantage of.

Looking more closely at the downtowns of the nine cities surveyed here, several things, many times contradictory in nature and often dealing with transportation, are apparent. For example, the 3½ million people who must be in these nine downtown areas to make a living are exposed daily to inordinately high levels of pollution in large measure caused by the automobile. Without an almost radical change in transportation policies—especially in regard to the use of the private automobile in the heart of downtown areas in large American cities—any other improvements to the downtown will be cosmetic at best.

Many cities of moderate size, like Minneapolis and San Francisco, have tried to ameliorate the negative impact of the automobile through urban design changes in the city's infrastructure. It was seen that Minneapolis prohibits the automobile on its main shopping street—Nicollet Avenue. And San Francisco has reduced the automobile capacity of Market Street. Despite Boston's stated program to ban the automobile from a 10-block area of its downtown, no American city, including Boston, has effectively placed restrictions on the use of the automobile downtown as have literally scores of European cities in their entire centers.

Ironically, the downtowns of the two largest cities in the United States, New York and Chicago—whose downtowns function only because 80 percent of Chicago's commuters and over 90 percent of New York's commuters use public transportation—have not closed one single street to traffic in their centers to benefit the high number of pedestrians and public transit users. Yet it is Chicago and New York, perhaps more than any other cities surveyed here, that desperately need a reorganization of surface transportation priorities to favor the pedestrian, public transportation, emergency services, and pick-up and delivery of goods. Considering that Midtown Manhattan is an area of only 1 sq mile (2.6 sq km) in a region of 12,000 sq miles (30,000 sq km), it would seem reasonable that a few streets in Midtown could be reserved primarily for the 1 million people who work in that tiny area, especially since over 80 percent of them arrive at work by means of underground transportation systems and once at street level must walk to their destinations.

Part of the reason for the dilemma is simple: more federal money is available to build highways than to improve public transportation. A lot more! Between 1956 and 1976, 38,000 miles (60,000 km) of interstate highways were built in the U.S., while from 1945 to 1970, less than 20 miles (32 km) of subways were built.[2]

According to John Hirton, deputy administrator of the Urban Mass Transportation Administration, "Since 1946, Federal, state, and local expenditures for highways and roads have totaled $361-billion."[3] Included in this figure is the $65 billion already poured into an interstate highway program that was originally estimated at $27 billion and will cost another $35 billion if the highway lobby gets its way. In 1973 alone, $24 billion was spent on highways. Hirton again: "More than one fourth of this was raised by property or general taxes (nonuser) and constitutes a clear public subsidy."[4] In contrast, federal grants for public transportation in 1973 totaled only $650 million.

The federal government is ultimately responsible for the short-sighted aspects of this one-sided program. Having helped hook Americans on driving to work, only the federal government has enough money to unhook them. Enforcing clean air standards coupled with more money for public transportation is one approach. But the fed-

eral government still has an inordinately strong bias toward funding highways. And the Environmental Protection Agency now says it has yielded to local pressures and will no longer try to enforce clean air standards. This might have been different had bus and subway riders been as an effective lobby as are auto manufacturers and oil companies.

In spite of all that has been learned about the problems and inadequacies of highways, several cities persist in continuing to investigate completing existing systems. But the lesson from viewing older cities—like Boston, Philadelphia, New York, and Chicago—is that the massive highways serve fewer than 30 percent of the incoming commuters at an overwhelming and unnecessary cost (dollar and environmental, which are not unrelated) that is rarely in the community's interest. Says William Ronan, former chairman of the New York Metropolitan Transportation Authority: "If the Long Island Railroad were discontinued, 29 one-way lanes of highway on Long Island running into New York would be required to handle the commuter load handled by the railroad."[5] Only a national program of conservation that simultaneously encourages the use of public transportation will help.

Los Angeles functions—barely—because it has multiple centers, avoiding the heavy concentrations of jobs at a single point, which is otherwise common to older U.S. cities. The intensification in recent years of certain of these centers in Los Angeles, including its "downtown," is the cause of concern to many planners who realize that with Los Angeles's almost complete dependence upon the automobile, the increased density might tip the balance and make the entire highway system—already at peak capacity—completely unworkable.

Quite the opposite of the situation in Los Angeles, New York and Chicago are absolutely dependent upon public transportation. It is therefore incredible that neither city has exclusive bus lanes in their respective downtown areas. Even Houston has exclusive bus lanes downtown! And, buses, as was seen, account for less than 3 percent of the vehicles on New York's streets, but they carry over 40 percent of the surface passengers. Still, they are forced to compete with the private automobile for space.

Another problem is that New York and Chicago's subways are among the darkest, dirtiest, dismally depressing subterranean environments ever created by man. And although many straphangers must ride them to and from work, they abandon what are multibillion dollar systems all other times mainly due to a perception that they are unsafe, which may be directly related to their foreboding appearance. While New York and Chicago do have a few modernized subway stations, steps must be taken soon to modernize their entire subway systems as Boston has already done. In fact, Mayor Koch of New York has committed the city in 1978 to just such a program. The expansive subway networks of New York, Chicago, Philadelphia, and Boston remain the key in these particular cities to a cleaner, healthier environment.

With a commitment to new and improved public transportation must also come programs to induce more drivers out of their automobiles and into buses and subways. Some of these inducements can be direct: increased taxes on gasoline and on downtown parking. Some can be more subtle: closing streets in the center to the private automobile. Attention, too, must be given to the role major employers can play, as programs initiated in Houston suggest.

An indirect approach can come directly from auto insurance companies. At present, auto insurance premiums in large cities are staggeringly high: Boston, $950 per year; New York, $720 per year; Chicago, $520 per year. Many who own automobiles in these cities have viable public transportation alternatives, but may feel obliged to use their automobile, having already spent so much money for insurance alone. Among other factors, insurance rates depend upon the type of vehicle being insured, the city in which it is driven, the age and marital status of the driver, and the driver's overall driving record. Given the fluctuating nature of insurance rates, it would seem that the rates could be substantially reduced for the automobile owner who uses public transportation during rush hours. That is, the insurance policy would not cover automobile use during those hours. This would be of

benefit to insurance companies and auto-owners alike. During the 5-day workweek, 40 percent of auto accidents—including 28 percent of fatal accidents—occur during the six hours that constitute the morning and evening rush hours (7:00–10:00 A.M.; 3:30–6:30 P.M.). Besides the increased protection of life and limb, the savings to the motorist should more than offset the cost of using public transportation.

As to other issues related to urban design, of the cities surveyed here, only Philadelphia has a comprehensive plan for the city's development, which it has clearly followed officially since 1961 and unofficially since 1947. And it shows. But that may be owing more to the vision and fortitude of one man—Edmund Bacon—than to the actual comprehensive plan.

With the exception of Lower Manhattan, New York and San Francisco do not have comprehensive plans. Instead, they have taken several urban design features typically illustrated in comprehensive plans and written them into zoning law. So even though many of the urban offices Mayor Lindsay set up were consolidated by Mayor Beame under budgetary cutbacks, the urban design controls remain legally binding on all new construction.

Zoning should be a creative tool for regulating new construction to ensure that future buildings are responsive to existing environmental conditions. It seems clear that many cities should re-evaluate their bonus systems to better correlate the zoning incentive to the true needs of the center. In many cases, though, cities ought to insist that a building have certain obligatory urban design features without resorting to incentives. In any case, the intent of zoning incentives only works when the zoning's basic limit is at a threshold where the developer wants to build more than the zoning allows. Of the cities surveyed here, only Boston, San Francisco, and New York have established clear zoning policies which work in this way: the developer usually builds according to the city's urban design criteria in order to get a bonus to build a slightly bigger building.

Zoning can also be instrumental in saving landmarks, but it is no substitute for a clear public policy to preserve the city's cultural and architectural heritage. Where local governmental interest or appreciation is lax, as in Chicago, citizens should have recourse to state and federal programs that are strong enough to prevent destruction of recognized landmarks.

Since it now appears that many center cities are reaching a sort of population equilibrium, at least for a few years, zoning can no longer be relied upon as a tool to create the kind of open space necessary in the center, and other, more direct means will have to be used to provide this needed space.

In the last 20 years, urban renewal—though harshly more disruptive than it needed to have been—has at least shown the willingness of middle- and upper-income groups to live in the city, especially near the downtown. While this may not be a consideration in cities like Houston [with control over 2,000 sq miles (5,000 sq km), middle- and upper-income groups are in the city by default], it is very much a part of the thinking in cities like Philadelphia, San Francisco, Chicago, Boston, and New York, where politicians seek middle- and upper-income housing as a way to increase the city's tax base.

In Philadelphia's Society Hill area (178) and San Francisco's Golden Gateway Center (249, 250), though the housing is affordable by middle- and upper-income groups only, the housing is nonetheless an integral part of a city fabric which is accessible to everyone. The Houston Center project (205–208) and Chicago's Lakepoint Towers (140), however, would portend of a future where middle- and upper-income groups live in fortress-like enclaves, often in locations which exploit the city's natural beauty and only serve to make the surrounding streets deserted and unsafe. In the absence of more humanistic attitudes of developers and their architects, zoning could be used to insist that future housing not be so exclusionary—at least in appearance and ground-floor use.

Battery Park City in New York, if ever built close to its original intent, will show how a city can provide a well-planned environ-ment accessible to, and inhabitable by, a diverse population.

No doubt the downtowns of the nine cities presented here as well as other American downtowns can be revived as attractive places for business if new opportunities are seized upon to establish an urban design structure that can give grace and beauty to the urban center, providing urban life with the dignity and amenity that characterizes so many cities outside the United States. American downtowns can become vital organisms that integrate shops, offices, and apartments with parks and plazas and a sensible transportation system that conveniently and comfortably moves passengers and allows for effective delivery of goods and services.

But if central cities are to become workable, livable places, politicians will inevitably have to make tough and costly decisions—many related to reorganizing transportation priorities. Implicit is the need for cities to exert more control over the estimated 50 percent of the land downtown, mostly in sidewalks, streets, and parking that the city directly administers. The cost of not making these decisions and establishing a coherent urban design policy for the downtown will be even greater, with a continued exodus of jobs and a continually deteriorating, demeaning, and unhealthy environment.

Notes

NEW YORK
1. Sibyl Moholy-Nagy, *Matrix of Man* (New York: Praeger, 1969), p. 227.
2. "Development Rights Transfer in New York City," *The Yale Law Journal* 82:338 (1972), p. 340.
3. Ibid.
4. Aline B. Saarinen (ed.), *Eero Saarinen on His Works* (New Haven, Conn.: Yale University Press, 1962), p. 16.
5. Paul Goldberger, "Grand Central Reinstated As a Landmark by Court," *The New York Times,* Dec. 7, 1975, p. 43.

CHICAGO
1. William A. Robson (ed.), *Great Cities of the World* (New York: MacMillan Company, 1955), p. 191.
2. Nory Miller, "Marble-Clad Carnival," *Architectural Forum,* January/February 1974, p. 45.
3. Ibid.
4. Interview with Jared Shlaes, Feb. 13, 1976.
5. Interview with John Costonis, June 16, 1975.
6. Interview with Robert DeVoy, July 21, 1976.
7. *Architectural Record,* May 1976, p. 34.
8. City of Chicago, Department of Development and Planning, *Illinois Central Air Rights Development,* May 1968, p. 6.
9. Alvin Boyarsky, "Lakefront Tower, Chicago," *AD,* March 1970, p. 158.

PHILADELPHIA
1. Richard S. Wurman and John Andrew Gallery, *Man Made Philadelphia* (Cambridge, Mass.: MIT Press, 1972), p. 26.
2. John Reps, *The Making of Urban America* (Princeton, N.J.: Princeton University Press, 1965), p. 160.
3. Interview with Edmund Bacon, Mar. 3, 1976.
4. Ibid.
5. Ibid.
6. Interview with Wilhelm von Moltke, Mar. 20, 1976.
7. Bacon, op. cit.
8. Bacon, op. cit.
9. Bacon, op. cit.
10. Interview with John Bower, Aug. 19, 1976.
11. Von Moltke, op. cit.

HOUSTON
1. Ada Louise Huxtable, "Deep in the Heart of Nowhere," *The New York Times,* Feb. 15, 1976.
2. Workers of the Writer's Program of the WPA in the State of Texas, *Houston: A History and Guide* (Houston: The Anson Press, 1942), p. 38.
3. Roscoe H. Jones, "City Planning in Houston without Zoning" (a report prepared by the director of city planning in the city of Houston to answer questions about nonzoning policies in Houston), 1976, p. 4.
4. Bernard Siegan, "Non-Zoning in Houston," *University of Chicago Law School Journal of Law and Economics,* April 1970, p. 133.
5. Ibid, p. 134.
6. Ibid, p. 73.
7. Ibid.
8. John Powers, "Tunnels and Air Rights: The Debate Continues," *Houston Business Journal,* Sept. 27, 1976.
9. Shadrach Woods, *The Man in the Street* (Baltimore: Penguin Books Inc., 1975), p. 70.
10. Huxtable, op. cit.

WASHINGTON, D.C.
1. John Reps, *The Making of Urban America* (Princeton, N.J.: Princeton University Press, 1965), p. 246.
2. Herbert Muschamp, *File under Architecture* (Cambridge, Mass.: MIT Press, 1974), p. 15.
3. Ben A. Franklin, "New Area Replaces Downtown," *The New York Times,* Dec. 28, 1975.
4. Wolf Von Eckardt, "Avenue Will Have Missing Tooth," *Washington Post,* Oct. 22, 1967.
5. Pennsylvania Avenue Development Corporation, *The Pennsylvania Avenue Plan, 1974* (Washington, D.C.: Government Printing Office, 1976), p. v.
6. Von Eckardt, op. cit.
7. Donald Canty, "How Washington Is Run," *Architectural Forum,* January 1963, p. 52.

SAN FRANCISCO
1. Mel Scott, *The San Francisco Bay Area: A Metropolis in Perspective* (Berkeley, Calif.: University of California Press, 1959).
2. Ibid.

BOSTON
1. Walter Muir Whitehill, *Boston: A Topographical History* (Cambridge, Mass.: The Belknap Press of Harvard University Press, 1975), p. 35.
2. Ibid, p. 202.
3. Ibid, p. 204.
4. Interview with Charles Hilgenhurst, Architect, Nov. 23, 1976.

ATLANTA
1. "Cooperating to Solve Problems," *Nation's Business,* April 1976.

Selected Bibliography

2. H. Randal Roark, "Atlanta: Urban Patterns," *The A.I.A. Guide to Atlanta,* 1975, p. 13.
3. Interview with Tom Shuttleworth, Nov. 3, 1976.
4. Joyce Leviton, "BIO: Architect John Portman," *People,* Aug. 11, 1975.
5. Robert Kiener, "John Portman: Architect/Visionary," *Hospitality,* September 1975.

EPILOGUE
1. Shadrach Woods, *The Man in the Street* (Baltimore: Penguin Books Inc., 1975), p. 90.
2. "Sic Transit . . . ," *The New York Times,* July 28, 1976.
3. John Hirton, "The Bias in Transit Planning," *Modern Railroads,* May 1975.
4. Ibid.
5. Ibid.

GENERAL

Bacon, Edmund N. *Design of Cities.* New York: The Viking Press, 1967.

Brambilla, Roberto G., *More Streets for People.* New York, IALF, 1973.

Cook, John W., and Klotz, Heinrich. *Conversations with Architects.* New York: Praeger, 1973.

Crosby, Theo. *Architecture: City Sense.* New York: Reinhold Publishing Co., 1965.

Davis, Kingsley, et al. *Cities.* New York: Alfred A. Knopf, 1966.

Giedion, Sigfried. *Space, Time and Architecture.* Cambridge, Mass.: Harvard University Press, 1963.

Goodman, Robert. *After the Planners.* New York: Simon & Schuster, 1971.

Hager, Rolf, ed. *The Zähringer New Towns.* Switzerland: Department of Architecture, Swiss Federal Institute of Technology, Autumn 1966.

Halprin, Lawrence. *Freeways.* New York: Reinhold Publishing Company, 1966.

Hirten, John E. "The Bias in Transit Planning." *Modern Railroad,* May 1975.

Institute for Public Transportation. *It's Up to You: A Citizen's Guide to Transportation Planning.* New York, June 1975.

Jacobs, Jane. *The Death and Life of Great American Cities.* New York: Vintage Books, 1961.

Jencks, Charles. *Modern Movements in Architecture.* New York: Anchor Press, 1973.

Meyerson, Martin; Tyrwhitt, Jacqueline; et al. *Face of the Metropolis.* New York: Random House, 1963.

Moholy-Nagy, Sibyl. *Matrix of Man.* New York: Praeger, 1969.

Muschamp, Herbert. *File under Architecture.* Cambridge, Mass.: MIT Press, 1974.

Rasmussen, Steen Eiler. *Towns and Buildings.* Cambridge, Mass.: MIT Press, 1951.

Redstone, Louis G. *The New Downtowns.* New York: McGraw-Hill, 1976.

Richards, Brian. *New Movement in Cities.* New London: Studio Vista, 1966.

Rotkin, Charles E. *Europe: An Aerial Close-Up.* New York: Bonanza Books, 1962.

Saarinen, Aline B., ed. *Eero Saarinen on His Work.* New Haven, Conn.: Yale University Press, 1962.

Spreiregen, Paul D. *Urban Design: The Architecture of Town and Cities.* New York: McGraw-Hill, 1965.

Tunnard, Christopher. *The City of Man.* New York: Charles Scribner's Sons, 1970.

Venturi, Robert. *Complexity and Contradiction in Architecture.* New York: The Museum of Modern Art, 1966.

Vernon, Raymond. *The Myth and Reality of Our Urban Problems.* Cambridge, Mass.: Harvard University Press, 1966.

Wolf, Peter. *The Future of the City.* New York: Whitney Library of Design, 1974.

Woods, Shadrach. *The Man in the Street.* Baltimore: Pelican Books, 1975.

NEW YORK

Books

Alpern, Robert. *Pratt Guide to Planning and Renewal for New Yorkers.* New York: Quadrangle, 1973.

Barnett, Jonathan. *Urban Design as Public Policy.* New York: Architectural Record Books, 1974.

Caro, Robert A. *The Power Broker.* New York: Vintage Books, 1975.

Okamoto, Rai Y., and Williams, Frank E., *Urban Design Manhattan.* New York: Viking Press, 1969.

Silver, Nathan. *Lost New York*. New York: Schocken Books, 1975.

Articles and Periodicals

Barnett, Jonathan. "Urban Design as Part of the Governmental Process." *Architectural Record,* January 1970, pp. 131–150.

"Can Fifth Avenue Be Saved." *The New York Times,* 1 March 1971.

"Charity Begins at Home." *Progressive Architecture,* February 1968.

"Development Rights Transfer in New York City." *The Yale Law Journal* 82 (1972): 338.

Elliot, Donald H. "The Role of Design in the Governmental Process." *Architectural Record,* January 1968.

Goldberger, Paul. "Grand Central Reinstated as a Landmark by Court." *The New York Times,* 17 December 1975, p. 43.

Huxtable, Ada Louise. "Concept Points to 'City of Future.' " *The New York Times,* 6 December 1970.

———. "Thinking Man's Zoning." *The New York Times,* 7 March 1971, p. 22.

"A New Set of Rules to Reshape New York." *Business Week,* 13 February 1971.

Van Ginkel, Sandy and Blanche. "Midtown Manhattan." *Architectural Forum,* October 1971, pp. 28–33.

Whyte, William H. "The Best Street Life in the World." *New York Magazine,* 15 July 1974, pp. 26–33.

———. "Please, Just a Nice Place to Sit." *The New York Times,* 3 December 1972, p. 20.

Public Documents

City of New York, Department of City Planning, Urban Design Group. *New Life for Plazas.* April 1975.

———, Department of City Planning. *Plan for New York City.* 1969.

———, Department of City Planning. *Zoning Ordinance.* 1976.

———, Office of Lower Manhattan Development. *Lower Manhattan Waterfront.* June 1975.

———, Office of Lower Manhattan Development. *To Preserve a Heritage: The Restoration and Utilization of Historic Sites in Lower Manhattan.* 1975.

———, Office of Lower Manhattan Development. *Proposed Municipal Building.* 1971.

———, Office of Lower Manhattan Development. *Special Greenwich Street Development District.* January 1971.

———, Office of Midtown Planning and Development. *Fifth Avenue.* 1970.

———, Office of Midtown Planning and Development. *Madison Mall.* 1971.

———, Office of Midtown Planning and Development. *Movement in Midtown* (Report prepared by Van Ginkel Associates). June 1970.

———, Office of Midtown Planning and Development. *Parking in Midtown* (Report prepared by Van Ginkel Associates). October 1970.

———, Office of Midtown Planning and Development. *Queensborough Bridge Area Study.* November 1970.

———, Office of Midtown Planning and Development. *Urban Design in the Bridge Area.* 1974.

———, Planning Commission. *The Lower Manhattan Plan* (Report prepared by Wallace-McHarg Associates; Whittlesey and Conklin; Alan M. Voorhees and Associates). June 1966.

Regional Plan Association. *The State of the Region.* March 1975.

Tri-State Regional Planning Commission. *Hub-Bound Travel.* February 1973.

Reports

Institute for Public Transportation. *Buy the 1973 Mass Transit.* 1973.

Midtown Task Force on Staggered Work Hours. *Staggered Work Hours in Manhattan.* 1972.

Mayor's Task Force. *The Threatened City.* 7 February 1967.

Pushkarev, Boris, and Zupan, Jeffrey M. *Capacity of Pedestrian Facilities.* August 1974.

CHICAGO

Books

Bach, Ira J. *Chicago on Foot.* Chicago: Follett Publishing Company, 1969.

Costonis, John J. *Space Adrift: Landmark Preservation and the Marketplace.* Urbana, Ill.: University of Illinois Press, 1974.

Mayer, Harold M., and Wade, Richard C. *Chicago: Growth of a Metropolis.* Chicago: University of Chicago Press, 1969.

Randall, Frank A. *History of the Development and Building Construction in Chicago.* Urbana, Ill.: University of Illinois Press, 1949.

Siegal, Arthur, ed. *Chicago's Famous Buildings.* Chicago: University of Chicago Press, 1969.

Articles and Periodicals

Architectural Forum, January-February 1974.

Boyarsky, Alvin, "Lake Point Tower, Chicago." *AD,* March 1970, p. 158.

"Chicago." *Architectural Forum,* May 1962, pp. 83-142.

"Chicago's Downtown Looks Up." *Inland Architect,* June 1958, pp. 16-23.

Commerce, November 1975.

Cooper, Richard T. "Wexler Stresses Need for Study of New Burnham Plan Elements." *Chicago Sun Times,* 10 October 1966, p. 6.

"Development Rights Transfer." *Planning,* July 1974.

Dixon, John Morris. "Marina City: Outer-Space Image and Inner-Space Reality." *Architectural Forum,* April 1965, pp. 68-77.

Gapp, Paul. "Taking a Critical Walk Thru Three Plazas: One Sweet and Two Sour." *Chicago Tribune,* 13 July 1975.

Goldberger, Paul. "Chicago's Stunning Architecture Lacks Diversity." *The New York Times,* 14 September 1976.

"Lake Point Tower: The First Skyscraper with an Undulating Glass Wall." *Architectural Record,* October 1969.

Newman, W. M. "Our 114 Year Lakefront War." *Chicago Daily News,* 24 September 1966, p. 3.

Shlaes, Jared B. "The Economics of Development Rights Transfer." *The Appraisal Journal,* October 1974, pp. 526-537.

"Transferable Development Rights." *ASPO,* report no. 304.

Public Documents

City of Chicago, Department of City Planning. *Development Plan for the Central Area of Chicago.* August 1958.

———, Department of Development and Planning, Department of Public Works, Chicago Transit Authority. *Summary of Transit Planning Study—Chicago Central Area.* April 1968.

———, Department of Development and

Planning. *The Comprehensive Plan of Chicago.* December 1960.
——, Department of Development and Planning. *The Comprehensive Plan of Chicago—Conditions and Trends: Population, Economy, Land.* August 1967.
——, Department of Development and Planning. *The Comprehensive Plan of Chicago—Volume 1, Analysis of City Systems: Residential Area, Recreation and Park Land, Education, Public Safety and Health.* October 1967.
——, Department of Development and Planning. *The Comprehensive Plan of Chicago—Volume 2, Analysis of City Systems: Business, Industry, Transportation.* May 1968.
——, Department of Development and Planning. *Illinois Central Air Rights Development.* May 1968.
——, Department of Development and Planning. *The Riveredge Plan of Chicago.* December 1974.
——, *Chicago Zoning Ordinance.* 1974.
——, Commission on Chicago Historical and Architectural Landmarks. *Chicago Landmarks.* 1975.
——, Commission on Chicago Historical and Architectural Landmarks. *Rules of Procedure.* December 23, 1969.

Reports

Chicago Central Area Land Use Trends (Report Prepared by Real Estate Research Corporation). October 1975.
——. *Chicago 21* (Report Prepared by Skidmore, Owings and Merrill; Real Estate Research Corporation; Alan M. Voorhees and Associates; Professor Morris Janowitz). September 1973.
——. *Planning Principles for the Chicago Central Area.* 1966.
Chicago Heritage Committee. *The Issue of the Lakefront: An Historical Critical Survey* (Written by Douglas Schroeder).
Johnson, Johnson, and Roy. Lakefront Study Progress Report to the Sub Committee of the Chicago Plan Commission. February 15, 1967.
Landmarks Preservation Council and Service. *Annual Report.* January 1, 1972–June 30, 1973.
——. *Annual Report.* July 1, 1973—June 30, 1974.
——. *Chicago's Landmark Structures: An Inventory.* December 1974.
Szujewski, Phil; Bellas, Jean; and Belding,

Daniel. ''A Slice of the Onion: An Urban Design Proposal for Chicago.'' Undergraduate thesis in the Department of Architecture, University of Illinois, Chicago. June 1975.
Weese, Ben, et al. *The Answers to the Lakefront Convention Hall.* November 13, 1957.

Unpublished Material

Pace Associates. ''Zoning Changes in the Central Area, Chicago.'' July 5, 1966.
Weese, Harry, and Associates. ''A Proposition for Settling the Issues of Grant Park.'' September 1968.

PHILADELPHIA

Books

Wurman, Richard S., and Gallery, John Andrew. *Man Made Philadelphia.* Cambridge, Mass.: MIT Press, 1972.

Articles and Periodicals

Bacon, Edmund. ''Downtown Philadelphia: A Lesson in Design for Urban Growth.'' *Architectural Record,* May 1961, pp. 131-145.
——. ''Time, Turf, Architects and Planners.'' *Architectural Record.* March, 1976.
Kling, Vincent. ''Penn Center and Its Progeny: The Growing Resurgence of Downtown Philadelphia.'' *Delaware Valley Industry,* September 1973.
''New Directions for Downtown and Suburban Shopping Centers.'' *Architectural Record,* April 1974.
''Post-Renaissance Philadelphia.'' *AIA Journal,* March 1976, pp. 31-49.
''Preserving Context at the Neighborhood Scale.'' *Architectural Record,* December 1974, pp. 88-89.
Stephens, Suzanne. ''Philadelphia Story.'' *Progressive Architecture,* April 1976, pp. 45-51.

Public Documents

Delaware Valley Planning Commission. *1985 Regional Transportation Plan.* 1969.
Philadelphia City Planning Commission. *Center City: Philadelphia.* 1960.
——. *Center City Redevelopment Area Plan.* 1976.
——. *Philadelphia: A City of Neighborhoods.* 1976.
——. *Planning in Philadelphia.*

Lectures

Edmund Bacon. ''Planning Philadelphia.'' Pratt Institute, 24 November 1975.

Unpublished Materials

Bacon, Edmund. ''Architecture and Planning'' (Talk given at the annual meeting of The American Institute of Architects, Philadelphia). April 27, 1961.
——. ''Planning, Architecture, and Politics in Philadelphia'' (Russell Van Nest Black Memorial Lecture, Cornell University, Ithaca, N.Y.), August 24, 1973.
——. ''Redesigning Downtown Philadelphia'' (Presentation given at the annual meeting of The American Institute of Architects, Philadelphia). April 27, 1961.

HOUSTON

Books

Big Town, Big Money. Houston: Cordoran Press, 1973.
Papademetriou, Peter C. *Houston: An Architectural Guide.* Houston: Houston Chapter of the AIA, 1972.
Workers of the Writers Program of the WPA in the State of Texas. *Houston: A History and Guide.* Houston: The Anson Press, 1942.

Articles and Periodicals

''An American Hybrid in Hotel Design.'' *Architectural Record,* May 1974, pp. 151-160.
Ashby, Lynn. ''The Supercities: Houston.'' *Saturday Review,* 4 September 1976, pp. 17-18.
Cuddy, Roxy. ''Broad Mixture of Merchants Maintain Bustling Business Beneath City Streets.'' *Houston Business Journal,* 27 September 1976.
Huxtable, Ada Louise. ''Deep in the Heart of Nowhere.'' *The New York Times,* 15 February 1976.
Interiors, April 1973, p. 78.
Powers, John F. ''Tunnels and Air Rights: The Debate Continues.'' *Houston Business Journal,* 27 September 1976.
Santamaria, Joseph W. ''Urban Dynamics of Non-Zoning.'' *AIA Journal,* April 1972.
Siegan, Bernard. ''Non-Zoning in Houston.'' *University of Chicago Law School Journal of Law and Economics,* April 1970, pp. 71-147.

Public Documents

City of Houston. *Car Share,* 1976.
Houston-Galveston Area Council. *Houston CBD Cordon Count,* 1976.
Houston City Planning Department. *Annual Report,* 1975.
———. *Land Platting Policy Manual,* 2 June 1976.
———. *Preliminary Houston Downtown Master Plan 2000,* October 1973.
U.S. Environmental Protection Agency. *Proposed Amendments to the Texas Hydrocarbon / Photochemical Oxidant Strategy,* 25 July 1975.

Reports

Houston Chamber of Commerce. *Houston: For Your Information.* July 1975.
———. *Houston Facts.* January 1976.
Rice Center for Community Design and Research. *Downtown Houston Transit Needs Analysis.* March 1976.
Texas Eastern Transmission Company. *Interesting Facts about Houston Center.* January 1971.

Unpublished Material

Jones, Roscoe H. "City Planning in Houston without Zoning." (The author is director of the Houston city planning department.)
Olson, William A. "Alternatives to Zoning: The Houston Story" (Paper read to the American Society of Planning Officials). April 3, 1967.
Warren David. "Public Transportation in Houston" (Intership Report). Summer 1976.

WASHINGTON, D.C.

Books

Cox, Warren, J.; Jacobsen, Hugh Newell; et al. *A Guide to the Architecture of Washington, D.C.* New York: McGraw-Hill, 1974.
McLaughlin Green, Constance. *Washington: Village and Capital, 1800–1878.* Princeton, N.J.: Princeton University Press, 1962.

Articles and Periodicals

AIA Journal, April 1974.
Architectural Forum, January 1963.
Bucks, Edward C. "Capital's Transit Is Using New Concepts." *The New York Times,* 10 September 1974, p. 37.

Conconi, Charles N. "Metro Is Coming! Metro Is Coming." *Washington Magazine,* May 1975.
Franklin, Ben A. "New Area Replaces Downtown." *The New York Times,* 29 December 1975.
———. "Washington's Subway Will Start Limited Service." *The New York Times,* 15 March 1976, p. 39.
Goldberger, Paul. "Washington's Buildings: Low Profile and Boxlike." *The New York Times,* 29 December 1975.
Hammer, Philip G. "The Planning of Washington as a City." *AIA Journal,* April 1974.
Lewis, Robert J. "Hoover Wins Fight on Arcades." *Washington Star,* 14 September 1967.
"Pennsylvania Avenue" (editorial). *Washington Post,* 21 September 1967.
Severo, Richard. "Plans Approved for FBI Building: Elimination of Arcade Stirs Furor." *Washington Post,* 15 September 1967.
Seymore, Jim. "Raise the Height Limit; A Washington Proposal to Bring Downtown Into the 20th Century." *Washington Magazine.*
Silha, Stephen. "Design Your Own City? Yes—Washington." *The Christian Science Monitor.* July 17, 1973.
Thiry, Paul. "The Planning of Washington as a Capital." *AIA Journal,* April 1974.
Von Eckardt, Wolf. "Avenue Will Have Missing Tooth." *Washington Post,* 22 October 1967.
———. "Metro: Example for the World." *Washington Post,* 20 November 1971.
———. "Why Are All These People Smiling." *Washington Post.*
Yudis, Anthony J. "Cambridge Firm Tapped for D.C. Downtown Face-Lift." *Boston Globe,* 10 June 1973.

Public Documents

Caemmerer, Paul. *A Manual on the Origin and Development of Washington.* U.S. Government Printing Office, 1939.
D.C. Zoning Commission. *Washington Building Height and Skyline Study.* May 1971.
D.C. Redevelopment Land Agency, and Ashley, Meyer, Smith, Inc. *User Consultation Process, Final Report.* February 28, 1973.
National Capital Planning Commission. *Downtown Design and Development.* 1974.

———. *F Street Plaza.* December 1971.
———. *L'Enfant's Methods and Features of His City Plan for the Federal City* (Excerpt from the Annual Report, National Capital Park and Planning Commission, 1930, by William T. Partridge).
———. *Planning Washington 1924–1976.* April 30, 1976.
———. *Policy Recommendations for the Location of Federal Work Facilities in the National Capital Region* (Prepared by George Schermer Associates). June 30, 1970.
———. *Washington's Central Employment Area: 1973.* May 1975.
Pennsylvania Avenue Development Corporation. *The Pennsylvania Avenue Plan 1974.* November 1974.
Smithsonian Institution et al. *The Federal City: Plans and Realities.* 1976.
Washington Metropolitan Transit Authority. *Metro Owner's Manual.* 1976.
———. *Metro Ridership.*
———. *Metro's Contribution to Environmental Improvement in the National Capital Region.*

Unpublished Materials

Ashley, Myer, Smith. *Downtown Streets for People.* May 29, 1973.
Letter from Jefferson to Washington, 14 September 1796. Library of Congress.

SAN FRANCISCO

Books

Brugmann, Bruce B.; Sletteland, Greggar; and the Bay Guardian Staff. *The Ultimate Highrise.* San Francisco: San Francisco Bay Guardian Books, 1971.
Scott, Mel. *The San Francisco Bay Area: A Metropolis in Perspective.* Berkeley, Calif.: University of California Press, 1959.
Vance, James E., Jr. *Geography and Urban Evolution in the San Francisco Bay Area.* Berkeley, Calif.: Institute of Governmental Studies, 1964.

Articles and Periodicals

Lathrop, William H., Jr. "San Francisco Freeway Revolt." *Transportation Engineering Journal,* February 1971.
Lindsey, Robert. "Mass Transit, Little Mass." *The New York Times Magazine,* 19 October 1975.

Marlin, William. "An Outside Inside." *Architectural Forum,* November 1973, pp. 47-55.

"Portman's Most Animated Atrium Yet." *Interiors,* October 1973.

Thompson, Elizabeth Kendall. "Dramatic Space for a New Hotel in San Francisco." *Architectural Record,* September 1973.

Webber, Melvin M. "San Francisco Area Rapid Transit: A Disappointing Model. *The New York Times,* 13 November 1976, p. 23.

Public Documents

City and County of San Francisco. *Administrative Code: Environmental Quality.* August 28, 1974.

——. *City Planning Code.* Part 2, Chap. 2. July 1, 1974.

San Francisco Bay Area Rapid Transit District. *Annual Report.* 1973/74.

——. *Chronology.* August 1974.

San Francisco Department of City Planning. *The Comprehensive Plan: Northern Waterfront.* April 1971.

——. *The Comprehensive Plan: Recreation and Open Space.* May 1973.

——. *The Comprehensive Plan: Residence.* April 1971.

——. *The Comprehensive Plan: Transportation.* April 1972.

——. *The Comprehensive Plan: Urban Design.* August 1971.

——. *Downtown Zoning Study.* July 1966.

——. *Downtown Zoning Study* (Case studies in Application of The Proposed Floor Area Bonus System). January 1967.

——. *Height Limits in Northeastern San Francisco.* October 1963.

——. *San Francisco Downtown Zoning Study* (Final Report). December 1966.

——, et al. *Transit Preferential Streets Program.* November 26, 1973.

——. *Transportation: Conditions and Trends.* August 1976.

——. *A Transportation System for the Embarcadero Area.* November 1974.

San Francisco Redevelopment Agency. *San Francisco Redevelopment Program* (Summary of Project Data and Key Elements). January 1975.

San Francisco Transit Task Force. *Market Street Design* (Reports #2, 4, 5 prepared by Mario J. Ciampi and Associates; John Carl Warnecke and Associates). 1965-1966.

——. *Summary Report.* November 1967.

Reports

Foundation for San Francisco's Architectural Heritage. *Heritage Newsletter.* May 1975.

San Francisco Planning and Urban Renewal Association. *Impact of Intensive High Rise Development on San Francisco* (Summary of Final Report). March 1975.

——. *Spur Report: Economics and Aesthetics in Union Square.* May 1975.

——. *Spur Report: Market Street Beautification: A Time for Decisive Action by the Private Sector.* January 1974.

Unpublished Material

San Francisco Department of City Planning. "Design Review Processes" (Memorandum from Dean L. Macris, Director of Planning to the City Planning Commission). March 13, 1975.

——. "Discretionary Review of Building Application No. 396943 for Southern Pacific Headquarters Block (One Market Plaza), Bounded by Market, Steuart, Mission and Spear Streets" (Memorandum from Allan B. Jacobs, Director of Planning to the City Planning Commission). May 27, 1971.

——. "Environmental Review Process Summary."

——. "Format and Guidelines for Materials Required for a Draft Environmental Impact Report." April 1975.

——. "Guidelines for Development: Market Street Frontage, South Side between 7th and 8th Streets." February 13, 1974.

——. "Requirements of the Market Street Special Signage District." May 1970.

BOSTON

Books

Whitehill, Walter Muir. *Boston: A Topographical History.* Cambridge, Mass.: The Belknap Press of Harvard University Press, 1975.

Articles and Periodicals

"Being Bold with the Old." *Time,* 5 July 1976.

"Boston Upgrades Its Ugly Subways: Setting New Standards for Transit Design." *Architectural Record,* February 1968.

Chermayeff, Peter. "Orientation in the Transit Environment." *Journal of Franklin Institute* 286, no. 5 (November 1968), pp. 477–490.

Fenton, John H. "Imported Ideas Improve Boston Subway." *The New York Times,* 27 November 1967.

Goodman, Robert. "New Face for a Very Old Lady." *Boston Globe,* 28 January 1968.

Huxtable, Ada Louise. "Why You Always Win and Lose in Urban Renewal." *The New York Times,* 19 September 1976.

Kay, Jane Holtz. "The Saving Grace." *Architectural Forum,* March 1973, pp. 52-57.

Kelly, Scott. "Boston Transit: Team Design and Fractions Fans." *Industrial Design,* June 1967.

Kifner, John. "A 'New' 1826 Market Joins Boston's Downtown Revival." *The New York Times,* 27 August 1976.

Moholy-Nagy, Sibyl. "Boston's City Hall." *Architectural Forum,* January-February 1969, pp. 40-58.

Pecker, Scott. "MBTA Adding Mileage 'N' Murals." *The Christian Science Monitor,* 6 November 1967.

Plotkin, A. S. "MBTA's Facelifting Plans Praised by Magazines and Museums." *Boston Globe,* 22 October 1967.

——. "Rumblings Underground: The Cambridge 'Intellectuals' vs. The MBTA Engineers." *Boston Globe Magazine,* 9 July 1967.

"Profile: Cambridge Seven Architects." *Progressive Architecture,* December 1972.

Schmertz, Mildred F. "The New Boston City Hall." *Architectural Record,* February 1969.

"Transportation: Subways Can Be Beautiful." *Time,* 20 October 1967.

Yudis, Anthony. "Boston's Pieces Coming Together." *Boston Globe Magazine,* 23 November 1975, p. 13.

Public Documents

Barrett, David R. *Incentive Zoning for Boston: A Report to the BRA.* July 1973.

Redevelopment Authority. *Boston's Adult Entertainment District.* January 1976.

——. *Boston's Office Industry, Office Space Demand and Supply, Past and Projected,* by Peter Menconeri. May 1974.

——. *Government Center.*

——. *Jordon Marsh/Lafayette Place.* April 1975.

————. Massachusetts Institute of Technology, Urban Dynamics Advisory Committee, Inc. *Boston's Transportation Program.* April 1974.

————. *1965/1975 General Plan for the City of Boston and the Regional Core.*

————. *Recycled Boston.* June 1976.

————. *Research Report: Government Center.* February 1970.

————. *Research Report: A History of Boston's Government Center.* June 1970.

————. *Research Report: The Prudential Center, Part One, Its Direct Impact on Boston.* September 1969.

————. *Research Report: The Prudential Center, Part Two, Its Effect on the Surrounding Area.* December 1969.

————. *The Tremont Street Special District.* January 1976.

U.S. Environmental Protection Agency. *Implementation Plans: Transportation Control Plan for Boston, Massachusetts.* June 12, 1975.

ATLANTA

Books

Boylston, Elsie Reid. *Atlanta: Its Lore and Laughter.* Doraville, Ga.: Foote and Davies (Printers), 1968.

Garrett, Franklin Miller. *Yesterday's Atlanta.* Miami, Fla.: E. A. Seeman Publisher, Inc., 1974.

Global Architecture: John Portman. Japan, 1974.

Marsh, Kermit B., *The American Institute of Architects Guide to Atlanta.* 1975.

Martin, Thomas H. *Atlanta and Its Builders.* Vol. I. Century Memorial Publishing Co., 1902.

Workers of the Writers WPA Program. *Atlanta: A City of the Modern South.* American Guide Series, 1942.

Articles and Periodicals

AIA Journal. April 1975.

Asher, Joe. "Atlanta Transit: MARTA Gets Moving, at Last." *Railway Age,* 8 December 1975.

"Atlanta Region: Unity in Diversity." *Atlanta Magazine,* 1975.

"Atlanta: Modern Transit for the New South." *Headlights,* January–February 1972, pp. 4-9.

Barnett, Jonathan. "What to Do for an Encore." *Architectural Record,* June 1976.

Carter, Ann, and Aeck, Antonin. "Acres of Entertainment." *Progressive Architecture,* May 1976.

"Cooperating to Solve Problems." *Nation's Business,* April 1976.

"Defying Tradition and Achieving Success." *Nation's Business,* August 1976.

"Downtown Is Looking Up." *Time,* 5 July 1976, pp. 46-54.

Galphin, Bruce. "John Portman of Peachtree Center." *Atlanta Magazine,* August 1967.

Gueft, Olga. "John Portman's Heaven under Glass." *Interiors,* July 1976.

Kiener, Robert. "John Portman: Architect/Visionary." *Hospitality,* September 1975.

Leviton, Joyce. "BIO: Architect John Portman." *People,* 11 August 1975.

Prugh, Jeff. "Underground Atlanta's Roof Falling In." *Los Angeles Times,* 17 March 1976.

Real Estate Atlanta 5, no. 1.

Stark, Al. "The Living Spaces of John Portman." *Passages,* May 1975.

Sutton, Horace. "The Supercities: Atlanta." *Saturday Review,* 4 September 1976.

Public Documents

Atlanta Regional Commission. *An Economic Base Study of the Atlanta Region.*

Atlanta Regional Transportation Planning. *MARTA: The Effect of Fare Reduction on Transit Ridership in the Atlanta Region,* Summary Report no. 1 (October 1973).

————. *MARTA: The Effect of Fare Reduction on Transit Ridership in the Atlanta Region,* Summary Report no. 2 (December 1974).

Metropolitan Atlanta Rapid Transit Authority. *Engineering Report Summarizing the Comprehensive Transit Plan for the Atlanta Metropolitan Area, Including the Short Range Transit Improvement Program* (Prepared by Parsons Brinckerhoff-Tudor-Bechtel). September 1971.

MINNEAPOLIS

Articles and Periodicals

Aschman, Frederick T. "Nicollet Mall: Civic Cooperation to Preserve Downtown's Vitality." *Planners Notebook,* September 1971.

Carpenter, Edward K. "Making Minneapolis Work." *Design and Environment,* Summer 1975, pp. 33-47.

"New Street Scene." *Architectural Forum,* January-February 1969.

Wascoe, Dan, Jr. "A New Life Style Walks into Minneapolis." *Passages,* August 1973, pp. 11-15.

Public Documents

City of Minneapolis, Heritage Preservation Commission. *Roots.* 1973.

————. Office of City Coordinator. *Loring Park Development.*

————. Office of City Coordinator. *Loring Park Development, Progress Report.* June 1975.

————. Office of City Coordinator. *Loring Park Development, Urban Design Plan* (Prepared by M. Paul Friedburg and Associates; Barton-Aschman Associates). November 19, 1973.

————. Office of City Coordinator. *Minneapolis People Mover.* April 1973.

————. Planning and Development. *Area Development Policies.* Fall 1971.

————. Planning and Development. *City Center '75.* January 1975.

————. Planning and Development. *Downtown Edges.*

————. Planning and Development. *Goals, Objectives, and Principal Policies.* May 1974.

————. Planning and Development. *Metro Center '85.* March 1970.

————. Planning and Development. *Minneapolis Skyway System.* January 1973.

————. Planning and Development. *Zoning Code.* December 1969.

Metropolitan Transit Commission. *Improving Transit Operations and Facilities in Downtown Areas.* May 22, 1975.

Minneapolis '76 Bicentennial Commission. *Minneapolis: Frontiers, Firsts, and Futures.* April 1976.

Illustration Credits

165	Photograph: Kenneth Halpern
166	Photograph: Marc Klaw
167	Courtesy Philadelphia City Planning Commission
168	Illustration: Wilhelm von Moltke. Courtesy Wilhelm von Moltke
169,170,171	Courtesy Bower and Fradley
172,173	Photographs: Tom Crane. Courtesy Bower and Fradley
174,175,176	Courtesy Bower and Fradley
177,178	Photographs: Kenneth Halpern
179	Courtesy Ueland and Junker
180	Courtesy Vincent G. Kling
181	Photograph: © Lawrence S. Williams, Inc.
182	Photograph: Kenneth Halpern
183	Photograph: Tom Crane
184	Photograph: Harper Leiper
185,186	Courtesy Houston Public Library
187	Photograph: Wallace Aerial Surveys, Inc.
188	Photograph: Harper Leiper
189	Illustration: Peter Musgrave-Newton
190,191	Photographs: Kenneth Halpern
192	Courtesy Philip Johnson and John Burgee
193,194	Photographs: Richard W. Payne. Courtesy Philip Johnson and John Burgee
195	Courtesy Skidmore, Owings and Merrill
196	Photograph: Ezra Stoller © ESTO. Courtesy Skidmore, Owings and Merrill
197,198,199	Photographs: Kenneth Halpern
200	Courtesy Koetter Tharp Cowell and Bartlett
201,202	Photographs: Kenneth Halpern
203	Photograph: Frank Lotz Miller. Courtesy Koetter Tharp Cowell and Bartlett
204	Courtesy Koetter Tharp Cowell and Bartlett
205,206	Courtesy Texas Eastern Transmission Corporation
207,208	Photographs: Kenneth Halpern
209	Photograph: Air Photographics, Inc.
210	Courtesy National Capital Planning Commission
211	Courtesy Library of Congress
212	Courtesy The National Archives
213,214	Photographs: Air Photographics, Inc.
215	Courtesy Library of Congress
216	Photograph: Kenneth Halpern
217	Photograph: Fred Figall. Courtesy D.C. Department of Housing and Community Development
218	Photograph: Charles E. Rotkin
219	Photograph: Kenneth Halpern
220	Courtesy Downtown Progress
221	Axonimetric illustration: Joe Passonneau
222	Courtesy Arrowstreet, Inc.
223	Courtesy Library of Congress
224	Photograph: Capitol Airviews
225	Photograph: Kenneth Halpern
226	Courtesy Pennsylvania Avenue Development Corporation
227	Photograph: Phil Portlock. Courtesy WMATA
228	Courtesy Joe Passonneau
229	Illustration: Laurie Olin. Courtesy Joe Passonneau
230	Photograph: Aero Photographers
231	Courtesy City of San Francisco, Office of Public Information
232	Courtesy San Francisco Public Library
233	Courtesy Victor Gruen Associates
234	Courtesy San Francisco Department of City Planning
235	Photograph: Kenneth Halpern
236	Courtesy San Francisco Department of City Planning
237	Photograph: Ezra Stoller © ESTO. Courtesy Wurster, Bernardi and Emmons
238	Courtesy Wurster, Bernardi and Emmons
239,240	Photographs: Kenneth Halpern
241	Illustration: Peter Musgrave-Newton
242	Photograph of model: Richard Karl Koch. Courtesy Welton Becket and Associates
243	Photograph: Kenneth Halpern
244	Photograph: Aero Photographers
245	Photograph: Mak Takahoshi
246	Illustration: Jacob van der Ploeg, Reed Rubey. Courtesy Foundation for San Francisco's Architectural Heritage
247	Photograph: Kenneth Halpern
248	Illustration: Peter Musgrave-Newton
249,250	Courtesy Wurster, Bernardi and Emmons
251	Photograph: Morley Baer. Courtesy Skidmore, Owings and Merrill
252,253,254	Courtesy John Portman Associates
255	Photograph: Ted Mahieu. Courtesy Bank of California

256 Photograph: Mak Takahoshi
257 Courtesy Market Street Development Project
258 Courtesy BART
259,260,261,262 Photographs: Kenneth Halpern
263 Courtesy San Francisco Department of City Planning
264 Photograph: Ed Brady. Courtesy Aero Photographers
265 Courtesy San Francisco Bay Guardian
266 Photograph: Aerial Photos of New England, Inc.
267 Courtesy New York Public Library
268 Courtesy Boston Athenaeum
269 Illustration: Peter Musgrave-Newton
270 Photograph: Aerial Photos of New England, Inc.
271 Photograph: Kenneth Halpern
272 Photograph: Aerial Photos of New England, Inc.
273 Photograph: Kenneth Halpern
274 Photograph: Cervin Robinson. Courtesy Kallmann and McKinnell
275 Photograph: Bo Parker. Courtesy Skidmore, Owings and Merrill
276 Photograph: Gorchev and Gorchev. Courtesy Edward Barnes
277 Photograph: Ezra Stoller © ESTO. Courtesy The Architects Collaborative
278,279 Photographs: Kenneth Halpern
280 Photograph: Aerial Photos of New England, Inc.
281 Photograph: Ezra Stoller © ESTO. Courtesy Kallmann and McKinnell
282 Illustration: William Fain. Courtesy William Fain
283 Courtesy Boston Redevelopment Authority
284 Photograph: Franco Romagnoli. Courtesy Benjamin Thompson Associates
285,286,287 Photographs: Kenneth Halpern
288 Courtesy Arrowstreet Inc.
289 Photograph: Harvey Hacker. Courtesy Cambridge Seven Associates, Inc.
290,291 Photographs: David Hirsch. Courtesy Cambridge Seven Associates, Inc.
292 Photograph: Dillon Aerial Photography, Inc.
293,294 Courtesy Atlanta Historical Society
295 Courtesy Emory University Archives
296 Courtesy Atlanta Chapter, American Institute of Architects
297 Photograph: Kenneth Halpern
298 Courtesy Atlanta Historical Society
299 Photograph: Kenneth Halpern
300 Courtesy Skidmore, Owings and Merrill
301 Photograph: Kenneth Halpern
302 Courtesy John Portman Associates
303 Illustration: Peter Musgrave-Newton
304 Photograph: Kenneth Halpern
305,306 Courtesy John Portman Associates
307,308 Photographs: Jerry Spearman. Courtesy John Portman Associates
309 Photograph: Alexandre Georges. Courtesy John Portman Associates
310 Photograph: Kenneth Halpern
311 Photograph: Jerry Spearman. Courtesy John Portman Associates
312 Courtesy John Portman Associates
313,314 Courtesy Thompson, Ventulett and Stainback, Inc.
315,316 Photographs: George Cserna. Courtesy Toombs, Amisano, and Wells
317 Courtesy MARTA
318 Photograph: Baureferat des Landeshaupstadt Munich. Courtesy Cooper-Hewitt Museum
319 Photograph: Thoen Photography. Courtesy Minneapolis Planning and Development
320,321 Courtesy Minnesota Historical Society
322,323 Courtesy Greater Minneapolis Chamber of Commerce
324 Courtesy Minneapolis Convention and Tourism Commission
325 Illustration: Peter Musgrave-Newton
326 Courtesy Greater Minneapolis Chamber of Commerce
327,328 Photographs: Kenneth Halpern
329 Photograph: Nathaniel Lieberman. Courtesy Philip Johnson and John Burgee
330 Courtesy Philip Johnson and John Burgee
331,332 Photographs: Kenneth Halpern
333 Photograph: Ezra Stoller © ESTO. Courtesy Kevin Roche, John Dinkeloo and Associates
334 Courtesy Philip Johnson and John Burgee
335,336,337,338 Photographs: Kenneth Halpern
339 Courtesy John Carl Warnecke and Associates
340,341 Courtesy Paul Friedberg
342 Courtesy The Partners
343,344,345,346,347 Photographs: Kenneth Halpern
348 Courtesy Greater Minneapolis Chamber of Commerce
349 Photograph: Kenneth Halpern
350 Courtesy Paul Friedberg

Index

Italicized numerals refer to illustrations.

A